Endo

"America is now descending into one of its most difficult hours since the Civil War. Americans sense out-of-control forces are now enveloping our culture. David Fiorazo now helps people understand the culture war with the release of his new book, *Canceling Christianity*. This book is required reading if you want to understand the difficult times that we are now living in as Americans, and what can be done to right the ship."
—**Dr. Andy Woods**, Pastor, Sugar Land Bible Church, President, Chafer Theological Seminary

"Men inspired by God made America great. Yet we have grown complacent and now even shun the biblical principles that made us One Nation, Under God. Fiorazo not only outlines the present spiraling crisis clearly, he also gives us a blueprint for fighting back that all true Christians should learn, pray over, and act on."
—**Pastor Steve Smothermon**, Legacy Church, Albuquerque

"David Fiorazo is well informed about the state of this nation and the state of Christianity in America. He deftly lays out the current situation, but he doesn't just point at the darkness. David also provides biblical solutions. Christians must realize they no longer have the convenience of being indifferent to civil government matters. They must engage those who possess civil authority with the truth of God's Word—and this book will strengthen Christian men to do so."
—**Pastor Matt Trewhella**, Mercy Seat Christian Church, Founder of Missionaries to the Preborn

"For years, I have been speaking to audiences about the critical need for God's people to 'get off the bench' and engage in the battlefield that is culture, but for generations, we have quietly allowed the cancel culture to strip us of our Judeo-Christian roots. A terrible price is being paid for our silence. In his newest book, author David Fiorazo offers an honest assessment of *why* we must engage the culture and *how* to begin moving from silence to strength in the battle for the hearts and minds of the next generation. If you're ready to walk boldly and bear fruit for the Kingdom, be encouraged! This book is for you!"

—**Heidi St. John**, Author, Speaker, Podcaster,
Mom Strong International

"*Canceling Christianity* is a must read for every person who loves God and appreciates the freedoms He gave us in America—freedoms which are being stripped away. David Fiorazo has done a masterful job of articulating the nature of the battle we are in. His analysis is straightforward, truthful, and Christ honoring. This book is a call to action and a warning to Christians of what will soon happen if we don't wake up, turn to God, and stand for His purposes.

—**Gary H. Kah**,
Former Europe & Mideast Trade Specialist,
Author of *The New World Religion*

"With the culture and some churches disintegrating before our eyes, we need 'watchmen on the wall' sounding the alarm. I have found David Fiorazo's insights the very best at that. If we don't push back against the radical left, very soon our country will be unrecognizable."

—**Jan Markell**, Founder, Olive Tree Ministries,
Understanding the Times Radio

"The release of *Canceling Christianity* could not be timelier. David Fiorazo reveals how a free and religious people have now come under demonically driven assault. He drives home the importance of actively being the *salt and light* in a decaying culture, thus reclaiming the mission of the true biblical church. As he writes, this truly is an 'epic battle for the nation's soul.' You. Need. This. Book.
—**Pastor Carl Gallups**, Hickory Hammock Baptist Church, Amazon Best-selling Author

"The cancel culture mob is not coming, it's here, along with 'wokeism' and a full-frontal assault on traditional values. My inbox is filled with examples from all aspects of society. In *Canceling Christianity*, David Fiorazo addresses these issues and gives some practical, biblical advice as to how the Church can engage the cancel culture mob in an effort to win souls and protect the flock from this assault. I would highly recommend that you read *Canceling Christianity*."
—**Pastor John Haller**, Fellowship Bible Chapel, Prophecy Expert

"David Fiorazo's work brilliantly exposes the soft totalitarianism permeating the Leftist woke-worldview, part of the cultural and political war to destroy our Republic under God. *Canceling Christianity* is a must-read analysis that not only critiques the madness of the Left but also gives us practical advice and hope in the battle ahead."
—**Dr. Jake Jacobs**, Author, Speaker, Teacher

CANCELING CHRISTIANITY

How the Left Silences Churches, Dismantles the Constitution, and Divides Our Culture

DAVID FIORAZO

Published by Freiling Publishing, a division of Freiling Agency, LLC.

P.O. Box 1264,
Warrenton, VA 20188

www.FreilingPublishing.com

ISBN 978-1-950948-77-2

Printed in the United States of America

Table of Contents

Introduction

Throughout the world for the last 2,000 years, societies have been trying to cancel Christians and even blot out God if that were possible. There is nothing new under the sun. But history has shown that the church has thrived where persecution exists. That's the good news.

Americans have been blessed to be the anomaly rather than the rule as Christianity has flourished here for centuries. The true church is essential to the health and strength of America, just as Christianity was pivotal to our freedoms and the foundation of this nation. As the church goes, so goes the country, they say.

The left, however, has been relentless in its commitment to destroy not only the church, but also the very essence of America. We have been under attack from within. Just as they used the COVID-19 crisis to restrict churches, suppress the truth, and advance their agendas, they will use the current cancel culture to silence those who have different views.

What is bewildering is they accuse those of us on the right of not being tolerant when they are the ones who are intolerant!

They are also using the breach of the US Capitol on January 6 to frame Christians, conservatives, and patriotic Americans as domestic terrorists. I have talked with several people who were there in D.C. that day, and the media propaganda is based on a false narrative. Did the complicit media frame all BLM protestors as arsonists, looters, and rioters? No.

Proverbs 14:34 states, "Righteousness exalts a nation, but sin is a reproach to any people." Anti-Christian movements are wreaking havoc across this land, and this book is another effort to wake up the remnant. It is not surprising that threats and hostility toward believers are ramping up. But the speed with which godlessness has infiltrated our culture and churches should alarm us.

This book will expose the enemy within and analyze what happened to the "United" States. We will address at least two causes of the ineffectiveness of our churches, the moral decline of culture, and the political divide:

1. the consistent agendas to erase God and eradicate Christian influence from society; and
2. the general apathy of the church that has allowed the immoral, leftist takeover.

We've been spoiled. Christians basically had home field advantage in America as believers permeated culture with light, salt, and truth. But now, we are clearly on the enemy's playing field. We lost our impact and surrendered territory while the enemy and his minions have advanced.

Practically every survey and cultural indicator reveals we have conformed to the world and shows a general failure of the church to disciple and equip believers. Too many Christians are complacent, confused, and disengaged. Some are not even saved! High numbers of young people have left the faith and we now see moral relativism on steroids in our society.

The stage had been set for nearly a century. The players were put in place decade by decade. What we see being played out before our eyes is part of the antichrist spirit of the age. Most would agree we are in a cultural crisis of rebellion against God to the point sin is openly celebrated.

Then along came 2020, a flashpoint in our short history.

When describing events of last year, the word "unprecedented" was used and overused so often it had to be retired. The country suffered greatly on many fronts. We became more totalitarian under emergency lockdown orders as rule of law was suspended. The church, however, was exposed, tested, and sadly deemed nonessential.

America will never be the same, but maybe that is okay. Though most of us now see this as an intensifying, uphill battle for America's soul, all is not lost. What took place, as well as what we are now going through, will be for our good (Romans 8:28). God is moving, and I believe we are on the brink of some universal shaking—starting with the church!

Prior to the great imposition of the coronavirus last year, the George Barna Group revealed some disturbing trends. First, do you know who they consider to be practicing Christians? Those who attend church at least once a month! Practicing? It is not surprising a key takeaway from the survey is church was not considered to be a major influence on society.[1]

Plus, only 27 percent of people agree churches have a very positive impact on the country. When singling out non-Christians, nearly 40 percent said the church in America has no impact on culture at all! And 18 percent see local church impact as either very negative or somewhat negative.

I share this, not that we should be too concerned about what people think, but because we were somewhat inconsequential last year. The nation reached critical mass with three major crises: COVID-19, Black Lives Matter riots, and the divisive buildup to a presidential election. Some churches jumped on opportunities to minister while others sheltered at home.

A new virus, a national health issue, was politicized—on purpose. From that point on, Americans were generally divided over what businesses were essential, shutting down the economy, mask mandates, social distancing, how to respond to racism, how to do church services, and politics.

We disagreed about the personalities of a bombastic, narcissistic Donald Trump and a condescending, hypocritical Joe Biden. But sadly, even professing Christians were divided over policies, party platforms, and procedures.

And while believers were debating political issues such as gender, murder, marriage, education, rioting, and socialism, the left kept up the pressure. For years, forces of evil have been working hard to purge the light and silence Christians. As a result, we live in a culture that calls evil good.

In this book, we will look at some of the key reasons we all but lost the culture and what can be done at this point. Be forewarned, it is not a pretty picture. This is an honest assessment of where we are and the daunting task ahead as a divided church navigates cancel culture.

Yes, we must keep fighting and preaching the Gospel, but for all practical purposes, the left controls the culture. Never surrender! But from this point on our focus must be to reclaim or reset a wayward church. I hope and pray it is not too late. While many churches refuse to address evil, some have aligned themselves with movements founded on worldly philosophies. Others have watered down the Word of God because they fear offending people.

If there was ever a time in American history the Christian Church needed to be a bold, active, gospel-preaching, fruit-bearing church, it is now. We were tested, pushed back, restricted, shut down, and discriminated against. And few of us resisted. Believers in various countries around the world are suffering real persecution, many have been killed for their faith in Jesus Christ—and we were afraid to open our churches.

When will we realize we are not here to make friends with the world, but to convert them? The sad reality, however, is the left is converting us! We no longer agree on social issues, which I call moral issues. Some avoid elections, voting, and government. Other believers are all in and become obsessed with politics, which sadly can be consuming.

Some saw the election of President Donald Trump in 2016 as a reprieve from the radical policies of the Obama-Biden years. Others could not get past orange man, bad to see the good fruit of Trump's policies. But now it is the O'Biden/Harris administration's turn to fundamentally transform the United States.

This is not to say Democrats are the enemy, nor is every one of them godless. Though the party has been sacked by social-ists and secular progressives and their platform is demonic, our struggle is not against flesh and blood, but "against the rulers, against the powers, against the world forces of this darkness, against the spiritual forces of wickedness" (Ephesians 6:12).

We are either influenced by the Holy Spirit of Jesus Christ or the satanic spirit of this world that is unleashing evil in our midst. Jesus once told some religious leaders, "…you are of your father, the devil" (John 8:44). The apostle John stated, "the one who practices sin is of the devil" (1 John 3:8), and that "the children of God and children of the devil are obvious" (1 John 3:10).

We must acknowledge the real spiritual war manifested in the natural realm, and though the battle is fierce and seems lost, an awakening or revival is not out of the question. I do not see that happening barring a miracle of God, but I hope I am wrong.

Many of those in the remnant of true believers are refusing to go down without a fight! We must never stop believing, pressing into Jesus, speaking up, and working to oppose evil agendas that are destroying our nation. We must battle against those who do evil and expose their deeds of darkness (Ephesians 5:11).

God's church desperately needs watchmen on the wall, not comfy CEOs and people-pleasing pastors more concerned about preaching happiness rather than holiness.

Dr. Owen Strachan, a professor at Midwest Baptist Theological Seminary, stated:

> "The greatest threat to biblical Christianity today is not atheism, militant Islam, the sexual revolution, or a hostile public square. The greatest threat to biblical Christianity today is weak, soft, man-centered, sin-affirming, ear-tickling, flesh-pleasing, self-help theology."

There are many threats to be confronted, including an infiltration of modern liberalism in our churches. But this feel-good, motivational, all-about-me, world-loving, best-life-now theology is another gospel that is powerless to save. But it sure does sell books and attract a crowd.

In our own churches, some are confused about absolute truth, creation, gender, marriage, family, and the separation of church and state. This must be remedied!

The left is after the youngest of our children and they are teaching there is no God so you can decide your own gender. We now have the most sexually explicit curriculum in public schools, the promotion of abortion, LGBT and drag queens being normalized, and biological boys using girls' bathrooms and locker rooms.

Have our churches prepared parents and Christian children for this unforgiving, unrelenting, immoral assault? We are almost out of time.

Pastor, I know your job is tremendously challenging, but no more 'cotton candy' messages or country club Christianity. No more capitulation to culture. Either hold the line, equip believers, and confront evil—or move to the back. Preach the unadulterated Gospel to a dying culture or let someone else lead. Please.

That lukewarm church in Revelation 3 was warned to repent. The Savior, the One who gave Himself for all mankind, the Cornerstone of the church, was on the outside looking in! And still is.

How did we get here? Part of the problem is we have forgotten our history. True Christianity has done much good for the world and this nation for a century or two, resulting in a respectable reputation. You would never know this from schools, history books, universities, government, media, and Hollywood.

The church was alive and active. But sadly today, we may also be compared to a few churches in Asia Minor in the days of the apostles. For example, Jesus rebuked the Church at Sardis and said:

> " 'I know your works. You have the reputation of being alive, but you are dead. Wake up, and strengthen what remains and is about to die, for I have not found your works complete in the sight of my God. Remember, then, what you received and heard. Keep it, and repent. If you will not wake up, I will come like a thief, and you will not know at what hour I will come against you' " (Revelation 3:1-3, ESV).

Strengthen what remains, brother and sister in Christ!

One of the most common calls, emails, or messages I receive is from sincere, Bible-believing Christians who have become disappointed with modern churches or their pastor. They desire meaty and expository teachings, discipleship, and a willingness to address Bible prophecy and current events in our culture.

I often tell people that they are not alone! We know something is missing, but what can we do about it? Get back to our foundations. Look at church history, American history, and then, get out of our comfort zones. The early church exploded in power and grew rapidly within godless societies not unlike ours that were hostile toward Christians.

We have the same Holy Spirit. What is our excuse? We stopped defending the truth, fighting to proclaim the Gospel, and protecting our freedoms. There are consequences for a nation when Christians take paths of least resistance.

In fact, after more than a year of COVID-19 chaos, too many churches and individuals reacted in fear of the virus instead of faith in our God. We trusted leftist, globalist news sources. We needed to gather for encouragement, prayer, equipping, communion, fellowship, and discipleship, but churches were closed.

On the holiest day of the year, Easter Sunday, Jesus' tomb was still empty, but so were most churches! Our doors were shut. For Christians, disappointment and anxiety were off the charts last year. For those outside the church, depression, fear, and hopelessness dominated as people turned to alcohol, drugs, pornography, entertainment, social media, and other temporary things.

What have we learned? Never again! We must never stop being the church. Online teachings are a tool that can be used, but videos can never replace church gatherings, worship services, and ministering to the needs of our communities.

This book is about the need for immediate change. It is about true Christianity in an anti-Christian culture. It is about course correction and rallying the troops for a fight to the finish.

We will discuss discernment in the church, politics, government, abortion, social justice, racism, the BLM global network, Big Tech, the one-party national media, progressive propaganda, the education system, the Great Reset, cultural Marxism, how a virus changed everything, the 2020 election, radicals now in power, and where we go from here.

This book is about influence, authority, redeeming the time, living our faith out loud, and working to maintain our first freedom. It is about preparing for persecution in America while resisting evil and those who would try to cancel Christianity.

We, believers in Christ, must fight through all the lies, confusion, counterfeits, double standards, opposition, and Big Tech turmoil. We must be reminded that Jesus, our Redeemer and King, is preparing His army. Judgment is coming. He is returning!

Breaking news: God is still in control; we have much work to do and saints to recruit!

Jesus is the only source of lasting peace, and our only real hope. Because He lives, we can face tomorrow with all its problems, possibilities, joys, and sorrows. This life is a vapor, but God chose you and me to be here for such a time as this.

I hope and pray this book encourages your faith, challenges your perspective, reminds you of our true history, provides insight, and strengthens your resolve to speak the truth about things that matter—no matter the cost.

1

Epic Battle for the Soul of America

"The strength of our country is the strength of its religious convictions. The foundations of our society and our government rest so much on the teachings of the Bible that it would be difficult to support them if faith in these teachings would cease to be practically universal in our country." —Calvin Coolidge

"The church needs to get back to the Bible, and the country needs to get back to the Constitution."
—Pastor Jack Hibbs

"America will never be destroyed from the outside. If we falter and lose our freedoms, it will be because we destroyed ourselves." —Abraham Lincoln

While campaigning against President Trump last year, Joe Biden's website displayed this interesting phrase in the upper-left corner: Battle for the Soul of the Nation. The implication was the soul or morality of America was at stake. We just define "soul" very differently because his values are not at all the same as Bible-believing Christians.

There has been a furious conflict in the spiritual realm over the United States since its inception. And the battle has never been more intense or misunderstood than it is today.

Biden's handlers tried framing that presidential campaign in 2020 as good vs. evil, as if Joe were the savior of a holy war that would ultimately save America. In many speeches, he referred to healing and light in this battle for the soul of the nation, giving the false impression Biden was the moral one to bring positive change and unity.

Due to the public being in constant crisis mode, the disruption of order, and planned civil unrest blamed on Trump, many Americans apparently bought it and voted for Biden.

We will dive into specific policies and party contrasts later and compare them with what the Bible teaches, but to associate President Trump and Republicans with darkness and evil is quite a stretch. It is clever marketing though. It is the Alinsky tactic of demonizing your opponent to distract from the real issues. The left has this down to a science.

Like the spiritual warfare over the souls of men, there are battles in heavenly realms over nations because of what they stand for as well as over the people in those nations. The enemy hates America because of the God we were once united under and the believers who represent Him.

Part of the epic battle manifests as hatred directed at Christians. There are cultural conflicts about worldview; heaven and hell, righteousness and unrighteousness, freedom and bondage, truth and lies, but it all comes down to three words: God or man. A person's foundational assumptions about God and man directly influence their philosophy of law and government.

This is why we see the intense, moral battle for America's soul and over whether or not to uphold the US Constitution as the law of the land. Though not perfect, America made it this far in history because we once sought to glorify the

Lord, obey His commands, and there was no resistance to advancing the Christian faith.

A few months ago, however, George Barna released yet another disturbing study finding that less and less people in America today believe in or support Christianity. The alarming title was:

"U.S. Moving Toward Elimination of Biblical Worldview as Cornerstone of Society"[2]

Stop for a few seconds and consider the word, "elimination." It took time to reach this point. While we were sleeping, the enemy of our souls and enemies of America have worked overtime to cancel Christianity. They have planted more weeds than we have seeds.

The left has used Hollywood to accomplish this progress for godlessness. They censor believers out of television programs while adding LGBT characters to most primetime programs. They only portray LGBT people in the best possible light while depicting Christians as narrow-minded, bigoted, and ignorant. They use TV and the media to ridicule God and the Bible, and almost never show Christians in a positive light; going to church, praying, doing Christian charity work, etc.

In 2020, the Cultural Research Center worked to uncover many concerns regarding morality and the spiritual state of the nation, as well as the beliefs of professing Christians. Surveys have found a majority of Americans think man is basically good, and that we do *not* have a sin nature.

This is unbiblical, problematic, and reveals our spiritual ignorance as a nation. Because our general theology is wrong, the country cannot help but be confused or divided over many issues.

Barna recently said most Americans are oblivious to the real civil war ravaging the nation. When we disagree about foundational issues such as God as Creator, gender—male and female, marriage, family, and the personhood and sanctity of preborn lives in mothers' wombs, where can you go from there? Moral relativism and cultural chaos.

Reports on last year's findings confirm a tragic trend:

Of all Americans surveyed in general, 58% agreed that "identifying moral truth is up to each individual; there are no moral absolutes that apply to everyone, all the time." One third, or 32%, disagreed, and one out of ten adults said that they do not know.

"The typical American believes, 'Truth is what I say it is, and no one can tell me otherwise,' " the Center mourns. "Americans believe that right and wrong can only be discerned by each individual, based upon their feelings and circumstances; and that what is right for one person might be wrong for another but each must have the freedom to make those choices without external judgment."[3]

Note the emphasis on our feelings. No absolutes, no judgment, it depends on the person. There is nothing new under the sun, and the rapid decline we are seeing shouldn't surprise us. It is just so disappointing for those who know Jesus, history, and the kind of country this used to be.

Jesus once responded to a question by saying no one is good except God alone, so if we want a good country, we must be a people who love Him and live by His laws. I believe we once did.

You've probably heard the following quote most often attributed to historian Alexis de Tocqueville (1805-1859) as he visited the US to find the reason for our national success. He looked everywhere, but:

> "Not until I went into the churches of America and heard her pulpits aflame with righteousness did I understand the secret of her genius and power. America is great because she is good, and if America ever ceases to be good, she will cease to be great."

True Christianity breeds strong families, and the Word of God boldly proclaimed in righteousness leads to a moral, stable, prosperous culture. We need to relearn this powerful point: our nation is only as strong as its churches and spiritual leaders.

Tragically, our country is suffering and our goodness has been decaying.

Last fall, I attended a pastor's conference in Dallas, Texas. I had grown weary fighting the good fight and at times, felt somewhat alone. I was trying to be a watchman on the wall at a time when church had been deemed nonessential and was going along with the pandemic charade.

The conference was put on by Liberty Pastors and was called "America at the Crossroads: a 911 Call to Patriot Pastors." It was exactly what I needed. Since that time, I have been blessed to get to interview many of those pastors and speakers on a podcast called *Stand Up for the Truth*.

I was encouraged to know there is a growing movement of godly men committed to sound doctrine, building the church, and to speaking the truth. They understand why we need to equip the saints while refusing to be silent about cultural evil.

Considering the battle we are in, I came across this quote again from John Calvin:

> "A dog barks when his master is attacked. I would be a coward if I saw that God's truth is attacked and yet would remain silent."

And yet, in America, God's Word, the truth, has been under constant attack, along with our faith, freedoms, and the US Constitution.

You may remember a scene from the Mel Gibson movie, *The Patriot,* where the preacher at church finished his Sunday message, took off his preaching robe to reveal a soldier's uniform underneath, grabbed his rifle, and asked men in the church, "Who's with me?"

Those brave men of God are referred to as the Black Robed Regiment. They were not only preachers but also prophets of liberty and truth. They bravely led men from their congregations onto the battlefield to face the dreaded Redcoats. They were hated and feared by the British because of their faith and their influence on thousands of men in small, country churches across the land.

These men were America's patriot preachers of the eighteenth century. Wearing black preaching robes, they boldly preached about biblical truth and civil liberty. When the inevitable clash with the British came, they courageously defended liberty and set an example of sacrifice and leadership.

Many of them died fighting for freedom to be a nation that freely honors the living God.

Times change but the battles remain the same. Our liberties are again at stake, but the threat is now from within! Enemies of Christ are in places of power in our own government while too many church leaders are unwilling to stand for righteous-ness and address First Amendment concerns.

If your pastor is worried about being politically correct and accepted by the world rather than being biblically correct and seeking God's approval, that's a problem. In addition to sound doctrine and the whole counsel of God, including Bible prophecy, if your pastor isn't talking about the importance of religious freedom, worldview, the role of government, and social issues from the pulpit, please ask him to do so.

Have we not been called by Christ to occupy lands and exalt the banner of His truth, or are we simply content to let those who have no reverence for the things of God to lie, gain power, influence culture, and rule over us?

We are at a very volatile point in history. Some say the election of Biden/Harris was the death of America as we have known it. Others have said that because of President Biden's allegiance to China, his inauguration was the funeral service for the nation. I disagree. We survived eight years of Obama/Biden, the most biblically hostile and corrupt presidency in American history.

Moreover, some important things were exposed by the presidency of Donald Trump, such as how deep the swamp in Washington is, how much power the Democrat media (propaganda) and big corporate tech (censorship, favoritism) have, how the left controls public schools, and how much influence communists and globalists have over the US.

Things are dark, but we are not yet down for the count. Christians must engage! It is not just your pastor's job. What are you and I doing Monday through Saturday?

I have been encouraged by a growing movement of Bible-believing Christians no longer willing to be the silent majority. It seems when enough people feel their backs are up against the wall, it is time to fight. It also seems more believers are refusing to fear being canceled by an intolerant leftist culture and social media mob.

We had nearly forgotten our mission and purpose, but now more of us are compelled to action. Next to loving God and preaching the Gospel, the highest calling of a Christian is not to be civil or even tolerant; it is to be salt and light. This is about godly influence in society.

Lots of churches do a great job attracting crowds and entertaining, while others virtue signal by claiming to love our neighbors through social justice activism. But many of these churches are producing ideologues of liberalism rather than disciples of Jesus.

We learned just how divided the church was when George Floyd was murdered in Minneapolis. I will never know what it is like to grow up being discriminated against because of skin color. I do know, however, the enemy will use anything to drive a wedge, even between Christians. As the media promoted mayhem on US streets, the left was thrilled to have an opportunity to divide us.

Another sad part of the story is many in the church joined a Marxist cause out of emotion or misplaced compassion. Why? Because the idea Black Lives Matter is so obvious, who would not get behind it, right? (Of course they matter.) But when rioting and vandalism spread like wildfire, most of us realized it was a tactic in the Democratic Party playbook.

Then came the election fiasco of 2020 that may forever have an asterisk next to it, which could go down as the final tipping point of a nation under attack from within. A nation that had abandoned God and a church that had been going through the motions. It was not only truth that had been under attack, but our very republic under God.

One underlying condition of a healthy national soul is the faith, morality, and virtue of children. Another study was released that should also concern us. According to Barna, 74 percent of young adults known as Generation Z at least somewhat agree with the notion that what is "morally right and wrong changes over time, based on society."[4]

As you know, this kind of thinking paves the way for the gender surrender we are seeing in our culture. By this reasoning, if God's laws now change along with right and wrong, then throw out the Ten Commandments. Wait— they already did that in the early 1960s. Thank you, government-run schools for contributing to the decay and moral decline of the nation, and instilling in children a godless, warped worldview void of truth.

More than ever before, we need Christian parents who have resolved to teach their children from the Bible and from unedited history books. We need to get back to teaching how our freedoms were obtained, and what is required to maintain them.

Too many Americans have no idea how close we are to losing not only our liberty but also our nation, which is why the battle is intense.

Author and pastor Dr. Richard Lee recently wrote about knowing who we are and what we're all about, suggesting more voters are waking up and realizing we're headed in a tragic direction. Lee states that we may be on the verge of a second American Revolution.

> "...not a revolution of guns and bullets this time, but a revolution in the voting booth and in the major forums of public opinion. It's a revolution of principle, demanding accountability from our public servants and everyone else that is engaged in government on any level. It's a revolution of faith and ideas, a new commitment to a higher cause."[5]

In this nation, we are blessed to have a voice. We have the right, privilege, and responsibility to engage in the process of electing leaders to represent us—who in turn pass legislation that will affect nearly every aspect of our lives.

Remember, social and political issues are moral issues, and the Bible has much to say to guide us about what to support, and yes, even about what to look for in electing government leaders.

Think about this: somewhere between 24 and 54 million Christians do not show up to vote in elections. We know there is some level of voter fraud and cheating every election. But even if just 3-5 million more believers voted according to biblical values, elections would not even be close. We are Christians first, American citizens second. But it is our duty to use the privileges we were given to move the country toward God, not away from Him!

Since we dropped the ball and practically backed out of the public square over a half-century ago, here are some tragic repercussions: Truth has been redefined, God is mocked, prayer and the Bible expelled from public schools, God's laws from the public square, but sin is celebrated, pleasure exalted, abortion legalized; we've seen the increase of adultery, divorce, homosexuality, rampant promiscuity, Hollywood poisoning the minds of children, public schools pushing a progressive godless agenda, a lack of integrity in government, a generation now endorsing socialism, record high suicide rates among young people, radical feminism, witchcraft, legalized same-sex marriage, government corruption, political gridlock, gender confusion, sexual anarchy, racial division, social justice apostasy, and riots in our cities paid for by power elites, globalists, and those who hate America.

Don't believe rewritten history that says our founders and pastors didn't intend to live in a country influenced by God and Judeo-Christian values. That's what our Constitution is based upon—the laws of nature and nature's God!

When we hold a true, biblical worldview, we see one side that generally rejects God, family, morality, self-restraint, and truth, but sees government as god. The opposite view understands God is our creator and authority, and society functions best with healthy families including a mom and dad; that loving God and neighbor and respecting the rule of law leads to blessing.

Should we expect favor and mercy from God rather than His judgment? Is there still a chance—in a nation that God had clearly shed His grace upon—that we might repent and be saved? It is sobering to recall the very first president of the United States declared that it is "impossible to rightly govern a nation without God and the Bible." And in his first inaugural address, President George Washington stated:

"The propitious smiles of heaven can never be expected on a nation that disregards the eternal rules of order and right, which heaven itself has ordained."

Have we not as a nation disregarded God and righteousness? How then can we expect Him to bless us again? Grace. Do we deserve it? Absolutely not. Will this great American experiment be prolonged and sustained for a little while longer for the sake of the elect, God's children, His prayer warriors, and for Israel? Perhaps.

His lovingkindness is everlasting, He is faithful to His Word, He is worthy of our praise, and His sovereignty rules over all. We also know Judgment Day is approaching.

To have a healthy nation and people, we need a strong, vibrant, influential church. Despite what public schools and universities now teach, we should not forget all the good that

Christianity has done for the world. This is one of the reasons we are hated. Because God has blessed us, we have blessed others.

Later in this book, we are going to look at the global agenda against America and those who have been working behind the scenes breaking down systems to form a one-world government. Some of them have been gleefully using the coronavirus to execute their plans to tank the economy and reset our free market system.

You may be familiar with the historical cycle of freedom describing how great nations have risen and fallen through the centuries.

"The people generally go from bondage to spiritual truth which leads to great courage; from courage to liberty, from liberty to abundance and prosperity; from abundance to selfishness, from selfishness to comfort and complacency, from complacency to apathy, from apathy to dependence, and from dependence back into bondage."

Millions of Americans do not vote. What might this indicate? Apathy. Then comes dependence on government. If more so-called believers actively worked to maintain and defend our precious liberties, we would be a much different nation.

Not surprisingly, according to Pew Research Center, the number of Christian voters in the U.S. is on the decline. The latest data found 64 percent of all registered voters surveyed in 2019 self-identified as Christian—down from nearly 80 percent just over ten years ago.[6]

Looking at each major political party, 73 percent of Democrats identified as Christian (confusing, I know) in

2008, but now that number is less than 52 percent! Remember when they booed the mention of God at the 2012 Democratic Convention? No surprise here.

In keeping up with a secularized culture, 78 percent of Republican voters identify as Christian, but this is a decrease from 87 percent in 2008. Though it is unclear if Christian voters means Bible-believing, converted disciples of Christ.

Now, with the cancel culture and discrimination against Christians and conservatives on the rise, expect fewer people to admit where their political allegiance lies. This will further skew the already inaccurate, confusing national polls.

The left gets away with padding the polls, lying, double standards, and hypocrisy. They also avoid any scrutiny for their unrelenting attacks and doublespeak because there is no accountability in the Democrat media any longer. Fair-minded people acknowledge the Trump administration endured relentless pressure and opposition from day one.

The fury of an ideologically driven media, godless socialist politicians, globalists, power elites, and a PC culture was poured out on one man. The mob—which includes Big Tech giants—is now going after those who supported President Trump, and of course, Christians.

But since Biden was *elected, the left says we must unite and work to heal America. Really?

WHEN THE LEFT MENTIONS UNITY, THEY MEAN SUBMISSION

President Joe Biden and many on the left called President Donald Trump a dictator for years, and yet, Biden issued more executive orders in his first week in office than any of the forty-five previous presidents. I bet you didn't hear that from the liberal media activists.

Joe Biden claims to want to heal and unite the country, but no one really believes him. He went right along with impeachment proceedings of President Trump. Make no mistake: the left doesn't want unity; they want submission. What have they been doing the past four years? Attack, obstruct, resist, oppose!

President Biden signed thirty-three executive orders in one week! For a little perspective, Bill Clinton signed two executive orders his first week in office. George W. Bush signed one. President Obama signed five, and President Trump signed four.

Democrats get away with hypocrisy because a friendly media covers them like a soft, cozy blanket.

One of the most concerning movements among the Democrat Party, however, is the growing idea that Christians, conservatives, and Republicans who supported President Trump need to be reeducated or deprogrammed. Some are openly talking like this now.

It's not only the rabid late-night comedians and mouthpieces on CNN and MSNBC, discredited former CBS News anchor Katie Couric rebuked Republicans who opposed impeaching President Trump, and suggested the 74 million Americans who voted for him need to be deprogrammed.

> "The question is how are we going to really almost deprogram these people who have signed up for the cult of Trump?"[7]

Some even implied he was a Nazi—but they should look in the mirror. Can you imagine if we started calling for reeducation camps for leftist Democrats in the cult of Liberalism?

One of the new radical party leaders, AOC, tweeted some words of advice for the Biden administration immediately following his inauguration. She said progressives "must begin creating justice, healing our planet, and improving the material conditions for all people."

This one statement is loaded with socialist jargon, but justice? Remember, when liberal Democrats use that word, it is not biblical or equal justice they want. Moreover, if you are creating justice, then you are talking about something that doesn't exist yet.

Also, in January, AOC gave orders to Abolish ICE (US Immigration and Customs Enforcement). Lest we forget after the November 2020 election, she implied Trump supporters, which she called sycophants, should be held accountable for supporting him. Let that sink in.

AOC wants an archive of records to be gathered on Republicans. Just like their pleas for unity, their idea of justice is just as empty and godless. Moreover, this sounds like communism.

The Biden/Harris Democrats are not concerned about finding common ground and uniting the country. They have complete control of all three branches of government. We will see how President Trump's SCOTUS picks and federal judicial appointments weigh in on upcoming court cases, especially those involving religious freedom. Ironically, the courts may now be one of our few saving graces.

The fake idea of unifying behind Biden was a ploy to get votes. His rhetoric about peace and healing the country was a hollow campaign slogan that went down the toilet as fast as his first executive orders were signed. And he campaigned to save America's soul?

The Biden White House executive orders killed thousands of jobs on the Keystone XL pipeline, halted oil and coal leases, rejoined the awful Paris climate accord and the World Health Organization, cut off funding on the border wall, stopped the deportation of illegal aliens, and declared special rights for anyone identifying as transgender.

According to one of the most divisive orders by a president, boys who identify as girls must now be allowed to compete in girls' athletic competitions, men who identify as women must be allowed in women-only spaces, health care plans must cover gender transition procedures, and doctors and hospitals must perform the surgeries.

You may find interesting what then Senator Joe Biden said just last October:

> "I have this strange notion, we are a democracy ... if you can't get the votes ... you can't [legislate] by executive order unless you're a dictator. ...We need consensus."

For those keeping score, President Biden signed a record forty-two executive actions, orders, or declarations his first ten days in office (currently over fifty)! Do what he says, not what he does.

This is not about politics; it is a worldview war. One with God, and the other, without God. What kind of country do you want to live in? Remember, the enemy of our souls hates America and the foundation she was built upon. That Rock was Christ. All other ground is sinking sand.

I realize it is difficult for many people to comprehend why people *within our own borders* would want a godless society and to sink this great nation. This battle is spiritual, first. Therefore, a big part of the solution must be the awakening, repentance, revival, and strengthening of the church.

But none of our efforts will stop the left. They have practically assembled a coalition of groups to unite for a common global, anti-American purpose: control over the United States of America.

Though not an exhaustive listing, the following groups and entities supported Biden/Harris for the White House and (now work together) for the ultimate prize. They include:

ABC, Abortion businesses, ACLU, Amazon, Antifa, Big Tech, Black Lives Matter, CBS, CFR, China, CIA, CNN, Communist Party USA, Corporations, Deep State, Democrat socialists, Dept. of Education, DOJ, Environmentalists, Facebook, FBI, Fox, Globalists, Google, Hollywood, International Bankers, Islam, Labor Unions, LGBT, Marxists, Mainstream Media, Muslim Brotherhood, NARAL, NBC, National Education Association, NBA, *New York Times*, NFL, NPR, Open Borders advocates, PBS, Planned Parenthood, Russia, SPLC, Socialists, Twitter, United Nations, Universities, WFTU, Witches/Occult, World Economic Forum, YouTube.

Many of these entities want a different kind of country. On the surface, they came against President Trump, of course, because he ruined their plans to coronate their elite, progressive queen, Hillary Clinton, in 2016. But they also oppose our Christian history, the Constitution, capitalism, and what America represents.

The spiritual forces behind them want change, and—just like the Fabian Socialists who came here in the 1930s and 40s—they have been hammering away at our founding principles and culture to mold the US in their image. The Pledge of Allegiance offends them, in God they do not trust, and the national anthem is not their anthem.

Many of them may not realize their unspoken allegiance is to communism, and the spirit that drives them is anti-Christ. The chaos we've seen on the news over the last five-plus years is all part of a smokescreen meant to distract people from seeing the truth. Much has been brought to light, however, in recent years, and more of us are catching on.

Enemies of America almost seem possessed to achieve their goals no matter the cost. They justify destroying life, property, societal structures, and authority to gain power for their evil lords. It is demonic at its core, and as we have seen, they will hold nothing back.

One problem is many people think this will somehow not affect them or their families personally. How unbelievably naïve and ignorant. It seems we have been fighting a war that a big part of the army does not know we are in.

We must follow the advice of the bold Christian preacher and evangelist, George Whitfield:

"Resolve for Christ, resolve against the devil and his works, and go on fighting the Lord's battles against the devil and his emissaries; attack him in the strongest holds he has, fight him as men, as Christians, and you will soon find him to be a coward; resist him and he will fly from you."

There are patriot pastors standing up for the truth across the country. There is also a growing movement of godly leaders, influencers, and believers actively living out their faith in every aspect of society. The work to preserve America and biblical values can be summed up in three words: Pray. Vote. Stand.

In 2020, then Senator Joe Biden declared the primary reason he decided to run for president was to reclaim the soul of America. But actions speak louder than words, and so do his controversial and divisive policies.

Our way of life in America and especially our freedoms are more precious and vulnerable than most of us realize. It has been said politics are downstream from culture, meaning culture influences government. Ideally, religion should be shaping culture, which in turn shapes politics.

If we love our God and our neighbors, we will naturally want to preserve the country we live in. The bigger task, however, is to spur into action those on the sidelines who claim the name of Christ. We must repent, confront evil in our nation, focus on Christ, and prepare for what is up ahead.

But too many Christians have been deceived to think the church should keep out of politics. We will address this next. The Lord has been patient with us, but His patience will not last forever.

2

The Second Biggest Lie in America

"The general principles, on which the Fathers achieved independence, were the only principles in which that beautiful assembly of young gentleman could unite… And what were these general principles? I answer, the general principles of Christianity, in which all these sects were united; and which had united all parties in America, in majorities sufficient to assert and maintain her independence. Now I will avow, that I then believed, and now believe, that those general principles of Christianity are as eternal and immutable as the existence and attributes of God…"[8]

—John Adams, 1813, letter to Thomas Jefferson

The principles of Christianity are eternal because the Lord Jesus Christ is the everlasting God and He once said, "Heaven and earth will pass away, but My words will not pass away" (Matthew 24:35). We live in a nation once founded on and influenced by the Word of God.

Too many Americans, however, have been duped into thinking God's Word and Christian influence must be kept behind church walls and out of government. This lie is parroted by the left and even many believers have fallen for it!

The second biggest lie ever told and believed by hundreds of millions over the last century is the separation of church and state. It is not found anywhere in the US Constitution. "Stay out of politics" they say, completely ignoring our history and founder's intent.

But wait, what is the biggest lie, you ask? Evolution—the theory suggesting there is no God or Creator, and that intelligent design is not plausible. Evolution holds that life suddenly began on its own, that something exploded out of nothing. Eventually, human beings evolved from a form of animal such as apes, which evolved due to a change in characteristics over many generations.

But this chapter will address the mission and role of Christians and our dual responsibility as citizens of heaven and citizens of America, especially relating to civil government and the Gospel.

Throughout church history going back to the first century, Christians believed religion and government (church and state) were two distinct entities. They also believed, as the apostle Paul wrote, that though they have completely different functions, these are not incompatible, and are both established by God.

In today's world and generally in America, however, we have come to accept the dangerous and unbiblical view that the state is the supreme social authority and therefore can control, regulate, or govern the church. Therefore, we have been debating about our complete submission to government and to what extent churches should obey state orders during the COVID-19 crisis.

It was not long ago that the church was considered part of the Kingdom of God. Like our founders, the great reformer Martin Luther looked at the church and state as two kingdoms, both having different authority. Some scholars have dubbed his view "The Two Kingdoms Doctrine," as Luther interpreted God ruling over the world through both the spiritual and the secular.

In 1523, Luther wrote "Secular Authority: To What Extent It Should Be Obeyed." This expresses the principle of Liberty of Conscience, forbidding human authorities from coercing or interfering in people's spiritual beliefs. Each kingdom should work for the glory of God, for the good of mankind, and the preservation of human life.

About the kingdoms of church and state, Luther wrote:

> "These two kingdoms must be sharply distinguished, and both be permitted to remain; the one to produce piety, the other to bring about external peace and prevent evil deeds; neither is sufficient in the world without the other."[9]

Knowing that "all Scripture is inspired by God," up until seventy-five years ago, men of God would rebuke, correct, and call out sin from the pulpit (2 Timothy 3:16). They were not afraid to apply God's Word to politicians and those in positions of power.

Luther also explained that the rebuking of authorities "is certainly not a revolutionary act when it is done at the Divine command and in accordance with the law of God, openly, fearlessly and honestly. It would, in fact, be much more dangerous," wrote Luther, "to the public weal if a preacher were not to rebuke authority for its injustices."

Today's church leaders generally do not practice church discipline, let alone rebuke someone for sin. Not too long ago in history, men of God would not rely on the media to hold politicians and those in power accountable. Why? Because the decisions of governing leaders affect the church!

And how do you separate your faith from what you do outside of church? Regarding the laws that are legislated—whether they are good laws or bad laws—do you not want to have a say? When you vote, do you leave Jesus outside the polling place just in case you want to support a candidate or a cause that goes against the Word of God and biblical teachings? How absurd.

> "In the total expanse of human life there is not a single square inch of which the Christ, who alone is sovereign, does not declare, 'That is mine!'"
>
> —Abraham Kuyper

Jesus is Lord of all. That means everything, every part of my life including how I worship, how I live, my family, what I do for work, how I respond to evil, and yes, what I approve of by voting in elections. What do you consider sacred or biblical? Then what do you consider secular or political?

For those who know the true history of America's founders and have read some of the early American writings and documents, these debates are tedious. In the abundant material and extensive documentation that we have available to us today, our founders wrote about, referenced, or quoted the Bible 92 percent of the time!

This reinforces the fact that the God of the Bible dominated early thinking and influenced government, laws, and society. Since most of those men were Christians, an overwhelming majority believed in the one true God of the Holy Scriptures.

We understand that the left (a term *generally* interchangeable with atheists, communists, Humanists, modern Democrats, socialists, Marxists, and/or globalists) has changed. Many values liberals held until the 1960s are now held by conservatives but scorned by leftists. These radicals want to keep Christ out of culture, Christians out of the public square, and God out of government. That is the essence of their thinking when it comes to the separation of church and state.

We are commanded to go into all the world and make disciples of all nations and preach the Gospel to all peoples. Knowing that our founders sought to influence society with biblical morality, righteousness, virtue, and Judeo-Christian values, do you honestly think those men would want to separate religion from politics?

Many Americans today think this is the case. How did they come to this conclusion? I will answer that with another question. Who controls the narrative, the education, and information in America? The left. And the father of lies.

As evidenced in his textbook, *History of the United States*, published in 1832, the great Noah Webster believed Christianity and government could not and should not be separated:

> "The religion which has introduced civil liberty is the religion of Christ and His apostles, which enjoins humility, piety, and benevolence; which acknowledges in every person, a brother or a sister, and a citizen with equal rights. This is genuine Christianity, and to this we owe our free constitutions of government."[10]

Even among Christians, many believe we should not get involved in what they consider political issues. This is often just an excuse for not wanting to engage. They think we must let government handle everything and we just need to quietly go about our business.

The truth is the two most important things we could talk about are religion and politics! Religion has to do with God, salvation, faith, worship, how we live this life and what happens in the next. Politics has to do with government, authority, who decides public policy, legislation, enforcing laws, keeping order, punishing evil, and rewarding those who do good.

One definition of politics is: "The science of government; that part of ethics which consists in the regulation and government of a nation or state, for the preservation of its safety, peace and prosperity; ...political activities characterized by artful and often dishonest practices."

As believers, what is our duty and responsibility to government as good citizens? Should we be informed and involved in the political process or just keep to ourselves? Are we to be concerned about our neighbors and community or are we to focus primarily on our own family and church? I submit to you we can and must do both!

When considering the declining morality of our culture, daily headlines, and pivotal issues that affect our lives and religious freedoms, here is an important question to ask: Is it biblical or political? For example, can we call abortion a political issue when we know a fetus is a human life with a beating heart, and that one of the Ten Commandments tells us not to murder?

Christians look to Scripture for our answers. We look at context for applications on how to live a godly life according to what the Bible teaches. God's Word explains His heart when it comes to our involvement, government, laws, and rulers in society.

BIBLICAL OR POLITICAL?

Let us go back in history to the year 1450 BC when Moses petitioned Pharaoh for the liberty of God's people, Israel. He even called down consequences when the pagan king failed to comply with Moses' demands.

In 870 BC Elijah challenged King Ahab and his advisors in the name of the Lord for their ungodly practices and policies. Should Elijah have overlooked evil and stayed out of it?

In AD 29 John the Baptist confronted King Herod about his sinful lifestyle and pointed to the Ten Commandments. It cost John his ministry and life. But too many Christians today would say he should have kept quiet. Was John the Baptist wrong for calling out evil?

Sometime between AD 30-33 the Roman governor, Pontius Pilate, took Jesus into the Praetorium the second time and said to Jesus,

> Do You not know that I have authority to release You, and I have authority to crucify You?" Jesus answered him, "You would have no authority over Me at all, if it had not been given to you from above; for this reason, the one who handed Me over to you has *the* greater sin" (John 19:10-11).

Was Jesus being political when He replied in this way, stating that there is a higher authority than Rome and implied there are consequences to sin? If your state governor were involved in an illegal trial with no evidence of guilt and no eyewitnesses to the charges, would you be bold enough to stand for truth and justice or would you avoid it because it's a political issue?

Approximately AD 32-33, two pillars in the Christian church, Peter and John, were told not to publicly preach (or speak!) in the name of Jesus. What would you do? Should they just have submitted to the governing authorities?

We know the end of the story. They refused to comply with the Jewish leaders:

> "But Peter and John answered and said to them, 'Whether it is right in the sight of God to listen to you rather than to God, make your *own* judgment; for we cannot stop speaking about what we have seen and heard' " (Acts 4:19-20).

Were Peter and John being too political? Should they have obeyed? We can answer this question by looking at verse 33:

> "And with great power the apostles were giving testimony to the resurrection of the Lord Jesus, and abundant grace was upon them all."

If God gave them power, blessed their efforts, and gave them abundant grace, who are we to say they should have obeyed orders and kept silent? And if there is any doubt that God wants His children to evangelize, notice He commended the apostles for their efforts. He also however, allowed them to be severely beaten (flogged). But upon their release, how did they respond?

> "So they went on their way from the presence of the Council, rejoicing that they had been considered worthy to suffer shame for *His* name. And every day, in the temple and from house to house, they did not stop teaching and preaching the good news of Jesus *as* the Christ" (Acts 5:41-42, NKJV).

Would we rejoice if we suffered shame for the name of Jesus? Do people outside church know we are Christians?

In AD 54 the apostle Paul preached the Gospel in Ephesus, a very pagan city, and he disrupted the business and politics in the region.

Jumping ahead to North America in the year 1775, should Christians not have literally fought for their freedom? Was it wrong of Pastor Jonas Clark in Lexington, Massachusetts, to lead his church and community to form a militia and face the British in the war for independence?

In 1830, Reverend Charles Finney preached about the holiness of God and stirred hearts of people during the second Great Awakening. Was he wrong to call for an end to slavery? Should he have kept cultural and social issues out of the pulpit?

In 1954, did you know Dr. George McPherson Dougherty preached a sermon convincing President Eisenhower to include the words "under God" in our Pledge of Allegiance? Oops! Separation of church and state! Take 'em out!

In 1963, was the civil disobedience of Dr. Martin Luther King Jr. wrong because he should have obeyed governing authorities at the time? The Baptist minister led civil rights marches and called for equal rights of all men. It cost him his life, and he is hailed a hero.

In 1973, was it wrong for people to protest *Roe v. Wade* and the legalization of abortion, also known as the murder of preborn babies? Was the decision of the Supreme Court sinful, or were those disputing the law sinning? Since that evil decision, Christian men and women have been fined and arrested outside clinics for protesting millions of babies aborted every year.

In 1986, just six years after the SCOTUS struck down a law requiring the Ten Commandments to be posted in

Kentucky public schools, the Court decided all restrictions on abortion were unconstitutional.

Would you consider these actions of Christians and Jews to be political or biblical? I believe we can walk and chew gum at the same time, or in this case, preach and protest. We must obey God's commands to make disciples by preaching the transformational Gospel of Jesus Christ, and only then can we make a dent in the current darkness.

Fast-forward to 2021.

In late February, the radical so-called Equality Act was being debated in Congress, and Florida Republican Greg Steube warned that passing the bill would go against Scripture. Kudos to him for pointing to the ultimate authority of the Bible. He said transgender individuals are implying God didn't know what He was doing when He created mankind. Steube added:

> "The gender confusion that exists in our culture today is a clear rejection of God's good design. Whenever a nation's laws no longer reflect the standards of God that nation is in rebellion against him and will inevitably bear the consequences," he said. "We are seeing the consequences of rejecting God here in our country today."[11]

Consequences indeed. But the headline here is how Democrat Jerry Nadler responded. Keep in mind, this was in the US House of Representatives, meaning Nadler represents his Democrat constituency. He retorted:

> "Mr. Steube, what any religious tradition describes as God's will is no concern of this Congress."

In other words, take your God and your worldview and leave them out of politics. If you've been paying attention in recent years, it's not surprising Nadler and the Democrats would attack someone espousing Christian principles, but take note how emboldened they have become.

Translation: the left can push their wicked worldview and legislate immorality, but we must keep our faith out of the halls of Congress, legislation, and the public square. This is another reason believers must refute this lie about separating church and state.

One of the most frequent comments or questions I receive from believers has to do with wanting their pastor to discuss political issues and confront evil when necessary. People tell me they are disappointed because they see it as fear of man or a failure to lead their congregations.

To be fair, some pastors and churches are out of balance and are too political. Some social justice apostates hated President Trump and let their congregations know. Others are Trump apologists and defended his every move while ignoring his personal faults. Most Christians could likely support his policies and decisions, but they had difficulty with his pride and abrasiveness at times.

The bottom line is Donald Trump was the man for the job. God anointed him for such a time in history—for His purposes. To me, he was a type of Cyrus, the pagan king God anointed and used greatly (see Isaiah chapter 45). He was a firewall preventing further weakening of America, globalism, and an end to religious liberty.

Avoiding anything deemed political is simply irresponsible. The separation of church and state is a lie from the pit of hell. Please stop believing it.

We need to talk about things from the pulpit such as abortion, creation (male and female!), secular education, transgender ideology, adultery, divorce, natural marriage between one man and one woman, homosexuality, LGBT issues, true equality, true justice, sex trafficking, idolatry, Islam, persecution, socialism, Marxism, communism, and more.

According to recent surveys, an overwhelming majority of Christians want their pastors to at least mention if not address these things on Sundays from the pulpit. Is it too much to ask of our spiritual leaders to connect the dots and help believers apply what the Bible teaches, especially regarding prophecy, current events, and what's going on around us?

With the Scriptures as our guide, we can accurately discern the times, know what was fulfilled by Jesus at His first coming, what world events are currently unfolding, as well as prophecies that are still to come. But it is beyond tragic that so many of today's American churches are uninformed about the end times, cultural issues, and the war on truth.

One report from last year was so out of balance it is heartbreaking. Church leaders were surveyed, and they admitted the Bible addresses these things and yet, most pastors avoid talking about them.

Writing for *Christian News Network,* Heather Clark pointed out that most believers want church leaders to address the role of civil government as well as tough topics.

> "Barna Research reports that more than 90 percent of theologically conservative pastors agree that Scripture addresses all aspects of life," the ministry outlined in a press release. "Yet just 10 percent said they were willing to speak to issues like abortion, religious liberty, and sexual identity from the pulpit."[12]

What happens when spiritual leaders avoid crucial issues? The people tend to do the same.

The subtitle of my 2015 book, *The Cost of Our Silence,* is "Consequences of Christians Taking the Path of Least Resistance." What we are seeing today is due in part to decades of Christians hiding their light, refusing to speak up, and keeping their faith out of the public square.

There certainly is a remnant of bold patriot pastors, but we desperately need some new, fearless men of God to come into leadership in our churches.

Think about the fact that in early church days when Christianity was new and unpopular, emperors such as Nero and others harshly persecuted followers of Jesus. Christians were jailed, beaten to death, and even used as human torches to light the streets of Rome. They knew their faith could cost them their lives. Many refused to deny Christ anyway.

And some of us are afraid of a virus, a state governor, a mocker, or an LGBT activist.

Have you ever found yourself wishing you had said something to someone, but didn't? Have you ever felt the urge to warn others, to cry out against wickedness, injustice, and the blatant promotion of sin in our culture? You are not alone! Don't beat yourself up. Ask the Lord to help you to follow through next time.

If your spiritual leader, your pastor, is not setting an example of faith over fear, teaching the whole truth, and engaging culture rather than ignoring evil, perhaps he has also believed the lie about keeping church and state separate. Perhaps it is time you approach him in love and truth.

We should mention the 1954 Johnson Amendment. This unconstitutional law paved the way for the squelching of free speech in America. How, you ask? The amendment was used to censor the political speech of conservative and anti-communist groups at the time who were speaking out against then Senator Lyndon Johnson. Sounds like what is happening today.

Johnson wanted to limit what could be said by churches and nonprofits. For whatever reason, many church leaders today are uncertain about the law and what it restricts, as well as the underlying (perceived) threat to a church's 501c3 nonprofit status. Due to confusion and misinformation, many religious leaders have been unnecessarily self-censoring for decades.

Naturally, the left has used the Johnson Amendment to bully Christians and churches to keep out of culture. They prefer we stay out of politics—and out of the public! Just keep your faith behind closed doors. For true, Bible-believing Christians, this is as unthinkable as it is impossible.

Time for a sobering moment of self-evaluation. If we are worried about the government, if we are concerned about the IRS revoking our church's 501(c)(3), then are we serving Caesar or Christ? Have we become that comfortable, and have we forgotten our persecuted brothers and sisters suffering in nations where the Gospel is forbidden and Christianity is restricted?

By the way, persecution is not on its way to America; it is here. More Christians are being banned, bullied, censored, discriminated against, fired from jobs, kicked out of schools, mocked, sued, and persecuted today. We were warned:

"Do not be surprised, brothers and sisters, if the world hates you" (1 John 3:13).

This is part of God's plan, and it is no reason to back down. Because most believers have been silent, the nation has suffered greatly. Moreover, the world is imploding, time is running out, and the door through which people can be saved is closing.

God rebuked the early church for being lukewarm and leaving their first love. What would He say to us today? We know Jesus is returning soon, but we don't know when. As sobering as it is, judgment will begin with the house of God.

Where is our faith?

If we do not inform more people and teach them the truth, the left will keep advancing in power. They will do everything they can to remove Christian influence from culture and government. You would think this would be an impossible task.

In the true history of America, there are countless examples of biblical declarations, speeches, quotes, and prayers offered by men who understood the importance and necessity of the Christian faith. But they are not handed down in families and taught in schools. The Bible, prayer, and politics often went together. They should go together today as well!

President John Quincy Adams stated:

"The hope of a Christian is inseparable from his faith. Whoever believes in the Divine inspiration of the Holy Scriptures must hope that the religion of Jesus shall prevail throughout the earth…"

It certainly seems obvious men in early government were not thinking about keeping Christianity separate from the state. For the honest researcher, there is overwhelming evidence. We must reeducate those willing to hear the truth as we teach or reteach our children.

The great impact of the Bible on America is an indisputable part of our history. God ordained the Church of Jesus Christ, and He also ordained civil government. Pilgrims arrived on these shores of North America with the stated goal of giving glory to God and advancing the Christian faith.

The separation of church and state would be a ridiculous, laughable concept to our founders and early patriots. It should be laughable to us as well. We will prove this as we explore the great impact Christianity has had on America and what made the church essential in the first place.

3

The Historic Impact of Christianity

"And as it is our duty to extend our wishes to the happiness of the great family of man, I conceive that we cannot better express ourselves than by humbly supplicating the Supreme Ruler of the world that the rod of tyrants may be broken to pieces, and the oppressed made free again; that wars may cease in all the earth, and that the confusions that are and have been among nations may be overruled by promoting and speedily bringing on that holy and happy period when the kingdom of our Lord and Savior Jesus Christ may be everywhere established, and all people everywhere willingly bow to the sceptre of Him who is Prince of Peace."   —Samuel Adams, 1797

Jesus Christ founded the Church on the Day of Pentecost and it has been going strong for over two thousand years! The overwhelming evidence for the tremendous, positive influence of Christianity worldwide is undeniable. And yet, some not only minimize Christianity's impact, but they also claim we would be better off without the church.

The truth is that no one has impacted and improved the world like Jesus Christ!

Satan has been successfully deceiving people into thinking Christianity is to blame for many of the world's problems.

Since people have fallen for such lies, how can this be overcome?

Like refuting the separation of church and state lie, we must replace what is false with truth!

This is not a PR problem for God, but a consequence of the truth war. Christians shaped America. Hundreds of millions of people have been transformed by Jesus Christ because the United States was built on, strengthened, and blessed by Christianity.

Some of these life-changing biblical principles include:

the value and sanctity of every human life, the abolition of slavery, the dignity and respect given to women, the stability of the family, advances in science, hospitals and health care, labor ethic and practices, economic freedom, educating the poor, feeding the hungry, caring for the sick, reforming laws to protect the weak, art, literature, architecture, education, philosophy, compassion, charity, justice, and equality.

You would have to be uninformed, in denial, or indignant to argue that the Christian church has not been a tremendous instrument for good or that Christians have not turned the world into a better place over the past 2,000 years. The church has its shortcomings, but they are heavily outweighed by its vast benefits to mankind through history. Now, what about the United States?

Anti-Christian and anti-American programming has led to people having a negative impression of God and the church today. For more than fifty years now, studies have concluded that fewer young people see the Christian faith in a positive light.

It seems the drastic decline in morality in America coincides with the all-out war on biblical values and rebellion in the culture. Why would people not appreciate teachings about loving God and their neighbor, compassion, forgiveness, family, generosity, respect for life, justice, hard work, sexual purity, thanksgiving, hope, and more?

Because they replaced God with one in their own image. It is vital we reeducate and inform others about the historical contributions of Christianity and show them how essential the church is to sustain a society like ours.

Let's start with the eternal and spiritual aspect of the Christian faith. Heaven and hell are in fact, real places, and destinations; this life is but a vapor. Because of the amazing love of Jesus, His sacrifice and offer of forgiveness, and the grace of God, it is remarkable more people are not pouring into churches.

Christianity is the only religion that offers real hope beyond this life, power in the present, everlasting peace, the assurance of salvation, and true joy regardless of circumstances.

Other religions say, "do, do, do," but Christianity says, "done," because Jesus completed the sacrificial work God, the Father, sent Him to do. It was finished at the cross. So then, we walk by faith, increase in spiritual fruit, and live in obedience to the Bible's teachings.

The early church and Christian movement was empowered by the Holy Spirit. Early Christianity grew in prestige and power by boldly and unapologetically preaching the Gospel. Christ's message of salvation and redemption was an individual responsibility and blessing. Individuals of faith make up strong, healthy communities.

The essence of a nation can be seen in the foundational building blocks of its principles, values, and institutions. Our growth, influence, and success as a nation are due to being established upon the Judeo-Christian worldview.

Communism, Marxism, Islam, and socialism do the exact opposite. In these kinds of societies, freedom is often hard to come by while women and minorities are discriminated against.

From Hollywood and the media to academia and Big Tech, the Christian faith is often maligned, mocked, and misrepresented. This caustic climate of humanism, secularism, socialism, moral relativism, and pluralism is dangerous for the church and the country.

In addition to vastly improving morality and enhancing human life, some of the fruit of Christianity and the Bible include: countless charities, relief organizations, missions, food programs, shelters, orphanages, recopying manuscripts, words, symbols, building libraries, music, the arts, and schools for the underprivileged.

Let's look at a few major areas in which Christianity had major worldwide impact. Sure, there are many topics such as education, the real liberation of women, marriage and family, sexual morality, and the dignity of labor, but I want to give special attention to our history involving the value of every human life, to slavery, to compassion and charity.

Some key principles were foreign to the Roman Empire in the first several centuries. One big difference between societies influenced by Christianity and others is a basic respect for life.

THE VALUE OF EVERY HUMAN LIFE

The conscience of Rome was dark and seared. They were executing Christian martyrs, assassinating kings or emperors, slaughtering gladiators in the games, supporting infanticide, and suicide was apparently encouraged. It was a heartless and calloused attitude toward life in general. Killing newborn infants soon after birth was quite common.

Gladiatorial games began in Rome around 264 BC and by the time the church was formed there, crowds had watched hundreds of thousands of gladiators and wild animals die brutal deaths for the cause of entertainment. Sometimes the shows lasted for months at a time. It took a few more centuries to reverse this bloodlust and disregard for life. It was the teachings of Christianity, including concern for the weak and oppressed, that led to the cancellation of the games.

The Bible and Christian church caused people to rethink the twisted morality, which supported such a low value of human life. Today, there are even native tribes in parts of the world who no longer subscribe to cannibalism thanks to the principle of the sanctity of human life. Humanity has made much progress through the centuries, but never without a fight.

As part of the worldview war, advocates of global warming and climate change suggest the environmental and social problems in the world are caused by overpopulation. They say we are breeding too many human beings for the earth to handle. Their agenda advocates controlling, regulating, suppressing, and even eliminating human beings.

Population control is nothing new. In America, Margaret Sanger's impact has been detrimental to life and has led to millions of abortions every year (an abortion every twenty-six seconds!). Sanger was an atheist, racist, eugenicist, and socialist who founded Planned Parenthood, coined the phrase "birth control," and placed her first clinics in black neighborhoods.

Sadly today, the whole abortion business thrives on murdering babies and making a profit. Planned Parenthood even sells aborted baby body parts to the highest bidder for research, vaccines, and other unjustifiable evils. Self is god, choice is a right, the Bible is irrelevant, and abortion is healthcare. This warped worldview literally prevents parenthood and justifies child sacrifice.

Christianity, on the other hand, teaches life begins at conception, every human being has value and is made in the image of God, and a pregnant woman is said to be with child. Biology and science back up what Scripture teaches about human life. The God of the Bible strongly condemns abortion, child abandonment, human sacrifices, infanticide, and suicide. Jesus, for example, said, "Let the little children come to Me, and do not hinder them" (Matthew 19:14).

Of the many verses differentiating Christianity with other worldviews, John 10:10 states:

"The thief comes only to steal and kill and destroy; I came so that they would have life, and have *it* abundantly."

Due to the influence of Jesus Christ, by the year 374, a Christian named Valentinian was the first Roman emperor to formally outlaw infanticide. The influence of Christianity on life continued and became the norm throughout Europe. This is one of the greatest legacies of the Christian faith. In much of the world today, anti-infanticide laws remain in effect—except for partial-birth abortion being a legal practice in parts of the United States and the West.

Christians in the Greco-Roman culture opposed the custom of child abandonment as well as infanticide. The church father, Clement of Alexandria, condemned the Romans for saving and protecting birds and other animals while abandoning their own offspring.

Talk about a disconnect. It reminds me of today's environmental crusaders wanting to save the planet and of course, protect animal life, while defending the brutal, life-destroying practice of abortion.

It is no surprise Christians were the first to take in human castaways and often adopt them. It must be stated that being pro-life is not just about exposing the evils of abortion, but actively protecting and supporting all life, including the elderly and disabled, as well as children of prisoners.

From bishops and emperors to church councils and historians, the public defense of preborn lives increased through the centuries and anti-abortion laws were established worldwide. Thousands of canons (rules) were issued by the church and many societal governments would then pass state laws banning abortion.

One issue Protestants and Catholics have historically worked together on was pro-life causes. Martin Luther used extraordinarily strong words condemning abortionists. Also, in 1945, Christian pastor, Dietrich Bonhoeffer declared:

> "Destruction of the embryo in the mother's womb is a violation of the right to live which God has bestowed…"

His words were typical of theologians and prominent men of God up until the 1970s when liberalism and secularism infected churches like a virus. Regarding abortion (murder), many mainline churches conformed to pop culture and rejected God's Word as well as the church's long-standing position on the sanctity of life.

The intrinsic worth of each individual man and woman, boy and girl, as a child of God and an immortal soul, was introduced by Christianity.

Until about seventy-five years ago, true feminists cared about the whole woman (spirit, soul, and body), and almost universally opposed abortion. Modern feminists, however, support sexual promiscuity, vulgarity, and abortion at any stage for any reason. The so-called Women's March in 2017 was a shocking display of open rebellion against God, Christianity, and of the proud celebration of sin.

Regarding abortion, the need for repentance is great. Both men and women in many churches across America could be free from the bondage of guilt and remorse if they confessed these sins. Encouraging or helping commit abortions is also a sin.

Finally, people are generally unaware of what Susan B. Anthony (1820-1906) said on the issue:

"I deplore the horrible crime of child murder [abortion]… No matter the motive, love of ease, or a desire to save from suffering the unborn innocent, the woman is awfully guilty who commits the deed; … but oh! Thrice guilty is he who for selfish gratification, drove her to the desperation which impelled her to the crime."[13]

ABOLISHING SLAVERY

Next, the abolition of slavery as well as the rejection of racism and racial segregation have their roots in Christian teachings. Throughout history, when human beings were treated harshly, unjustly, and without dignity, Christians were the ones who spearheaded reforms. Jesus offered Himself to all individuals, classes, nations, and tribes.

No people, nation, organization, or religion has done more regarding the freedom, social reform, and education of minorities than the Christian church. At a time when slavery was a common practice, it was the Bible that revolutionized people's thinking about equality. In Galatians 3:28, Paul declared individual believers are all one in Christ Jesus, and further stated, "there is neither Jew nor Greek, slave nor free."

Writing to church leader, Philemon, the apostle Paul made an appeal for his son in the faith, a runaway slave named Onesimus. He had run away, received Christ, and was ministering to Paul in prison. Paul sent him back with the letter to Philemon, his owner, asking him to treat Onesimus as he would treat Paul, and to consider Onesimus,

> "no longer as a slave, but more than a slave, a beloved brother, especially to me, but how much more to you, both in the flesh and in the Lord. If then you regard me *as* a partner, accept him as *you would* me" (Philemon 1:16-17).

This was a radical shift in thinking at that time, especially in a culture that had such a low value of human life in general and in which slavery was widely accepted.

Written as a poem and put to music around the 1840s, "O Holy Night" was the first Christmas song to be played on the radio (1906). Describing the thrill of hope when Jesus became flesh and appeared to mankind, a weary world rejoiced in the redemption offered to all people.

But note the third verse proclaiming in Christ, the slave is our brother, and the end of oppression. This comes from the biblical application of Paul's letter to Philemon describing how we ought to acknowledge every believer. We are all members of the family of God.

"Truly He taught us to love one another;
His law is love and His Gospel is Peace
Chains shall He break, for the slave is our brother
And in His name, all oppression shall cease"

In Luke chapter 4, Jesus read from the scroll of Isaiah about releasing the oppressed. God sent Jesus to preach the good news to the poor and to proclaim freedom to the captives (Luke 4:18-19). These were important causes for the church to take up.

Christians who led reforms include Basil of Caesarea, also known as St. Basil the Great (330-379), a theologian who preached against wealthy people who had no concern for the poor. He established centers to distribute food to the needy and set up places to provide both lodging and medical care.

Bartolome de Las Casas (1484-1566) traveled to the West with Columbus but ended up settling in Hispaniola (the Dominican Republic) and spent five decades fighting for the rights of indigenous people of the Americas.

Puritan minister, Roger Williams (1603-1683), was the founder of Rhode Island, one of the first abolitionists, and a religious freedom advocate.

Philosopher and Quaker, William Penn (1644-1718), founded the Commonwealth of Pennsylvania and believed in treating the Indians and minorities with charity and justice. His deep faith and dedication to God's Word drove his life and must be remembered.

"I do declare to the whole world that we believe the Scriptures to contain a declaration of the mind and will of God in and to those ages in which they were written; being given forth by the Holy Ghost moving in the hearts of holy men of God; that they ought also to be read, believed, and fulfilled in our day; being used for reproof and instruction, that the man of God may be perfect. They are a declaration and testimony of heavenly things themselves, and, as such, we carry a high respect for them. We accept them as the words of God Himself" (*Treatise of the Religion of the Quakers*, p. 355).

William Wilberforce (1759-1833) was a Christian abolitionist who also served as a member of England's House of Commons. He spent forty-four years working tirelessly to abolish slavery. Just before his death, Parliament passed the Abolition Act, resulting in 700,000 slaves being set free. Seven years after he died, the British Empire abolished slavery for good. (The 2006 movie, *Amazing Grace*, chronicles Wilberforce's efforts.)

These achievements are even more astounding when you consider the fact that prior to Jesus Christ, slaves made up about 75 percent of the population in Athens, Greece, and over half of the population in Rome. And contrary to modern revisionist history and the media, long before Columbus arrived in the New World of America, slavery was practiced by many Indian tribes.

Sadly, even after slavery was outlawed in the United States in 1865, the practice continued in other countries for another hundred years.

According to the human rights organization, You Can Free Us, over 45 million people are enslaved in the world today! Women and children make up 95 percent of modern-day slaves, and 80 percent are used in sexual exploitation. Houston is one of the busiest hubs, and human trafficking has surged to over a $150 billion industry.

According to author and former professor, Alvin J. Schmidt, people's general ignorance on this topic is due to the mainstream media's refusal to report the truth about slavery, and due to deconstructed history in public school textbooks. Schmidt writes:

"Ethiopia had slavery until 1942, Saudi Arabia until 1962, Peru until 1964, and India until 1976. Moreover, it still exists to this day in Sudan, Africa's largest country.

"Politically correct media and school textbooks give the impression that slavery has primarily been a sin committed by white people who enslaved blacks. The fact that only about 25 percent of Americans in the South had slaves before the Civil War is commonly not mentioned, nor is the fact… 407 black Americans in Charleston, South Carolina, alone owned black slaves."[14]

In his incredible book, *How Christianity Changed the World,* Schmidt goes on to explain how the media also refuses to report the amazing work Christian Solidarity International is doing in Sudan. They literally buy slaves to set them free! Tragically, more than three million Sudanese Christians—mostly slaves—have been executed in recent decades.

But America is evil and racist? It is true some pagan societies and even church fathers continued to condone slavery, and the practice was revived in various countries, but for Christians there is no biblical justification to support it.

Christianity was the foundation for the American civil rights movement, court decisions, liberating laws of the 1960s, as well as efforts spearheaded by Martin Luther King Jr. The

Bible supports the protection of the weak, innocent, and vulnerable, including rules about the treatment of employees, orphans, widows, and foreigners. Because human beings are made in the image of God, they have eternal worth.

More influential men and women in these areas should be noted before concluding this chapter:

Constantine, Licinius, Theodosius II, Justinian, and Afra of Augsburg (former prostitute who became a Christian and ministered to abandoned children), St. Augustine, St. Chrysostom, Norway's King Magnus, John Calvin, evangelist George Mueller (established orphanages and cared for more than 10,000 children in sixty years), Amy Carmichael, and Robert Raikes.

Others deserving of mention include clergyman Elijah Lovejoy (the first martyr of the American abolitionist movement 1837), Eric Liddell, Irene Webster-Smith, Mother Teresa, Edward Beecher, Charles Finney, Charles Torrey, William Garrison, and Julia Ward Howe (wrote "Battle Hymn of the Republic" in 1862).

Harriet Beecher Stowe (1811-1896) wrote the classic book, *Uncle Tom's Cabin*, a vivid portrayal of slavery that caused President Abraham Lincoln to remark in jest, "So this is the little lady that started this great war." Her father, Dr. Lyman Beecher, was a minister and founder of the American Bible Society.

Though it is hard to ignore its Scripture references, redemptive theme, and the main character clinging to the promises of Christ, we rarely hear about the Christian inspiration for Stowe's famous book. The popularity of the novel worldwide led to the thinking that abolishing slavery would be inevitable.

About *Uncle Tom's Cabin*, Harriet Beecher Stowe once stated, "God wrote it. I merely did his dictation."

COMPASSION AND CHARITY

> " 'For I was hungry, and you gave Me *something* to eat; I was thirsty, and you gave Me *something* to drink; I was a stranger, and you invited Me in; naked, and you clothed Me; I was sick, and you visited Me; I was in prison, and you came to Me.' 'Truly I say to you, to the extent that you did *it* for one of the least of these brothers *or sisters* of Mine, you did *it* for Me' " (Matthew 25:35-36, 40).

The words and example of Jesus Christ as well as His true followers through the ages have led to the loving ministry to those in need in our own communities as well as worldwide. Caring for the poor, weak, handicapped, and needy is a direct result of the Christian faith in action.

So many churches, charities, nonprofits, and charitable organizations could be noted here, some of which include Samaritan's Purse, World Vision, Food for the Hungry, Lutheran World Relief, Mercy Ships, Compassion International, and Medical Teams International.

Throughout American history, the church of Jesus Christ has done more than any other people group and institution in history to alleviate poverty and care for those in need. Space and time do not permit me to detail many of the advancements in education, medicine, science, and the reforming of child labor laws resulting from Christian influence.

The Salvation Army is a Christian international charitable organization reporting a worldwide membership of over 1.7 million. Founded in 1865 in London by Methodist preacher

William Booth and his wife, Catherine, they sought to bring salvation to the poor, destitute, and hungry by meeting both their physical and spiritual needs.

Present in 131 countries, the Salvation Army runs charity shops, operates homeless shelters, and offers disaster relief and humanitarian aid to developing countries. Their doctrine focuses on Jesus, holiness, and the Wesleyan-Arminian tradition. The Army's purposes are "the advancement of the Christian religion ... of education, the relief of poverty, and other charitable objects beneficial to society or the community of mankind as a whole."

Next, the YMCA was founded in the 1840s and has served more than 20 million people worldwide. Established for the purpose of "winning young men to Jesus Christ and building in them Christian character," the YMCA combined physical activities with educational and religious activities.

According to Rose Publishing,[15] dozens of Christian relief organizations do so much good for America and the world employing more than 30,000 humanitarian workers, shipping more than 225 metric tons of food, and handling disaster relief for millions of people annually. They serve the needy with food, clothing, medical care and supplies, small loans, drinkable water, and shelter.

We could also list deserving Christians through the centuries who have greatly blessed society and were influential in education, science, medicine, arts, literature, philosophy, and more:

Johannes Gutenberg, Boethius, Martin Luther, John Calvin, Friedrich Froebel, Robert Grosseteste, Nicolaus Copernicus, Galileo Galilei, Blaise Pascal,

Johannes Kepler, Isaac Newton, George Washington Carver, Florence Nightingale, Henry Dunant, and Louis Pasteur.

CONCLUSION

We have touched on a handful of biblical values, world-impacting influential Christians, and charitable organizations that made the church essential. Someone once said, "The hinge of history is on the door of a Bethlehem stable."

Writing by the influence of the Holy Spirit of God, the apostle John stated that Jesus was and is eternal; that He, the Word, was with God at the beginning of time and became flesh to dwell on earth at a specific point in history (John 1:1, 14). He stepped out of eternity into time so that He might offer Himself to save fallen, helpless mankind and to bridge the gaping chasm between sinful man and holy God.

Jesus Christ was not a political figure and had no affiliation with kings, governors, or religious leaders of His day. He made no demands, lived in poverty, taught with authority, and His followers were mostly uneducated. And yet, they as well as those influenced by them impacted millions more than Alexander the Great, Muhammad, and Napoleon put together. Jesus changed history and turned the world right side up.

Imagine the worldwide darkness without Him and His Holy Spirit. From His earliest disciples who were transformed by His life, death, and resurrection, to His followers today, the world has truly been dramatically and fundamentally altered for the better. Christ's resurrection compelled their faith and gave them hope; it does the same for us today. As a result, the fruit of Christian teachings have produced revolutionary changes in every way imaginable.

Christianity has made the world a better place, and so has America. We dropped the ball big-time last year in the face of a virus and closed our life-preserving churches leading to the label of "nonessential." What a lie. We must reverse that narrative by being the true church, preaching the Gospel, working to demonstrate God's love, and showing the church is alive, well, and vital.

4

Did the Church Pass the COVID Test?

"In this you greatly rejoice, even though now for a little while, if necessary, you have been distressed by various trials, so that the proof of your faith, *being* more precious than gold which perishes though tested by fire, may be found to result in praise, glory, and honor at the revelation of Jesus Christ" (1 Peter 1:6-7).

"For God has not given us a spirit of fear, but of power and of love and of a sound mind" (2 Timothy 1:7, NKJV).

Toward the end of 2020, *Merriam-Webster's Dictionary* announced the word of the year: "pandemic." "Panicdemic" might be more accurate. The word has now come to be associated with an extended period of time rather than just a technical term or health threat.

Last year began one of the most difficult years for many Americans and people around the world. We were pressed and refined to the point of practically being forced to let go of any resemblance of "normal" life—if such a thing even existed. I believe the church was tested big-time. How do you honestly think we responded to the COVID test?

To those who abide in Him and bear fruit, Jesus said He will prune us so we can be even more fruitful (John 15:2). James encourages believers to understand the testing of our faith produces endurance (James 1:3-4). Peter said to rejoice in trials that prove our faith genuine (1 Peter 1:6-7). And Paul told Timothy to suffer hardship as a good soldier of Christ Jesus (2 Timothy 2:3-4).

I believed at the time and still believe this was and is good for us, and we know God causes all things to work together for the good of those who love Him (Romans 8:28), and for His glory.

Jesus will ultimately be glorified by the true church as He seems to be separating the sheep from the goats. We often consider normal to be good, but it is not always best. People have said they cannot wait to get back to the "new normal."

According to *Webster's Dictionary*, normal is defined as: "conforming to a type, standard, or regular pattern; characterized by that which is considered usual, typical, or routine." A routine often turns into a rut, and prior to last year, I think the church had generally been in a rut.

Clearly, 2020 was anything but usual, typical, and routine. We had and maybe still have a God-given opportunity to break free from normal. The Christian faith is not and never has been normal! This time in history has been one of the biggest tests of the American church. Biblical morality, our influence, and faith in God had already been on a rapid decline over many decades.

Some pastors did their best to navigate COVID-19 and made some creative efforts so they could hold services. Kudos. But too many pastors neglected to address the demonic, global influence that drove the shutdowns worldwide.

The conflicting opinions by the "experts" must be mentioned here. Some doctors said one thing, some said another, and then they contradicted themselves! This happened more than once and Dr. Fauci was one of them. It was a confusing time. For nearly every new development on handling the virus, there was an accompanying conspiracy theory. Some of them were true.

The COVID crisis was used as a springboard to strangle America and implement evil. The left made it about President Trump. Joe Biden and others blamed Trump for the deaths in the US but somehow did not blame NY Governor Andrew Cuomo, whose policies led to the highest number of nursing home deaths in the country.

Sadly, many believed the Democrat media narratives and jumped on the blame-Trump bandwagon. The American economy was booming and here came a virus out of Wuhan, China. This, after more than three years of relentless opposition and resistance to President Trump, including crude jokes, personal attacks, impeachment efforts, obstruction, and accusations of bigotry and racism.

Think about this war of words for a moment. Even as Christians, when we hear something repeated over and over, then hear it from multiple sources, we tend to believe it. Do you not think it is important for church leaders to speak some clarity and truth to crucial national events?

How did the church react to a new virus, to the fearmongering of the liberal media, medical expert contradictions, church restrictions, reports of people dying from COVID-19, nursing home horror stories, and to governor's heavy-handed lockdowns, ordinances, and mask mandates?

How did the world generally react? Fear and panic. Why? All they have is this life. Death, to them, is the end. Christians, on the other hand, are to trust God and have no fear of death. Jesus overcame death and the grave. Because of Him, our faith overcomes this world!

I think of the wonderful song, "In Christ Alone." Note the third verse:

No guilt in life, no fear in death
This is the power of Christ in me
From life's first cry to final breath
Jesus commands my destiny
No power of hell, no scheme of man
Could ever pluck me from his hand
'Til he returns or calls me home
Here, in the power of Christ, I stand

But how did we generally respond to the Rona? If we are being honest, I am not sure we passed that test. Some pastors stayed the course, but overall, I think we caved. We all but surrendered our religious freedom under the guise of obeying those in authority. But does Scripture teach *unlimited* submission?

If the Christian church in America is vital to the overall health of the nation and if we have the answer to sin, man's greatest problem, then why didn't we act like it? The virus also revealed what many of us already knew: the unbelieving world sees the church as nonessential. They told us by their words and their policies.

In our short history, there have been few times that people needed God and the good news of Jesus Christ more—and most churches had closed their doors. Tragically, some are still closed! Others are not operating at full capacity due to state restrictions, lawsuits, and people choosing to stay home and watch online teachings.

Have we lost or forgotten our mission? Have we failed to trust a known God with an unknown future? The Bible says we have not been given a spirit of fear! And yet, too many professing Christians went right along with the world in part because liberal media activists told us to be afraid. Fear the unpredictable virus and that crazy orange man!

Individual believers in Christ are to be sanctified and set apart from this world, to live holy lives pleasing to God. You and I are the temple of the Holy Spirit, meaning that every believer is indwelt with the Spirit of God. For the record, we are talking about the same power that raised the Lord Jesus from the dead.

Holy Spirit! Nothing should stop us from preaching the Gospel, praying with others, speaking the truth, having communion, standing for righteousness, meeting together, and ministering to the saints of God!

The church is not a building, a program, or a place. The Greek word for church is *ekklesia* or *ecclesia*, which is defined as "a called-out assembly or congregation." It is vital we understand that the church is a gathering of like-minded believers.

We are to meet regularly for the teaching of God's Word, fellowship, communion, prayer (Acts 2:42), and to encourage one another. The saints must be equipped (Ephesians 4:12) and then commissioned to ministry. Videos are useful tools, but how do we do all this by watching an online sermon or service? The writer of Hebrews told Christians to "draw near to God with a sincere heart in full assurance of faith…" and adds:

> "Let us hold fast the confession of our hope without wavering, for He who promised is faithful; and **let us consider how to stimulate one another to love and good deeds, not forsaking our own assembling together,** as is the habit of some, but encouraging one another; and all the more as you see the day drawing near" (Hebrews 10:23-25, emphasis added).

We must be the church, all the more as we get closer to Jesus' return! We need to be there for each other, and whether they realize it or not, the world needs the Christian church! The real danger to America, however, is not a virus or a physical health issue; the danger is spiritual. If you have not noticed, warfare is off the charts and the enemy has pulled out all the stops.

If the church is not open, what hope is there for people struggling with depression and anxiety or suffering from despair, loneliness, or mental health issues? It is no surprise we have seen suicide rates skyrocket and calls to help lines shoot up 600 percent or more in the last year.

People are seeking answers. Medication, illegal drugs, pornography, entertainment, gaming, and alcohol prove to be horrible comforts. 2020 helped us understand the repercussions of isolation, excessive fearmongering (media panic porn), seclusion, covering our faces with masks, heightened levels of anxiety, and even limited physical contact through social distancing.

Human beings were not meant to live this way. The enemy knows this. We need personal interaction, love, physical touch, relationships, and fellowship. At a time when more people were faced with extreme levels of stress, major life adjustments, financial hardship, and even their own mortality, many have not only felt helpless but also hopeless.

Did we miss an opportunity? Now more than ever, more people are looking for answers, they are open to prayer, and are seeking spiritual things. But some churches never opened back up.

To be fair, some people have legitimate and serious health concerns such as compromised immune systems, but others who are avoiding church have no excuse. I hear people admit they enjoy staying home and watching a teaching online. You can watch a video anytime! If your church is open, get back into fellowship. If it is not, find a biblical church that stayed open.

Be wise, take precautions, and be responsible. But do not give in to fear of the Rona.

We have the right to worship our God however and whenever we chose to do so. Freedom of religious expression is one of our first and most basic rights under our Constitution. The God who gave us life also gave us liberty. America is the first republic in world history to declare in a governing document that rights come from God, *not* from government!

If government does not provide our rights, how can that government take them away? Last year, many of us watched helplessly as Christian pastors across the country were threatened and fined for holding in-person church services. Then came the glaring double standards.

Recall at that time Black Lives Matter riots (the liberal media referred to them as "peaceful protests") in many cities, businesses were destroyed, and even Bibles and American flags were burned in the streets of Seattle and Portland as Antifa mobs took over public property.

Abortion businesses and liquor stores were not restricted and remained open. At one point last year, you could still take the life of an unborn baby—legally—but you could not go to the dentist unless it was an emergency. Many bars, pot distributors, and hardware stores stayed open. Governors shut down private businesses and public facilities, but abortions continued.

When a handful of conservative state governors issued orders to stop surgical abortions, Planned Parenthood and other facilities refused to comply and remained open, defying health concerns as well as federal guidelines at the time.

Leaders in the abortion industry told clinic workers they were staying open and would disobey orders.

What did most pastors across America do? They told their congregations they had to close because, you know, the virus and the governor! What was the message to Americans? Abortion is essential; the church was not. Public events and gatherings were closed along with schools, restaurants, businesses, and other nonessential services.

Why did Planned Parenthood abortion businesses get a pass? They are an affiliate of the Democrat Party. Let us clarify, then, exactly what is essential. Food, water, electricity, hospitals, gas stations, public safety, counseling services, law enforcement…and abortion?

I even saw a big banner outside one Planned Parenthood that read, "Our Doors Stay Open." While most of the world—including hospitals and the actual medical profession—were doing whatever was necessary to save lives and stop the spread of the virus, abortion advocates insisted on destroying lives.

To remind young people that sex, pregnancy, and abortion are essential, they even placed an ad campaign on Facebook saying:

> "Planned Parenthood's top priority is ensuring that every person can continue accessing essential health care, including abortion. We know your health care can't wait."

How many pastors and churches put ad campaigns on social media saying something like, "The church is essential, and our top priority is to ensure everyone hears the good news of Jesus Christ? And every person who needs hope can access prayer or counseling because we know your salvation and spiritual life can't wait"?

It has been well established that a fetus, a preborn life in a mother's womb, is a human life at conception. How then, is abortion a necessary, health-related medical procedure? A couple hundred years ago, we would not even be having this conversation!

But kudos to the small number of churches out of more than 300,000 that did not close their doors and remained open. Kudos to those who closed at first for a few weeks or so, but then opened back up. Thank you to those bold, faithful men of God who recognized how vital the Christian church is to the health of Christians, our communities, and our country.

Admittedly, in some states, churches were severely handicapped by government. But even in California where restrictions on Christians are the harshest and churches were ordered to shut down, several pastors fought back. Some are involved in lawsuits and are still battling Emperor Gavin Newsom's draconian orders.

Thanks to godly men, including pastors Jack Hibbs, John MacArthur, Mike McClure, Shane Idleman, Rob McCoy, and others who decided to have church and found ways around the restrictions. At Grace Community Church, for example, they gathered with a full house in obedience to the Word of God, after which Pastor John MacArthur received a letter from Los Angeles county officials threatening fines and possible arrest.

We are talking about fines of $1,000 a day if the church did not comply—for holding a worship service. In America. MacArthur responded by saying, "It has never been the prerogative of civil government to order, modify, forbid, or mandate worship." Amen!

Fox News host Shannon Bream asked him about the seriousness of COVID-19. Part of his reply was that in a state with 80 million people, 9,000 had died *at the time* related to the virus, which has a 99.98 percent survival rate! MacArthur added:

> "We feel like we are the most essential reality in the world. Look, Jesus is Lord … He is the head of our church. Governor Newsom is not the head of the church. [Los Angeles] Mayor [Eric] Garcetti is not the head of the church."[16]

Fact: The Constitution does not give government power to regulate church services.

ROMANS 13 AND THE RONA

We are to submit to government, its laws, and those placed in authority, and yes, according to Scripture, all authority is established by God (Romans 13:1). Christians must be known for respectfully obeying authority. The short answer is, however, we do not need government permission to have church and worship the Lord as He commanded.

Since the Bible is our ultimate authority, then we also must ask why there are so many examples of disobeying government in the Bible. In fact, those who defied authority or broke laws for godly purposes were commended by God. Here are a few examples:

- The Hebrew midwives "feared God and did not do as the king of Egypt commanded them." They ignored Pharaoh by saving the Jewish baby boys—including Moses's parents saving him (Exodus 1:15-21, 2:1-10).
- Rahab disobeyed a command from the king of Jericho, was spared, and is even listed in the great Hall of Faith in Hebrews chapter 11.

- Moses refused Pharaoh and sided with the Jews because he feared God. In Hebrews 11:27 it states, "By faith he left Egypt, not fearing the wrath of the king...."
- Queen Esther approached the king uninvited to save the Jewish people from annihilation (Esther 4:10-16).
- Shadrach, Meshach, and Abed-Nego refused to bow to the golden image of Nebuchadnezzar (Daniel 3:1-23).
- Daniel defied the king's ordinance when he refused to stop praying to the God of Israel (Daniel 6:1-13).
- Jesus did not obey the Jewish Sabbath laws (Matthew 12:1-14, John 18:31).
- The apostles and early Christians refused orders to stop preaching the Gospel (Acts 5:27-29, 12:1-4, 16:19-24).
- More believers through the ages defied ungodly authorities, knowing they would endure harsh treatment (Hebrews 11:35-38).

Christians are to resist a government or authority that commands or compels evil. In the case of America, we can work within the laws of the land to elect godly leaders and when necessary, change any government that permits evil.

Civil disobedience is allowed when ordinances or laws violate God's law and commands. But when we disobey an evil government, we should also be prepared to accept possible punishment for our actions.

If you are still wondering if these kinds of actions and words conflict with Romans 13 and 1 Peter 2, the Bible does teach obedience to kings, governors, police, and employers. They must not, however, try to use their authority over church services or forbid our obedience to God's law. Scripture does not grant ruling authorities jurisdiction over the church!

Jesus declared that "all authority in heaven and on earth has been given to Me" (Matthew 28:18). When government places restrictions on believers such as church attendance, singing, and social distancing, it makes it difficult to worship freely, minister to people, and participate in communion.

We have been so blessed in America. Government interference or intrusion into our churches is quite foreign to us. Rather than the exception to the rule, persecution of the church has been the norm throughout the ages. Remember this as we move through uncertain times in our country and endure more leftist tyranny.

> "Blessed are you when *people* insult you and persecute you, and falsely say all kinds of evil against you because of Me. Rejoice and be glad, for your reward in heaven is great; for in this same way they persecuted the prophets who were before you" (Matthew 5:11-12).

The early church had to deal with harsh and hostile rulers just for claiming the name of Christ. Two main persecutors of Christians have historically been government and false religions. So, we must strive to find that balance of "we must obey God rather than men" (Acts 5:29), and, "if they persecuted Me, they will persecute you also" (John 15:20).

God is faithful, Jesus is King, and we do not need the government's permission to worship Him. Since blue-state governors came down hard on Christians and churches, few were surprised late last year when they turned to restrict Thanksgiving and Christmas gatherings. Their main message? Fear the virus, avoid people, and stay home.

Just a week or so after the November 2020 election, Joe Biden voters gathered on various city streets and other places to celebrate the Marxist coup. At the time, we were told not to gather with family for Thanksgiving. Celebrate Democrats, good; be with family or go to church, bad.

Apparently, the virus was awfully intelligent and selective. It knew not to infect any Black Lives Matter protesters, Antifa thugs, or to bother leftists crowding together to celebrate. But for everyone else, it was time for Lockdown 2.0, the holiday edition.

Democrat governors in CA, WA, MI, WI, VA, IL, NY, and others laid out detailed (some suffocating) restrictions on holiday gatherings. Basically, emperors Newsome and Cuomo said church, Thanksgiving, and Christmas were not essential. The CDC warned at that time for people to avoid in-person gatherings and—(ready?)—to celebrate virtually (online).

Like her tyrannical Democrat colleagues, Michigan governor Gretchen Whitmer issued rules and recommendations for residents who gathered for holidays including:

- If you get together inside, include no more than two households or ten people.
- Wash hands regularly and try not to share utensils.
- Wear a mask. Take it off when you eat or drink, then put it back on.
- Keep six feet apart as much as you can.
- When possible, keep voices down.

Wisconsin governor Tony Evers signed an executive order advising people to stay home and save lives! Message: Fear the outside world. Be responsible and don't kill people!

Previously, Evers boasted that Wisconsin contained the virus. It was under control around July of 2020, but cases surged in the fall. This happened after he already locked down businesses, public places, and imposed church restrictions, including mask mandates.

The logical question is, if masks and mandates work, why weren't those measures effective? Same story in a few other blue states with the tightest public lockdowns. Excuses were the irresponsible citizens, or a second wave, or that darn president who, according to Joe Biden, killed over 200,000 Americans with the virus.

Governor Evers said that every day "this virus goes unchecked is a setback for our economic recovery." It is interesting he did not seem to care as much about the economy prior to the election. He said, "Businesses, families, and farmers will continue to suffer if we don't take action right now."

But action was taken months earlier! Apparently, it did not work. The CDC also said people should bring their own food to holiday gatherings. Right. Follow the science.

In California, they have endured Democrat-dominated government for decades. For holidays, the CA Department of Public Health stated that "all persons planning to host or participate in a private gathering" must comply. To what, you ask?

Governor Newsome's mandatory restrictions included:

- No more than three households are permitted, including hosts and guests.
- The host should collect names of all attendees and contact information in case the state or local county wants to contact trace the guests later.
- Thanksgiving must be held outside.
- Food or beverages must be in single-serve disposable containers and those serving food must be in masks.
- The gathering may only be two hours or less.
- Attendees may briefly go inside to use restrooms if the facilities are frequently sanitized.

What happened to the land of the free and home of the brave? How did so many people put up with this in states across the country? What would our great grandparents think? What would our Founding Fathers think?

About California's restrictions, Liberty Counsel founder Mat Staver said:

"The same Governor Gavin Newsom that has encouraged thousands of total strangers to protest together in the streets now wants to impede upon the freedom of families and friends to enjoy their Thanksgiving holiday. For some families, Thanksgiving will not include Grandma and the children or siblings.

"Imagine family members traveling for hours only to be restricted to a two-hour outdoor gathering without physical contact! What if the weather is too hot or cold or it rains? For Governor Newsom to think he has authority to micromanage a private family Thanksgiving dinner is the height of hubris. These restrictions are ludicrous."[17]

IT CAME UPON A COVID CHRISTMAS

In another glaring example of government overreach, New Mexico's radical governor, Michelle Grisham, penalized two churches for holding Christmas Eve services and for having too many worshipers. Legacy Church and Calvary Church in Albuquerque were fined $10,000 each for not following state mandates!

Grisham (D-NM) condemned Christian leaders as pro-virus, rebuked churchgoers, and called them selfish. But months earlier, she praised Black Lives Matter protests, naturally, and was unconcerned about laws or viruses.

Grisham had banned Christians from corporate worship by mandating that churches limit attendance to 25 percent of building capacity. The churches were fined for not turning away those who chose to voluntarily attend services.

Regardless of how your church handled meetings and services, government penalties for worshiping Jesus Christ should alarm us and be opposed by all Christians. Grisham and other Democrats clearly violated the constitutional rights of believers by mandating how, when, and where Christians can practice their faith.

In a sermon in January 2021, Pastor Steve Smothermon of Legacy Church encouraged believers to persevere and fight the good fight of faith! He declared the role of pastors is to lead by example and to stand up to tyranny. He is a rare gem that certainly has had an opportunity to do just that.

Responding to the governor's criticism for operating his church during the pandemic, he stated:

> "I knew that during this time, we needed to be the Church more than ever. Some people decided to slow down, but we decided to speed up. We didn't want to let this (COVID-19) shutdown, shut us down. We will never stop being the Church."

The governor hypocritically said church gatherings directly contribute to more suffering and illness, but she took the opposite view last year. During Black Lives Matter protests when rioting and vandalism broke out in New Mexico and in many US cities, she went on record saying:

> "I want to wholeheartedly commend the thousands of New Mexicans who peacefully protested in Albuquerque."

Pastors, take note: What did Steve Smothermon do at Legacy Church? They began referring to their services as protests. Brilliant! He said they will never close their doors again and added:

"We will continue to conduct peaceful protests against this Governor's orders."

Elections have consequences. Most Americans would not have put up with this just decades ago. Politics and power structures have changed in part because the people have not held their government accountable. Integrity matters. This goes for the state level up to the presidency.

Yes, people have died from COVID. Millions more die each year from many other things. How about some perspective? Are all the lockdowns, mandates, rules, and restrictions constitutional? Are they justifiable? We saw how easy it was for them to keep moving the goalposts.

Most people agree the virus is real, but the concern of freedom-loving Christians is the stability of our economy as well as religious freedom. We have allowed our lives to be drastically altered—including how we do church.

Facts are funny things. Shame on the malignant media and their peddling of panic porn. There was and is an agenda behind much of what they report. Look for stats and studies, for missing context, death rates, percentages, and overall perspective.

John MacArthur reminds us the church always refines its convictions under duress. This is not a problem to be feared. He said this is a triumphant hour for the church to be the church, adding:

"I really believe that people are searching for something that transcends the circumstances of their life, of culture, of even what's going on in our nation, especially when things are being tossed to and fro with waves of difficulty and challenges."

Especially during these trying times, the church should be coming to the rescue because we have Jesus. Our Lord said we Christians are the light of the world and must be set on a hill, not hiding at home or behind closed church doors.

In Revelation 2, Jesus commended the church in Ephesus for their faith and perseverance under hard circumstances. Then He continued by saying what should also be a warning for us today:

"But I have this against you, that you have left your first love. Therefore remember from where you have fallen, and repent and do the deeds you did at first; or else I am coming to you and will remove your lampstand out of its place—unless you repent" (Revelation 2:4-5).

A lampstand means influence and place in society. Looking back, we know from history the lampstand at Ephesus was removed. We do not know all the reasons, but the remains of ancient churches should remind us that we do not live forever and we must make sure we are doing Kingdom work.

The true church needs to be visible. Jesus is also the only hope for sinners to be saved and have eternal life. People have been concerned about physical health. The church must remind them of their most important need, spiritual life and health. In these exciting last days, most of us would acknowledge we are living in quite prophetic times. Repent, church! Mobilize and evangelize!

If you love Jesus and know the power of the Holy Spirit as well as how the early church began, what we saw last year and are still seeing is unfortunate and embarrassing. I understand the unknown virus factor at first, but sadly, we witnessed one of the greatest, most influential (at one time) institutions in world history cave under pressure.

Every aspect of our culture keeps moving further away from biblical principles, but God's Word has not changed. As lawsuits and more political pressure come against believers, however, it is probable that the Lord will use these things as a means of discipline to refine the true church.

We need to return to bold allegiance to God. The world may not appreciate the value of Christianity, and part of that falls on us. But the hour is late, and it is time to recognize evil agendas are advancing, and globalists are plotting their next moves.

It is not just about attacking Christians; their plan is to destroy, then remake America in their image. Does this sound grandiose? Keep reading.

5

The Great, Godless, Globalist Reset

"The pandemic represents a rare but narrow window of opportunity to reflect, reimagine, and reset our world to create a healthier, more equitable, and more prosperous future."   —Klaus Schwab

"Now we take Georgia, then we change America."
                              —Senator Chuck Schumer

"We need change. The pandemic brought our organizational and developmental models into a crisis. It exposed many injustices."   —Pope Francis

"The fault lines that emerged in 2020 now appear as critical crossroads in 2021. The time to rebuild trust and to make crucial choices is fast approaching as the need to reset priorities and the urgency to reform systems grow stronger around the world."
                              —WEF website

The left must be thinking, *That was easy*, as American citizens have generally allowed governing authorities to control the most basic aspects of our lives. Is this really about a virus, or is there something more diabolical behind all this?

You may have heard the following saying attributed to a Marxist leader in the 1960s: "The issue is never the issue. The issue is always the revolution."

A revolution has been underway for some time. The left is using the issues of COVID-19, racial division, church restrictions, environmental extremism, transgender ideology, hatred of Trump, immigration, and identity politics to further their godless takeover.

What are their goals and how will they succeed? Crush the middle class in America. Reset capitalism. Destroy freedom. Cause chaos, confusion, and distractions (such as a sham impeachment trial). They are patient and persistent, content to make incremental progress.

Globalists today are thrilled with everything that is going on in America. In recent years, capitalism has come under attack here as socialism and Marxism are heralded. These are but symptoms of the progressive push to overhaul the entire world economy.

Those behind the agenda to overthrow the governing system in America have been emboldened, and it goes back more than fifty years. The revolution did not begin in 2016. For example, at the United Nations Business Conference in 1974, David Rockefeller said:

"We are on the verge of a global transformation. All we need is the right major crisis and the nations will accept the New World Order."

By now, most people have heard about the Great Reset. Every year, rich and powerful elites meet in Davos, Switzerland, to plan ways to reset what they believe are antiquated systems in need of revamping. Their targets are capitalism, industry, laws, education, societies, and even people's current way of thinking and behaving.

That is a nice way of saying they want to take over the world. And this is not an exaggeration.

In fact, the purpose of the Great Reset is to use the pandemic to justify radical measures to shift the US and global economies and force a one-world government. The left has used uncertainty, fear, and unrest to their advantage while distracting most people from what they are really doing.

These measures include the apparent suspension of our constitutional rights, and if you resist, you are censored or shamed. This doesn't seem like something Americans would allow. But we did.

We have had political gridlock and division for decades, but the left ignited a well-funded and organized rebellion in 2016 that became a Marxist coup. The issue is never the issue.

In 2017 and again in 2021, the issue was impeaching President Trump. In 2020, the issue was the coronavirus. On Memorial Day weekend 2020, the issue became police brutality, Black Lives Matter, and systemic racism. The underlying cause, according to the left, is that America is an evil country that needs to be reconstructed and reimagined.

How much more could we take? Only power elites know how to fix all our problems. In the early days of the most corrupt administration in US history, Rahm Emanuel (President Barack Obama's Chief of Staff) said in an interview:

"You never let a serious crisis go to waste. And what I mean by that is it's an opportunity to do things you think you could not do before."

After eight years of Obama/Biden overreach, we understood some of what they wanted to do—and ended up doing—which is what opened the door for American citizens to want a change. That change was Donald Trump.

The left thought Hillary Clinton had it in the bag and would usher America into a global and socialist utopia. But the people intervened. The Democrat Party is a far-left extreme version of your great-grandparents' day. Ignoring half of the country, they went into attack mode, throwing everything in their arsenal at President Trump and his administration.

Leaders in today's Democrat (globalist, leftist, socialist) coalition include Barack Obama, Bernie Sanders, AOC, Kamala Harris, Nancy Pelosi, Hillary Clinton, Chuck Schumer, Joe Biden, Elizabeth Warren, Adam Schiff, Maxine Waters, Keith Ellison, Gretchen Whitmer, Ralph Northam, Jay Inslee, John Kerry, Diane Feinstein, Andrew Cuomo, Gavin Newsome, and more.

They give marching orders to the media, to their base, and to whomever is useful to the cause. Their goal is power at any cost, even if it causes suffering or death of American citizens. And it has.

In addition to defunding the police, which leads to more lawlessness, Minnesota's Democrat Rep. Ilhan Omar called for the dismantling of the United States economy and political system.

Seattle City Councilwoman Kshama Sawant said they are preparing the ground for a different kind of society:

"Because we are coming for you and your rotten system. We are coming to dismantle this deeply oppressive, racist, sexist, violent, utterly bankrupt system of capitalism. This police state. We cannot and will not stop until we overthrow it, and replace it with a world based, instead, on solidarity, genuine democracy, and equality: a socialist world."[18]

A Marxist-inspired Black Lives Matter leader said in an interview they would burn the system down if they don't get what they want.

So, what do they want? Power, compliance, obedience, submission, and surrender. They smell blood in the water. For decades, they have controlled the deep state, entire education system, the entertainment industry, unions, universities, government, corporations and sports, the liberal media, and even half the churches in the country.

If this were not enough, most millennials are now willing to vote for socialist candidates. Government education is producing pawns for the Democrat Party. The country has changed.

Five days prior to being elected in 2008, Barack Obama said the left was ready to fundamentally transform the United States of America. He meant it, and then went on to prove it.

Following the Obama/Biden administration, we had more division, more abortion, class warfare, more debt, discrimination against Christians, higher taxes, more racism, more regulations, less freedom, pro-China, pro-Islam, more illegal immigrants, more socialism, more citizens relying on government, a gutted, weakened military, and less support for our great ally, Israel.

This is the fruit of progressive policies.

So, in 2020, few Americans seemed to notice that Joe Biden's campaign slogan, "Build Back Better," was used by globalists at the World Economic Forum! Biden's campaign website openly stated part of his plan to supposedly help the economy is a bailout for state and local governments, which would force taxpayers to bail out mismanaged blue-state budgets.

Do the Democrats want to build the USA, or do they want to weaken us and build a global system? Biden, Harris, and the left say they will restore the economy by massive tax hikes, raising corporate taxes and reversing GOP tax reform (which made America competitive again internationally, thanks to President Trump).

Biden plans to extend the super-charged unemployment benefits, which could briefly help economic output in the short term, but the Congressional Budget Office concluded it would cause higher unemployment. Biden/Harris do not seem too concerned about hamstringing big business and killing jobs.

The existential threat to the world, however, according to Biden Democrats, is climate change, formerly known as global warming, formerly known as global cooling. One of the top priorities of the Biden administration has always been the environmental crisis, also known as blaming mankind and America for climate change.

And guess who was tapped as climate czar? Former Obama Secretary of State, multimillionaire globalist, John Kerry. He is now a member of the National Security Council with the Biden administration. Along with Benghazi propaganda specialist, Susan Rice, and others, it is just more of the same.

How does Kerry feel about Trump supporters and those who vote Republican? Shortly after the 2020 election last November, he was part of a panel discussion at the World Economic Forum (formerly, European Management Forum). Kerry said he was astounded that many people "voted for the level of chaos and breach of law and order…"

No mention of breaching law and order last summer as violent riots spread nationwide. Like a good Saul Alinsky Democrat, Kerry accused others of doing exactly what his own party did: cause chaos and disrupt peace on US city streets by attacking police, stirring up public fear, and vandalizing small businesses.

European Commission president, Ursula von der Leyen, was on the panel that saw Joe Biden as a key part of the agenda to transform world economic systems. John Kerry said he believes the Great Reset is more important than ever, and that "we're at the dawn of an extremely exciting time."

Kerry also touted Biden's decision to rejoin the Paris Climate Agreement, which, according to many sources, could eliminate over a million jobs in America. This could be part of the downward spiral that global bureaucrats were waiting for to bring on a New World Order.

The European Commission is thrilled to have a friend in the White House. Those pulling the strings behind the Biden/Harris administration know they can wield more power with a cooperative American government.

Ursula von der Leyen emphasized the priorities of their global agenda and the most pressing issues include COVID-19, climate change, and technology, the digital society. She added:

> "So, covering everything from data to infrastructure, but also talking about security and democracy, technology to fair taxation—all of these topics are on the table with digital change. So ladies and gentlemen, the need for global cooperation and this acceleration of change will both be drivers of the Great Reset... [T]his as an unprecedented opportunity."[19]

Let's be blunt here. When America's own leaders and citizens betray the US Constitution and work with foreign leaders to empower entities other than our own country, it is a form of treason. Imagine what our founders would do to the traitors.

In June 2020, John Kerry reveled in the possibilities the coronavirus could bring. Last June, he gleefully stated, "This is a big moment," when considering the power shift globalists could enforce using the pandemic. In fact, the WEF openly encouraged taking advantage of fearful people to change governments and economies.

In the forum's Great Reset series last summer, the WEF session was entitled, "Redesigning Social Contracts in Crisis." Wealthy, elite business and government leaders had gathered in the hopes of progressing toward a one-world government; to reset capitalism and the global economy. But a strong America and free markets have always been in the way.

President Donald Trump was also a major roadblock. Most Americans were proud of our president in September of 2019 when he spoke at the United Nations General Assembly meeting in New York City as he promoted nationalism, renounced globalism, and scolded China for unfair trade, Iran for aggression, and open border activists.

President Trump talked about the privilege he had of addressing the assembly as "the elected leader of a nation that prizes liberty, independence, and self-government," and said others seek conquest and domination.

He added that the United States "vigorously defends the traditions and customs that have made us who we are." President Trump continued:

"The free world must embrace its national foundations. It must not attempt to erase them or replace them... Wise leaders always put the good of their own people and their own country first.

"The future does not belong to globalists. The future belongs to patriots. The future belongs to sovereign and independent nations who protect their citizens, respect their neighbors, and honor the differences that make each country special and unique."[20]

Amen! He said what few have dared say in recent memory: the future does not belong to globalists! That speech spoke volumes and triggered the radical left. Game on!

Think about this for a minute. Are we to believe it was really a coincidence that at the end of 2019, unleashed by China was a virus that wreaked havoc on the world and was used to usher in suffocating restrictions on America?

The goal to reset capitalism was decades in the making, but to create a breakthrough, our economy had to be crushed, and at the same time, the country's social order needed to be destabilized. A new strain of virus out of China was just the ticket. Globally funded, Antifa and Black Lives Matter were simultaneously given marching orders.

You may have heard the Great Reset is being rolled out under the guise of a Fourth Industrial Revolution in which older enterprises are to be driven to bankruptcy or absorbed into monopolies. This would result in economies tanking, which is part of the plan.

In early 2019, *Time* magazine's cover pictured a robot with Klaus Schwab, founder and executive chairman of the World Economic Council. The issue was titled, "Your Move, Humans," and featured articles by Al Gore, Melinda Gates, Justin Trudeau, and other globalists. A key element of their agenda is the fusion of man and machine.

Just prior to the 2020 Election, *Time* magazine partnered with the WEF and promoted The Great Reset to usher in world socialism, and on the cover was a sort of reconstruction of the world. The issue was unashamedly anti-American and featured rich elites admitting the pandemic provided "a unique opportunity to think about the kind of future we want."

Notice this is about what *they* want, hammering and fashioning the world how they see fit. I am quite certain at least half of US citizens do not share the same vision or worldview. Professor Klaus Schwab was named on the cover and wrote a featured article inside.

Born in 1938, Klaus Schwab is a child of Adolf Hitler's Germany, a police-state regime built on fear and violence, on brainwashing and control, on propaganda and lies. He is schooling the world with his fascist vision, which, according to Schwab will, "create a more inclusive, resilient, and sustainable world going forward."

The WEF is described as the global platform for public-private cooperation and brings together rich and powerful leaders in society, including businessmen, politicians, and intellectuals, to advance key issues in the global agenda. It seems these partnerships are aimed at establishing handpicked and unelected individuals to lead the world and to impose the rule of the 1 percent on the rest of us.

This is about governments taking over businesses and industries, running economies; this is about serving the elites who, of course, know better than the rest of us. Schwab talks about "the fundamental lack of social cohesion, fairness, inclusion, and equality," and insists now is the "historical moment" to fight the virus as globalists "shape the system."

The thinking is that everything would be wonderful if progressive power players had control over people and production. Environmental laws, regulations, and taxation would skyrocket, but that lacks sex appeal and has been difficult for them to sell—even with the help of Hollywood actors and Greta Thunberg.

Schwab loves Thunberg, and he played a part in using her like a political pawn. But despite the media darling's popularity, climate change seemed to have lost some luster. Now with COVID-19, however, they found a new reason to call for businesses, citizens, and industries to participate in a time of healing and uniting the world as one.

Sound familiar? Imagine world peace, unity, and values. Encouragement. Pass it on!

Since the US must be canceled, some demand we have a better national anthem and suggest John Lennon's "Imagine," describing the utopian vision. No heaven, no hell, people living for today, not worrying about the future (or facing judgment for their sins). Imagine no God, no country, no borders, a one-world government, no religion, too—and "imagine all the people living life in peace."

Apart from Jesus Christ, there is no true peace. Life is temporary, man-centered, and fleeting. Jesus told His followers they would have trouble in this short life, but in Him we have peace (John 16:33).

The apostle Paul wrote to believers saying the day of the Lord's return would surprise a lot of people, and come "just like a thief in the night." First Thessalonians 5:2-5 states:

> "While they are saying, 'Peace and safety!' then destruction will come upon them suddenly like labor pains upon a woman with child, and they will not escape. But you, brethren, are not in darkness, that the day would overtake you like a thief; for you are all sons of light and sons of day. We are not of night nor of darkness."

Before 2020, people thought of safety in terms of national security or personal protection from an enemy, but some are now obsessed with masks, vaccines, and social distancing.

Take heed. It has been rightly said those willing to trade their liberty for temporary peace and safety will eventually have neither. But I fear we may have done just that.

Activists and radicals are wrecking this country, but American patriots who love religious freedom, self-government, the Constitution, and individual liberty will likely resist. Will the Democrats and globalists be able to deceive and manipulate enough people into giving up their freedom in exchange for dishonest promises of peace and health that will never be fulfilled?

Because most citizens value Americanism, they cannot be sold on Democrat policies, so the only ways to get what they want are to lie and cheat or by force. Who can forget last year's so-called peaceful protesters causing destruction and rebellion?

Remember, the issue to them is the revolution.

Under the O'Biden administration, the COVID crisis will inevitably lead to a weaker economy, increased debt, and calls for nationalized healthcare. Expect more government control and less personal freedom. With tighter restrictions and the push toward a centralized global system will come a targeted persecution of those who stand in the way.

We have witnessed some drastic measures to advance the global socialist agenda. How far are they willing to go? Just because Klaus Schwab and company tell us the world is now entering the Fourth Industrial Revolution does not mean that it is true. We do not have to accept their new normal or give in to the fearmongering.

Author, journalist, and educator, Alex Newman, wrote about the clear and present danger to our liberties that the Great Reset presents. The WEF made some predictions that people in other countries being displaced by climate change will be deported to America. Another concerning part of the agenda is no more ownership of private property. (But apparently, we'll be happy.)

Newman writes:

"Accomplishing that goal on a worldwide level will require eliminating or discrediting the American system of God-given rights protected by government. And thus, other WEF predictions include the United States losing its status as the leading superpower, with a new order featuring 'a handful of countries' that will 'dominate' taking its place. ...That is accelerating now. Even 'Western values' will be 'tested to the breaking point,' the WEF video says."[21]

Our national Judeo-Christian foundation and principles that still permeate much of our society have been chipped away. The left does not value or appreciate who we are and what we stand for, which is why they are all about faux hope and extreme change.

Last year, Joe Biden said he wanted to transform America—again! Fasten your seat belt. Christians must be prepared. Be in prayer, put on the armor of God, and stay strong in the Word!

On the surface, the left works to force change in culture and politics, but the root cause is spiritual. These forces of darkness seem almost possessed to achieve their goals. It is demonic at its core and we now know they will hold nothing back. They are ultimately against Jesus, Christianity, the Bible, and naturally—against America.

It reminds me of the Pharisees and Sadducees described in the gospels. Before Christ arrived, the two groups were enemies. But Jesus was a threat to their way of life, so what brought them together was the common goal to destroy Him and save their religion and temple.

A similar pattern is occurring today. How else do we explain, for example, both Islam and LGBT advocates supporting the Democrats? Homosexuals are often executed in Muslim countries. Hollywood typically rails against Wall Street and the rich, but in this case, both supported Joe Biden. We could list more examples of uncommon bedfellows, but you get the point.

Writing at Rapture Countdown, Keegan Fernandes warns about what he calls the imposition of a health dictatorship that will be used to advance the technological aspect of globalism. Many share his concerns about increased surveillance and contact tracing, for example.

Fernandes suggests the progressive left will fool people by promising things such as universal incomes and canceling individual debt. He adds:

"The price of these concessions from the International Monetary Fund will be the renunciation of private property and adherence to a program of vaccination against COVID-19 and COVID-21 promoted by Bill Gates with the collaboration of the main pharmaceutical groups. Beyond the enormous economic interests that motivate the promoters of the Great Reset, the imposition of the vaccination will be accompanied by the requirement of a health passport and a digital ID."[22]

Remember Bible prophecies about the increase of knowledge in the end-times? We used to wonder why more knowledge would be a bad thing and now we are finding out. Just look at our universities and the science community. The most educated and intelligent people on earth are some of the most wicked, worldly, and ignorant about spiritual things.

The last days are here and the end is coming soon—perhaps in our lifetimes. This can be both exciting and nerve-racking. This means the seven-year tribulation is approaching faster than we can imagine. Satan and his demonic forces are rushing the world toward the fulfillment of end-times prophecies involving the beast described in Daniel and Revelation.

Sadly, many things have changed forever due to COVID-19 and the advance of globalism, but one thing we must guard against is division among brothers and sisters in Christ over nondoctrinal issues. Let us keep the main thing, the main thing, and not be like the world. God has allowed this great imposition on America and the world for His purposes.

Useful idiots and globalist minions, both human and demonic, will continue working toward a new world order, basically another Babel, and rebel against the God of heaven. We know how the story ends. The stage is set; pieces are in place and moving quickly. God only knows where we will be, what will happen with America, and when Christ will return.

Here is one more excerpt from President Trump's UN Speech referenced earlier.

"The true good of a nation can only be pursued by those who love it: by citizens who are rooted in its history, who are nourished by its culture, committed to its values, attached to its people, and who know that its future is theirs to build or theirs to lose. Patriots see a nation and its destiny in ways no one else can.

"With God's help, together we will cast off the enemies of liberty and overcome the oppressors of dignity. … My fellow leaders, the path to peace and progress, and freedom and justice, and a better world for all humanity, begins at home. Thank you. God bless you. God bless the nations of the world. And God bless America. Thank you very much." (Applause.)

The ultimate agenda to rule the world will eventually fail. Moreover, it profits nothing to gain the world but forfeit your soul (Mark 8:36). Threats against Christians and the church, however, will continue as enemies of God convert more social justice radicals in the US and around the globe.

But their pathways end in emptiness, darkness, and death. Jesus is the only Way, the true light that shines in the darkness. This generation desperately needs Him. In fact, a lot can happen in just one generation and we should have learned from the past instead of repeating it.

6

It Just Takes a Generation

"For no man can lay a foundation other than the one which is laid, which is Jesus Christ" (1 Corinthians 3:11).

"Blessed are those who hear the word of God and keep it" (Luke 11:28).

"What one generation tolerates, the next generation will embrace."
—John Wesley

One thing we have learned from history is people rarely learn from history! Enemies of God have always existed, and it is not always demonic agendas that destroy godly societies. People often destroy themselves. It only takes one generation or less for a people or nation to let down their guard, relax their disciplines, become comfortable, and fall away from God.

America is in trouble in part because we have not raised up younger generations of God-fearing Christian children. Parents and pastors have not been bold leaders and teachers, our churches have not discipled effectively, and the saints have not preserved and impacted culture for Christ.

We are warned throughout Scripture to guard against apathy, deception, and the seductions of the world. The New Testament is filled with admonitions and instructions such as:

> Contend for the faith, run the race with endurance, obey God rather than man, make disciples, set our minds on things above, resist the devil, train ourselves in godliness, be disciplined as good soldiers of Christ, walk by faith not by sight, grow in the knowledge of Christ, speak the truth in love, produce lasting fruit, endure hardship, watch and pray, test all things, press on, fight the good fight of faith, and many others.

Why so many warnings, rebukes, and strong encouragements in the pages of Scripture? Because God knows human nature and the heart of man. It is easy to let up, get comfortable, become distracted or busy, pursue leisure, love this world, and slowly fall.

We often rise to the challenge during times of trial, spiritual warfare, or the extreme highs and lows of life we sometimes go through. What seems to get the best of us, however, is the everyday, mundane, uneventful routines in life.

In the Old Testament, it happened to God's chosen people even after all He had done for them. The children of Israel were living life—and an entire generation had gone by.

British evangelist, pastor, and author, Alan Redpath, offers some insights on this:

> "The best test of sincerity is not always the open hostility of foes, for this often braces up the energies of combat, while at the same time it makes the path of duty clear. Still less is at the hour of triumph over our foes, then there is no temptation to rebel. The real

test of our faithfulness to God is in most cases our power to continue steadfastly in one course of conduct when the excitement of conflict is removed, and the enemies with which we have to contend are the insidious allurements of ease or custom amid the common place duties of life."

Much of what people hear in American churches is about God's blessings and grace. It seems we have been sold on Christian life as a cruise ship when in fact it is a battleship.

Conforming to the world and allowing our faith to become lukewarm happens over many years. When this occurs, we are much less concerned about spiritual things let alone obedience to God. We can still be saved perhaps but are ineffective or unproductive as well as terrible witnesses.

Jesus taught His disciples about the challenge of seeking temporary things and losing sight of the Kingdom of God. Our biggest challenges in the Christian life are being consistent in daily Bible reading and cultivating an eternal perspective.

We must be diligent, set apart for Christ, and intentional about living for the Lord.

Joshua was a famous leader who is recognized as a great man of God. Some of his last words challenged the people of Israel to love the Lord and reject idolatry. He pleaded with them to "serve the Lord in sincerity and in truth," and to put away gods of their ancestors. He challenged the people to "choose for yourselves this day whom you will serve."

And in Joshua 24:15 comes his famous declaration of faith:

"But as for me and my house, we will serve the Lord."

To their credit, look at how the people responded immediately to his challenge.

"So the people answered and said: 'Far be it from us that we should forsake the Lord to serve other gods; for the Lord our God is He who brought us and our fathers up out of the land of Egypt, from the house of bondage, who did those great signs in our sight, and preserved us…' " (Joshua 24:16-17).

Notice that generation swore to serve the Lord God and acknowledged what He had done for them. With all they knew and saw, it was unthinkable for them to reject God and serve any other.

That is exactly how early American pilgrims and patriots must have felt in this new land. They could not imagine being back in England or turning away from the God who brought them so far. How could they forget His faithfulness?

But you know how Bible history goes. Joshua died. Then came the unfaithfulness of Israel. In our case, Joshua might be compared to Washington, Adams, Jefferson, or Lincoln; or perhaps Spurgeon, Edwards, Whitefield, or Graham.

The Bible indicates Israel forgetting their history and falling away was gradual. Also, the people did not educate their children to the extent necessary or warn them convincingly. They neglected to pass down the vital historical accounts and spiritual truths about God, about who He is and what He did for them.

Sound familiar? Volumes have been written about changes in America since 1776. To the credit of our founders and those who came shortly after, the dedication to God and the Gospel of Jesus Christ remained a focus for nearly two centuries. Just like freedom, which needs to be fought for and maintained, we must strive to obey the law, beginning with the first commandment.

In the second chapter in Judges, after stating that the people served the Lord all the days of Joshua, the author of Judges emphasizes that they also remained faithful through all the days of the elders who outlived Joshua! This was a good thing.

But the summary of what happened next includes some of the most sad, sobering words in all of Scripture. It came after documenting that Joshua died when he was 110 years old. The elders soon died as well.

"When all that generation had been gathered to their fathers, **another generation arose after them who did not know the Lord nor the work which He had done for Israel.** Then the children of Israel did evil in the sight of the Lord, and served the Baals; and they forsook the Lord God of their fathers; ...and they provoked the Lord to anger" (Judges 2:10-12, emphasis added).

Who is responsible for younger generations regarding what they know or do not know about God and history? Parents, spiritual (church) leaders, and educators.

If it can happen to His chosen people, Israel, why would we think it could not happen in America? Sadly today, the largely secular nation of Israel has still rejected Jesus, the true Messiah. Bible prophecy, however, indicates all will not be lost.

It is vital to note the progression here one more time, and God willing, learn this lesson that we might make immediate changes. The younger generation did not know the Lord, the God that their parents worshipped, nor what He did for the nation. What happens then?

The very next sentence tells us that as a result, they "did evil in the sight of the Lord" and served other gods! Know the Lord and do good; know not God and do evil. Pretty simple.

What are some of the gods or idols in America served by this generation? Heck, there's even a show called *American Idol!*

A short list may include Hollywood, entertainment, sports, travel, technology, iPhones, selfies, social media, worldly celebrities, athletes and preforming artists, sexuality, liberalism, politics, materialism, work, career, family, children, houses, cars, and more.

I told you this was sobering. But if the church is still alive and the Constitution is still the law of the land, we can learn from past mistakes and sound the alarm.

We should take a few minutes and recall history so we can analyze how tremendous progress and success was achieved here. They could not have done it without God's help!

Brave pioneering men and women risked everything to get to North America and live for the one true God, free from religious persecution. And today, we are seeing the church threatened and Christians discriminated against.

In a few generations, the left has nearly achieved their goal to eradicate Christian influence from the culture. But be assured that by the grace of God, the earliest settlers on these shores had the very opposite goal: to freely live out their Christian faith in a land where Jesus is glorified.

In 1620, it was William Bradford who wrote about their safe arrival to these shores. What was the first thing they did? The people made it across the perilous, "vast and furious ocean" and right there on the beach they "fell upon their knees and blessed the God of heaven" who delivered them.

Bradford documented the fact that they undertook such a journey to plant the first American colony, "for the Glory of God and advancement of the Christian Faith…" This is something you rarely hear mentioned anymore. Why? It is minimized or has been edited out of US history.

In the 1600s, ministers such as John Harvard established Harvard University and taught theology. Harvard College was founded under the banner, "In Christi Gloriam," as its founders believed: "All knowledge without Christ was vain."

The early Motto at Harvard in 1692 was "Veritas Christo et Ecclesiae," which means Truth for Christ and the Church. Great men of God such as John Quincy Adams, Samuel Adams, and others, graduated from Harvard. Fifty percent of graduates became ministers!

This may surprise and even shock some who were not taught the truth about America. When the Continental Congress first met on September 5, 1774, at Carpenter's Hall in Philadelphia, they all knew that their mother country, England, which had the greatest army on earth, was sending troops to America to force the colonies into submission.

They counted the cost and they turned to God, asking Him to plead their cause and fight against them. They read Psalm 35 to begin their session and John Adams wrote to his wife Abigail saying, "…it seemed as if Heaven had ordained that Psalm to be read on that morning."

Fifty-six delegates from the colonies were present to witness one of those magnificent moments in history that captured the moving of God's Spirit. Oh, to have that on video! George Washington, Patrick Henry, John Randolph, Richard Henry Lee, and John Jay were there, along with John and Samuel Adams of Massachusetts.

John Adams continued:

"After this, Mr. Duche unexpectedly to everybody, struck out into extemporary Prayer, which filled the bosom of every man present; It had excellent effect upon every body here."

At 9 o'clock a.m., September 7, 1774, Reverend Jacob Duché, Rector of Christ Church of Philadelphia, PA, offered the very first prayer of the Continental Congress:

"O Lord our Heavenly Father, high and mighty King of kings, and Lord of lords, who dost from thy throne behold all the dwellers on earth and reignest with power supreme and uncontrolled over all the Kingdoms, Empires and Governments; look down in mercy, we beseech Thee, on these our American States, who have fled to Thee from the rod of the oppressor and thrown themselves on Thy gracious protection, desiring to be henceforth dependent only on Thee. To Thee have they appealed for the righteousness of their cause; to Thee do they now look up for that countenance and support, which Thou alone canst give. Take them, therefore, Heavenly Father, under Thy nurturing care; give them wisdom in Council and valor in the field; defeat the malicious designs of our cruel adversaries; convince them of the unrighteousness of their Cause and if they persist in their sanguinary purposes, of own unerring justice, sounding in their hearts, constrain them to drop the weapons of war from their unnerved hands in the day of battle!

"Be Thou present, O God of wisdom, and direct the councils of this honorable assembly; enable them to settle things on the best and surest foundation. That the scene of blood may be speedily closed; that order, harmony and peace may be effectually restored, and truth and justice, religion and piety, prevail and flourish amongst the people. Preserve the health of their bodies and vigor of their minds; shower down on them and the millions they here represent, such temporal blessings as Thou seest expedient for them in this world and crown them with everlasting glory in the world to come. All this we ask in the name and through the merits of Jesus Christ, Thy Son and our Savior. Amen!"[23]

Thank God this was documented! A spontaneous prayer following the Scripture reading that inspired a group of patriots who began deliberations on their knees.

Now consider those we have elected to government over the last seventy-five years who legislate and run our country. How badly do we need repentance! Only by the Spirit of God can we ever hope to have revival, drain the swamp, and elect Christians to as many offices as possible.

It truly is astounding this nation has lasted as long as it has with most of our freedoms and founding documents intact. There are however, a few major indicators that reveal how evil had invaded this land virtually unchecked.

In the 1800s, Christianity was growing, and believers were gaining influence in society. That may have been the greatest missionary century in history. Unlike today, major institutions, our laws, businesses, and society in general, were influenced by Christians. Even while this was happening, however, truth was being attacked.

Back to Harvard University's beginnings. Samuel Langdon was a colonial chaplain and pastor before becoming president of Harvard in 1776. One year earlier he spoke to the Massachusetts Provincial Congress:

"We have rebelled against God. We have lost the true spirit of Christianity, though we retain the outward profession and form of it."

What happened? He seemed to be calling out hypocrisy in the church. Some men were being watchmen on the wall, warning the people about rejecting God!

As it often happens, liberal administrators and professors gradually infiltrated Harvard, leading to a change in its motto. No longer would they educate by the standard of "Truth for Christ and the Church." They decided to remove "Christ" and the "Church," which left only "Veritas" in 1836.

And just a few years ago, the word of the year, according to Oxford dictionary, was "post truth."

Harvard, along with most public universities in the land, would journey down the path of compromise, diversity, moral relativism, and political correctness, to the point that today, college freshmen can register as one of dozens and dozens of gender options.

In March of 1863, President Abraham Lincoln, with full agreement and support of the US Senate, declared a national day of fasting and prayer to God. This was only eighty-seven years after celebrating America's independence, and Lincoln was concerned about the country's pride, financial blessings, and comfort, which go hand in hand with spiritual apathy.

Part of his national proclamation and call to repentance stated:

"[W]e know that, by His divine law, nations like individuals are subjected to punishments and chastisements in this world; ...We have been the recipients of the choicest bounties of Heaven. We have been preserved, these many years, in peace and prosperity. We have grown in numbers, wealth and power... But we have forgotten God.

"We have forgotten the gracious hand which preserved us in peace; ...and we have vainly imagined, in the deceitfulness of our hearts, that all these blessings were produced by some superior wisdom and virtue of our own. Intoxicated with unbroken success, we have become too self-sufficient to feel the necessity of redeeming and preserving grace, too proud to pray to the God that made us! It behooves us then, to humble ourselves before the offended Power, to confess our national sins, and to pray for forgiveness."[24]

The 1900s saw unprecedented economic success and industrial growth. The population was growing, churches were growing, families became busier, and worldly temptations skyrocketed.

From the creation of government-run public schools and the Roaring Twenties, to the Great Depression, two World Wars, and the sexual revolution of the sixties, there is so much more we could say. But one Bible verse keeps coming up, as it is quite relevant and appropriate. It is a time-proven warning revealing the heart of mankind and a shift in morality. Isaiah 5:20 states:

"Woe to those who call evil good, and good evil, and those who substitute darkness for light and light for darkness…"

Do you agree that in the rebellion against God today, sin is being openly promoted? Where is the warning or voice of the essential church?

Remember this: man cannot make moral what God declared to be immoral. Either believe the Bible or believe the liars, deceivers, and antichrists. True disciples of Jesus should not be duped and go along with the left, the pop culture crowd, or the media mob.

Public opinion sure has shifted in the last fifty-plus years, but truth has remained the same. What changed? Did Almighty God, Creator of heaven, earth, and all things, change? Nope. The people; and worse, the churches of America.

It just takes one generation for a decline to become a falling away.

Remember the verses we read earlier from the second chapter of the book of Judges? Let's change a few words to remind us of the parallel between ancient Israel and the US today.

When God provided for the early settlers and the population grew, the Constitution of the United States was established and religious freedom was assured. Christians were elected to office, the Gospel was preached, life was enjoyed, and the pursuit of happiness was a basic blessing. As centuries went by, people placed happiness over holiness. After earlier generations had died, other generations arose who did not know the Lord Jesus or what He had done in our history.

Then citizens of America did evil in the sight of the Lord, and served other gods, such as self, leisure, money, politics, entertainment, sex, sports, and abortion; and they forsook the

Lord God of their fathers, who had delivered them from the land of England. They allowed the living God to be banned from their schools, universities, and mocked in the public square. Fewer people read the Bible and instructed their children, and they followed other gods, cults, and false religions—and they bowed down to them, provoking the Lord to anger.

Time is rapidly running out! So, what now? Look to the timeless principles in the Bible.

> "Therefore say to them, 'Thus says the LORD of hosts, "Return to Me," declares the LORD of hosts, "that I may return to you' " (Zechariah 1:3).

Yes, we are surrounded by evil. There is a war on truth. This nation's moral and spiritual foundations have been altered, culture is collapsing, and our defenses need reinforcing. But God!

We must overcome the temptation to seek our own comfort or desire worldly success. We must overcome evil with good (Romans 12:21). And, just like Joshua, just like many early American pilgrims and patriots, no matter how others choose to live, may you and I declare, "But as for me and my house, we will serve the Lord."

Are we willing to fight for our families, our children, and the next generation? Then we must fight for truth to prevail, resist worldly philosophies, and strive to protect and value every human life made in the image of God.

7

*Lives That Matter to God:
Christianity vs. Marxism*

"And He has made *from one blood every nation* of men to dwell on all the face of the earth, and has determined their pre-appointed times and the boundaries of their dwellings" (Acts 17:26, emphasis added).

"The problem is not with the quest for social justice. The problem is what happens when that quest is undertaken from a framework that is not compatible with the Bible. Today many Christians accept conclusions that are generated from madness machines that are wired with very different presuppositions about reality than those we find in Scripture." —Dr. Thaddeus Williams

"The lives of black people matter very much, but 'Black Lives Matter' is an evil Marxist cult whose far left agenda destroys Black families and their neighborhoods."   —Dr. Scott Lively

We must not forget what was permitted to happen during the summer of 2020. And why.

America was on fire. Buildings were destroyed, cars were firebombed, businesses were boarded up and closed, lawlessness reigned, lives were threatened, four dozen citizens were killed, looting was permitted, police were assaulted, churches were vandalized, statues were torn down, and the livelihoods of many—including inner-city black Americans—were lost.

The season of protesting and rioting was promoted by the liberal media, approved of by Democrat Party leaders, carried out by the Marxist Black Lives Matter Global Network Foundation (BLM), funded by progressive power elites, and endorsed by pro sports leagues.

BLM is a far left-funded, global movement supporting abortion, transgenderism, environmental justice, Marxism, racism, homosexuality, Democrat policy, and the LGBT agenda. According to its own website, BLM is working to dismantle white privilege, frowns upon male leadership roles, law enforcement, the traditional family, and worked to remove President Trump from office.

Our concern is not only public safety and the preservation of law and order under our constitution, but also, what role is the church playing in this historical moment in the country? How did Christians respond—and how are we dealing with the aftermath of social justice infiltration?

No matter how they spun it, what we witnessed in 2020 was lawlessness: murder, physical assault, theft, destruction of property, vandalism, death threats, and general violence. This is not to suggest everyone who sincerely marched in the streets or protested in peaceful ways was complicit in the death and destruction, but when Christians lock arms with those who carry out evil, it sends a confusing message.

The Bible warns not to be unequally yoked with unbelievers or approve of things that contradict Scripture. In their own words, two lesbian cofounders of BLM are trained Marxists. Karl Marx hated Christianity. How could we in good conscience partner with this movement?

Before we dig into the roots of BLM, Critical Race Theory, and the contrasting worldviews of Christianity and Marxism, we need to recognize lawlessness as a symptom of a deeper problem in the heart of man: sin. The only cure is the saving Gospel of Jesus Christ, whose red blood cleanses people of any color who repent and put their trust in Him.

As believers and as citizens of a heavenly Kingdom, our obedience to God's law and His Word is what truly matters. Everything we do and say must spring from the foundation of loving the Lord above all things and then loving our neighbors.

In his gospel, Matthew witnessed the following interaction:

" 'Teacher, which is the great commandment in the law?' He said to him, 'You shall love the Lord your God with all your heart and with all your soul and with all your mind. This is the great and first commandment. And a second is like it: You shall love your neighbor as yourself. On these two commandments depend all the Law and the Prophets' " (Matthew 22:36-40).

When we love God, we also love those who are made in His image.

So much happened in 2020, but the crisis that broke the proverbial camel's back was not the China virus, political division, the millions in taxpayer dollars spent on the failed impeachment and investigations of President Trump; it was not governor power grabs, discrimination against churches, Big Tech censorship, the 2020 election, or even racial injustice.

It goes back to the decline of morality and the gradual grinding down of our nation. We were primed for cultural Marxism. The left is working their agenda in five key areas of America: social, political, education, religion, and the traditional family. We have not fought back effectively against this all-out assault on Christianity.

There has been an obvious attack on the family. In fact, on the BLM website, it reads: "We disrupt the Western-prescribed nuclear family structure." BLM also fosters "a queer-affirming network." This global organization using a great slogan is founded upon Marxist principles.

In the name of social justice, BLM uses victimology, guilt, and accusations of racism to pit people against each other. They claim to be helping black (lives) people, but we've heard it all before.

Decades have passed, programs were put in place, and many politicians and administrations have come and gone. The problems are worse and their solutions have not helped. Lyndon Johnson's Great Society for example, was one of many efforts that ballooned the federal government but promised to eradicate poverty. It failed miserably, not helping the black community.

In an interview last summer, retired US Army lieutenant Col. Allen West said using the name "Black Lives Matter" is very oxymoronic because they are not focused on the issues that are confronting the American black community. He said you do not hear BLM talking about fatherlessness, for example. West was born in 1961, and regarding that time, he stated:

> "[T]he traditional two-parent household in the black community was nearly 77%. There were thriving black-owned businesses throughout our community. Today, only 24% of black kids have mom and dad in the home. We can have all the conversations about racism you want, but we will just keep whistling past the graveyard."[25]

West said BLM is a Marxist mob and that they do not address "the genocide of 20 million black babies murdered in the womb since 1973." He concluded by saying BLM does not stand for school choice or vouchers, and educational freedom, which he declared the "biggest civil rights issue in the black community right now."

Instead, BLM raised over a billion dollars from corporations, international organizations, political fundraisers, private leftist donors, and funneled money into the campaigns of Democrat Party candidates. For the better part of 2020, when you clicked on "Donate" on the BLM website, it redirected you to ActBlue Charities, a fundraising arm of Democrat campaigns.

Scrolling down on their site to where you donate, you saw that the fundraising was managed by NARAL (Pro-Choice America). Wait, wasn't this about helping blacks and injustice?

And sadly, you cannot hold them accountable. Further investigations revealed the ActBlue site takes a 3.95 percent fee off the top of each contribution—if it meets specific criteria—and naturally, ActBlue reserves the right to redirect donations to ActBlue charities they choose.

Writing for *Red State*, Elizabeth Vaughn concluded what other true journalists have: the Democrat Party was hijacked by the left, and the left is being run by extremists. In an article last June, she said we witnessed events that only months earlier would have been inconceivable. Why mention this? Not only to expose the fraud, but also to alert Christians who still support the cause.

"How many people suffering from white guilt over their white privilege have donated to ActBlue believing they were making a contribution to Black Lives Matter? ...The Democrats have set up a well-organized, highly-developed and exceptionally effective fundraising system which allows them to escape accountability."[26]

Christians should not be indifferent towards racism, discrimination, or bullying regardless of the form it takes. But wisdom and discernment are needed regarding who to give money to and what causes to support.

According to Scripture, every single person is created in God's image and has value, as He is the Creator of us all. The Bible speaks to bloodlines and nations, and seeing that the Lord is sovereign, He has ordained when in history we live, how long we live, and where.

The Bible further holds that "we are the offspring of God" (Acts 17:28), descendants, though the New Testament makes it clear *not* everyone is His child. Made in His image, yes, but we must by faith be born again of His Spirit and adopted into the family of God.

The apostle Paul explains that we are individually accountable to Him. In Acts 17, it states:

"Truly, these times of ignorance God overlooked, but now commands all men everywhere to repent, because He has appointed a day on which He will judge the world in righteousness by the Man whom He has ordained. He has given assurance of this to all by raising Him from the dead" (Acts 17:30-31).

These certainly are times of ignorance perhaps like none other in history, but God's patience means salvation, and the door is open for the unsaved to repent before it is too late. Judgment is coming.

It is counterproductive to divide people by nation or origin, sex, race, or skin color—especially for those of us already in Christ. Our identity is in Him. Groupthink and political correctness have fractured our country—on purpose. The father of lies is having a field day, as deception is rampant.

We must not compromise our biblical worldview on race, gender, sexual preference, or any issue! Those of us trying to remind Christians about this responsibility to God's Word have been accused of being insensitive to the cultural moment. I was called tone-deaf and ignorant.

I am not sure we can put this any clearer: We do not have a skin problem; we have a sin problem. This is our biblical worldview, like it or not. There are two kinds of people in the world—forgiven and unforgiven; saved or unsaved. This perspective must be reinforced!

The Bible has many reminders of how we are related, and how believers have an amazing inheritance as we wait for the return of our King.

> "After these things I looked, and behold, a great multitude which no one could number, of all nations, tribes, peoples, and tongues, standing before the throne and before the Lamb, clothed with white robes, with palm branches in their hands, and crying out with a loud voice, saying, 'Salvation belongs to our God who sits on the throne, and to the Lamb!' " (Revelation 7:9-10).

All means all. Nations, tribes, peoples, tongues. Believers will stand, all unworthy, before the Lamb of God. The heart of the matter is a matter of the heart—the inner man. Not skin color.

One thing that was alarming and disturbing last year was seeing laws going unenforced. If you break the law, there should be consequences. Paul wrote to Timothy about the fact the law is good if it is used lawfully, and "that the law is not made for a righteous person, but for the lawless and insubordinate, for the ungodly and for sinners" (1 Timothy 1:8-9).

The condition of humanity is clearly described by Jeremiah and others. Man needs redemption.

"The heart is deceitful above all things, And desperately wicked; Who can know it? I, the Lord, search the heart, I test the mind, Even to give every man according to his ways, According to the fruit of his doings" (Jeremiah 17:9-10).

Revealed throughout Scripture is the fact the heart of man is wicked, and without Christ it is beyond cure. The Bible completely rejects the notion that man is basically good! Rather, there are none who are righteous, not one (Romans 3:10).

If you need some proof regarding the heart of mankind, think about the fact that in World War II, 85 million people were killed. Talk about an indictment of the human race. Some estimates suggest 60 million of those deaths were civilians. As previously mentioned, another 60 million human lives have been aborted since 1973's *Roe v. Wade*.

We have seen the dismantling of biblical values and are living with the rotten fruit. There are consequences when evil is allowed to go virtually unchecked, but what happened to the restraints?

The Ten Commandments are a good place to start for basic guidance. The church, the body of believers, should be impacting society by following God's laws and letting our lights shine. But instead, there is an onslaught of immorality, the destruction of the family, attacks on authority, and the capitulation of the Christian church to the culture.

This brings us to the question of how evil is to be managed or mitigated in society. I was encouraged by a 2020 summer sermon by Pastor John MacArthur called, "Who's to Blame for the Riots," and want to discuss his thoughts here.

Four restraints to evil include our conscience, family, government, and the church.[27]

GOD HAS GIVEN US:

1. Conscience: the law of God has been written on the heart of every human being, and we do have the knowledge of right from wrong. Every one of us. The conscience is our warning device from God. But what happens is a person overrides that law justifying immoral behavior by training the conscience to ignore it.

If you train the conscience to ignore itself because you don't want to feel guilty or you just want to do whatever you want, damn the consequences, then you've just wiped out the personal restraint.

2. Family: raising godly children; parenting, passing down righteousness, goodness, truth, and discipline to the next generation. By removing the traditional (nuclear) family like BLM advocates, and by removing its influence, you wipe out the second restraint. We need healthy families!

Think of adultery, abortion, cohabitation, divorce, same-sex marriage, Hollywood, pornography, poverty, progressive sex education, fatherlessness, technology, television, gaming, and social media. All these things negatively affect families in some way.

3. Government: an ultimate authority designed by God to protect those who do good—and punish those who do evil. It's quite simple. When law, government rule, is completely broken, rejected, and vilified as we saw last year, another major restraint of lawlessness is erased.

We briefly mentioned Romans 13 earlier, but in light of the godless rebellion and anarchy displayed in our cities, look at the first four verses.

"Let every soul be subject to the governing authorities. For there is no authority except from God, and the authorities that exist are appointed by God. Therefore whoever resists the authority resists the ordinance of God, and those who resist will bring judgment on themselves. For rulers are not a terror to good works, but to evil. Do you want to be unafraid of the authority? Do what is good, and you will have praise from the same. For he is God's minister to you for good. But if you do evil, be afraid; for he does not bear the sword in vain; for he is God's minister, an avenger to execute wrath on him who practices evil" (Romans 13:1-4).

Everyone should obey God-ordained authority. Government (law enforcement) was attacked by criminals or enemies of good. Politicians failed in their role to serve the people in their cities. They ordered the pullback (stand-down) of those who protect the innocent and punish those who practice evil. As a result, the third restraint was removed.

4. Church: the final restraint in society! Granted, there are problems in today's church beginning with false teachings that have infected our congregations and denominations. The body of Christ was supposed to be a flavoring, preserving salt and a bright light exposing darkness. The cultural confusion, however, has resulted from the church conforming to worldly ideas and philosophies.

These four main restraints of evil have been breached. This helps us understand the trajectory of the country and immorality in general. What happens when you remove God's Word, family values, Christian influence, respect for authority, truth, and fixed moral absolutes? Anything goes. Remember, it just takes one generation for a nation to fall away from God.

There is an excellent passage in Paul's letter to the church at Galatia that further confirms that everything changes once we are justified by faith in Christ and become part of the same family. It is very appropriate to discussions about BLM, racism, and cultural Marxism.

"But the Scripture has confined all under sin, that the promise by faith in Jesus Christ might be given to those who believe. But before faith came, we were kept under guard by the law, kept for the faith which would afterward be revealed. Therefore the law was our tutor to bring us to Christ, that we might be justified by faith. But after faith has come, we are no longer under a tutor. For you are all sons of God through faith in Christ Jesus. For as many of you as were baptized into Christ have put on Christ. There is neither Jew nor Greek, there is neither slave nor free, there is neither male nor female; for you are all one in Christ Jesus" (Galatians 3:22-28).

God provided the law to teach us that we need to be saved from our sins. But once we believe Jesus and receive His offer of forgiveness and salvation, we become part of God's family! And once we are in Christ, we no longer identify with external descriptors.

CUTTING THROUGH THE NOISE AND EMOTION WITH FACTS

The frenzied reaction to the tragic killing of George Floyd by a police officer in Minneapolis was fueled by the left who were more than willing to use it for their campaign of chaos. Along with COVID, globalists and socialists had another opportunity to instill fear into people.

Any death in the public spotlight is a sad reflection of the heart of man, but when race is involved, it makes it even more divisive and toxic to the healing of our fractured nation. We can be upset at injustice, but our reactions must still be within biblical parameters. If not, what makes us different from the world?

Most would admit that not all law enforcement do things by the book and there has been plenty of abuse. It is also important to keep the numbers of these cases and deaths in perspective. I believe this is important due to our lack of truthful information from most media.

America's population is approximately 329 million. According to *Law Enforcement Today*, there are 900,000 sworn law enforcement officers and an average of just under one thousand incidents per year in which police have used deadly force. Of these cases, 95.3 percent of suspects were armed.

According to the FBI's Uniform Crime Report, there were 58,627 assaults against law enforcement officers in 2016, and most likely that number skyrocketed in 2020.

Officers come into contact with the population 55.8 million times per year. There are about 26,000 complaints of excessive force, but only 8 percent of these were sustained (proven or legitimate), equaling 2,080 cases. That's .0039 percent (excessive force) out of over 55 million interactions.

Kyle S. Reyes, national spokesman for *Law Enforcement Today*, declares that by looking at the numbers and facts over feelings and emotions, people will get a clearer, accurate perspective and understanding of what is really happening. He states:

"Seems to me like the real problem here is socio-economic disparities along with a public perception issue thanks to biased reporting. And let's not forget the huge role that social media plays in disseminating false narratives and creating emotional, knee-jerk reactions."[28]

By listing facts and numbers, some will say I am insensitive, but I am not denying racism still exists. Police brutality is not out of control, however, and police reforms such as situational training should be discussed as new policies are implemented.

Reform is good. The heart of man, however, is still wicked, which is our underlying problem.

In the cultural upheaval that some people think was a spontaneous reaction to George Floyd, there were countless casualties, including police officers and black business owners. Then, corporations, Big Tech, professional sports, and the entertainment industry locked arms in protest and solidarity, virtue signaling, wearing masks, and taking knees.

Sports and entertainment leagues, the National Basketball Association (BLM-NBA), National Football League, and others, generally blamed it all on America, our history, Trump, and white privilege. Athletes making millions of dollars a year and many earning hundreds of thousands protested police brutality and inequality by refusing to stand for the national anthem. The few players who did stand with a hand on their hearts were criticized.

China controls the NBA, which is basically the marketing department of Nike. The shoe giant rakes in $40 billion a year. Nike bows to red China and is silent on human rights abuses and slave labor. Its spokesmen include LeBron James & Colin Kaepernick. James went on record saying blacks couldn't leave their houses because police were "hunting us down" on the streets.

The National Basketball Association Players Union even promoted the clenched Communist fist of power last year with the phrase, "The Revolution Will Be Televised." They planned on pushing the social justice narrative all season long—and they did.

Remember the days of Tim Tebow taking a knee to pray to God while on the sidelines or after scoring a touchdown? The activist media and others on the left criticized him at the time. Today, Christian and/or patriotic athletes standing for God and country during the national anthem at sporting events are considered courageous.

New Orleans Saints quarterback Drew Brees was even forced to apologize for being proud of his family's military service and for defending the national anthem. He backed down as both he and his wife bowed the knee to PC and BLM pressure. Saul Alinsky would be thrilled.

Also in 2020, dozens of pro-life protesters in various states were arrested outside abortion clinics. In at least one case, a woman wrote "Black Pre-born Lives Matter" in chalk on a public sidewalk. Democrat mayors essentially said, "That is not the proper narrative, arrest them." But vandals and rioters were free to spray-paint or burn buildings and public property.

In what society does this make sense?

Double standards abound. In case you had not noticed, the left has been undermining their own country by sowing division and discord. Moral decay, cultural decline, hate, accusation, political divisiveness; and the complicit Democrat media keeps stoking the flames of racism.

Many Christians went so far as to march with BLM protesters, but it wasn't long before Antifa infiltrated the marches and public protests. Even some religious leaders and pastors marched, some of them perhaps for a photo op or to be people pleasers. A progressive view of justice or of a secular social theory is held by many young people today.

We want to be compassionate, loving, and empathetic, but too many well-intentioned people quickly jumped on the BLM bandwagon not knowing what they were all about. Christian friend, be careful who you align yourself with because if it is not biblical, it sends mixed messages to an already confused world.

If you are still defending BLM, you are espousing the values of a worldview in conflict with your own—if you're a Bible-believing Christian. In essence, who would not agree with the obvious? Black lives do matter. But prior to supporting BLM, did you do an Internet search on the background of this organization or did you read their statement of faith? Before you champion any cause, do some research.

You would have found a far-reaching agenda going beyond black equality or justice; their main goal is political power. The cofounder admitted they want socialism. On national television, another BLM representative said they will "burn the system down" if they do not get what they want. Imagine if a Republican said that.

CHRISTIANITY VS. MARXISM AND CRITICAL RACE THEORY

Can you support this global movement and follow Jesus Christ at the same time? Too many Christians are falling into a trap of joining or endorsing popular ideas that are completely antithetical to the teachings of Jesus.

Here are three possible reasons Christians feel pressured into repeating or supporting the beliefs of BLM, a neo-Marxist, collective guilt ideology that is incompatible with the Gospel:

1. Fear of not going along; peer pressure
2. A misunderstanding of what they've signed onto
3. An authentic conversion to the radical cause

Joshua Lawson, managing editor of *The Federalist*, made some important points in an article last year concluding that you can be Christian or Marxist, but you cannot be both.[29]

The grand unifying principle for the Marxists behind the Black Lives Matter movement is everything can be reduced to oppressors versus the oppressed. Have you noticed the left in America pitting people against each other and claiming we were and are a racist nation? They have had success pushing this narrative.

Collective guilt is not biblical. Romans 8:1 reminds us, "There is no condemnation for those who are in Christ Jesus." Part of the BLM agenda is to judge white people today for the sins of the past, even though we were not born yet and many of our ancestors weren't even in America!

Whether the sins were committed yesterday, last year, or 400 years ago, the far left insists that all Caucasians must bear the guilt for sins committed by *other* Caucasians. In contrast, Christianity teaches we are accountable to God alone for our sins, individually. The person who sins must go to Jesus for atonement.

Both the New and Old Testaments support this doctrine.

"Yet you say, 'Why should the son not bear the guilt of the father?' Because the son has done what is lawful and right, and has kept all My statutes and observed them, he shall surely live. *The soul who sins shall die.* The son shall not bear the guilt of the father, nor the father bear the guilt of the son. The righteousness of the righteous shall be upon himself, and the wickedness of the wicked shall be upon himself" (Ezekiel 18:19-20, emphasis added).

Just as the individual soul who sins is accountable for that sin, those who believe Christ as Lord and Savior are saved personally, not collectively with others. Universal repentance is not biblical, and neither is universal salvation.

Next, Christianity rejects historical Marxism, which peddles the materialistic notion that if everyone could just be wealthy enough, economic status would be meaningless. Christ teaches us not to concern ourselves with questions of wealth, who has it, who owes us, and how we can reclaim more of it for ourselves. Jesus said, "...seek first the kingdom of God and His righteousness and all these things will be added to you" (Matthew 6:33).

By demanding things others have earned or worked for, Marxism also fuels covetousness and envy. God said we should not covet anything belonging to others. The neo-Marxists running the BLM movement have cultivated anger, entitlement, and resentment. Instead of preaching love and contentment, they cause people to covet their neighbor's status or things.

Conversely, the Bible teaches thanksgiving and contentment.

"Not that I speak in regard to need, for I have learned in whatever state I am, to be content: I know how to be abased, and I know how to abound. Everywhere and in all things I have learned both to be full and to be hungry, both to abound and to suffer need. I can do all things through Christ who strengthens me; And my God shall supply all your need according to His riches in glory by Christ Jesus" (Philippians 4:11-13, 19).

Christians are to work and trust the Lord for provision while being content with what they have.

The Bible also has answers for every need or problem about life, including the four main questions of mankind: origin, meaning, morality, and destiny.

Marxism has no answer for questions of purpose, meaning, and eternity. To them, everything is a struggle for power, to be resolved either by redistribution or the sword.

Marxism seeks to tear down and divide; Christianity seeks to build up and unify. Marxism produces angst, hatred, more oppression, and victimology. True Christianity produces the fruit of the Holy Spirit (Galatians 5:22).

Jesus has already done the work of erasing all cultural or ethnic barriers to God. Grace is available to all those who put their faith in Him!

Regarding Critical Race Theory (CRT), one of the most prominent expressions of Marxism in American culture today, it is being taught in many universities and is seeping into public school curriculum. It is a racist ideology that is incompatible with Christianity.

This is from the UCLA School of Public Affairs:

"CRT recognizes that racism is engrained in the fabric and system of the American society. The individual racist need not exist to note that institutional racism is pervasive in the dominant culture. This is the analytical lens that CRT uses in examining existing power structures. CRT identifies that these power structures are based on white privilege and white supremacy, which perpetuates the marginalization of people of color."

Since kids have learned revisionist history for many decades now, and since many students probably think white men are to blame for the world's problems, when they go to college these lies and fabrications become a permanent part of their belief system.

Does this help you understand why young people are so anti-Trump, anti-Republican, and against putting America first? They believe this nation prospered by taking advantage of blacks and minorities. Some suggest at least one-third of our population has never been taught about what truly made America a great, blessed, strong, and prosperous nation.

Critical Race Theory advocates the judging of people by their group identity rather than their individual character, behavior, and merit. CRT training sessions have already been held in many public agencies. CRT establishes division by claiming the underlying problem is structural or systemic racism rather than individual racism, which does exist.

They claim white people, more specifically white males, are the oppressors, and all the oppressed groups are linked together: blacks, women, Indians, Muslims, homosexuals, transgenders, and workers. America is evil, they suggest, because of our whiteness, and our founders, of course.

CRT fails to recognize there are ninety-four countries with no freedom laws and no constitution protecting the rights of citizens, and in those countries there are today approximately 40 million slaves. The difference is in America we have a representative republic founded on the truth of God and that our rights come from Him. Therefore, every human being has individual rights.

CRT seeks to deconstruct the foundation and system of freedom, government, justice, and equality in Western society. CRT is a theory made to sound good, and even some pastors have been deceived by its teachings, but the Bible clearly rebukes this thinking. CRT promotes partiality and discrimination, the very opposite of what the Bible teaches.

The Dialectic Process is a set of very well-crafted steps designed to move a person from a belief in absolute truth to relativism. Have they ever been successful! (I met Dr. Marlene McMillan in Dallas last year and thank her for some of this information.)

The first step of the Dialectic Process is identifying areas of discontent. In order to get people in America (who have more liberty than anywhere in the world) to become discontented, they must be told how bad their life is or how unjust. One of the methods of the Dialectic Process is using the same words and giving them different meanings while constantly changing the definitions.

Political correctness also uses language to control culture and sell lies as acceptable, or even as truth. The goal of CRT was not truth, but revolutionary action. So, CRT is built on a false framework that is strengthened by unrelenting, destructive criticism with the aim of taking down societal structure. Some have accepted James Cone's theories of systemic racism, concluding that the whole system has to be destroyed to eliminate racism.

One simply has to do some digging into our unedited American history to find abolitionists, most of whom were

Christian, who hated slavery because of what the Bible teaches. The 2 percent of the population who owned slaves prior to the Civil War do not justify accusations of rampant racism. Abolitionists had support from most of the US population. Christians taught slaves to read and write, and many risked their lives to help them escape!

To summarize, Critical Race Theory is an unbiblical, worldly philosophy that divides church and culture, opposes the Gospel of Jesus, and judges society through a lens of power. Rather than addressing individual sin, the problems are whiteness and systems that oppress people of color. Rather than producing godly sorrow and repentance, CRT produces animosity, guilt, and resentment. Its focus is the flesh while God emphasizes the heart.

We cannot conclude this chapter without mentioning the latest assault on history and Middle America, the *New York Times'* 1619 Project, part of a deliberate effort to undermine education. It picks up on the Marxist theme of oppressed and oppressor groups, suggesting the US was born when slaves were first brought here, and not in 1776.

The 1619 Project has already been adopted in high schools. It has been already implemented in higher education as the next step for universities having already welcomed CRT. Explaining why the left is working to rewrite this settled national history, Brenda Hafera (Director of International and Continuing Education Programs at The Fund for American Studies) states:

"America's founding principles are the source of our unity. The ideas of the Constitution and the Declaration, along with our shared history, language, land, and institutions, forged us into one people.

"If Americans are taught to reject our founding principles, that leaves room for us to be defined and shaped by new ideas and theories. Coincidentally, the 1619 Project proposes an alternative founding principle: identity politics. America…was born out of a conflict between free and enslaved peoples and is defined to this day by struggles between men and women, straight and gay, black and white, etc."[30]

Clearly this is another attack on Christianity, biblical values, actual history, and the unifying principle of We the People.

Jesus Christ is the only solution to sin, which includes inequality and injustice (actual or perceived). Only He can atone for sin and unite a community or a people. The demonic and divisive doctrine of CRT has also crept into the Christian church. It is essential we teach the truth, expose deception, and root out anything that tickles people's ears while having no power to save!

Like Satan himself, Karl Marx claimed, "My object in life is to dethrone God." This is not a man Christians should have anything to do with. In addition, in every nation that adopted Marxism as its ideological model, Christians have been oppressed, sin runs rampant, and millions have died.

I wish BLM and promoters of CRT were just as angry and passionate about all black lives. For example, there was a wonderful life-affirming story last year about the youngest surviving premature baby. He was born in Georgia at twenty-one weeks, weighed thirteen ounces, and spent months in the hospital. And he's black.

Made in God's image, this is a powerful story in support of life; birth, motherhood, pregnancy, humanity—and the fact every life matters! His name is Jemarius Jachin Harbor, Jr., and was sent home last June from Emory Decatur Hospital.

More black babies are aborted than born in NYC. Abortion takes the lives of 360 black babies every single day across America where Margaret Sanger's mission is being accomplished. Why no outcry from the left? You know why.

What about black-on-black crime? Last summer, Chicago broke its own weekend records for the most shootings and murders in the city's history. It happens every weekend in major cities, but why is there no media attention or public outcry? You know why.

Finally, videos from last year showed people being asked to apologize for their white privilege, for slavery, and other injustices of past generations. Some were told to bow down and repent.

Abortion survivor Gianna Jessen refers to her cerebral palsy as a gift from a loving God who helped her fight for life. She responded with truth in that cultural moment of intimidation:

"i will listen. but i will not bow and kneel in humiliation for injustice i am not guilty of. i will not apologize for the color of my skin. i will not be ashamed of the founding of this country. i will kneel before only One. i will bow before Jesus Christ. along with my brothers and sisters of all tribes, color and nations. we will magnify His Name together.

"i will not kneel to agree with manipulation and control. i will not bow before the accuser of the brethren. i will stand, in Triumph, before the Lord of Hosts, who alone, weighs justly the Hearts of men."

One day, every knee will bow, and every tongue will confess that Jesus Christ is Lord (Philippians 2:10-11). No other allegiance will matter! The foundation of His throne is righteousness, justice, and truth (Psalm 89:14). A good God would be just, and would judge evildoers. He will not let sin go unpunished, and His judgment will not be held back much longer.

John writes in Revelation about Jesus sitting on a great white throne. It will be a time of great fear and judgment, when the dead, small and great, will stand before God and be judged according to their works (Revelation 20:11-12). But the most sobering part of what John saw was this:

"And anyone not found written in the Book of Life was cast into the lake of fire" (Revelation 20:15).

Call on Jesus while there is still time! Every human being will stand before God one day and see that the cross is the great equalizer, and salvation has nothing to do with skin color.

To our Creator, every human life matters, but there is a dark, deadly evil in our land that we have become desensitized to, and the blood of the innocent cries out to God. Christians should not approve of BLM and we should not approve of abortion.

8

If You Can Kill Babies, You're Capable of Anything

"People need to be brought back to thinking correctly, by building their thinking on the only true foundation—the Creator of all things. I call this 'Thinking Christian.' There is a correct Christian way of thinking about geology, biology, astronomy, physics, chemistry, art, music, psychology, history, language, politics, etc. And this correct way must start with the revealed Word of the Creator God and this His foundational principles."
                                                    —Ken Ham

"If the unborn is *not* a human person, no justification for abortion is needed. If the unborn is a human person, no justification for abortion is adequate."
                                                    —Greg Koukl

Has the conscience of our nation become seared? In my lifetime, abortion has gone from something spoken about in hushes and whispers and embarrassment—to something many women are proud of and that young people overwhelmingly support. Big abortion business, Planned Parenthood, still receives our tax dollars to the tune of over half a billion dollars a year. An essential church would speak out regarding human lives in mothers' wombs.

One of my favorite podcast guests is Steve Smothermon, pastor of Legacy Church in Albuquerque, New Mexico. I met him in September of 2020 at the Liberty Pastors conference I mentioned earlier. It truly inspired me to press on the rest of the year. I appreciate pastors who teach sound doctrine and take bold stances on the inerrant truths of Scripture. I admire men of God even more if they speak out against abortion, one of the great evils of our lifetime.

I will never forget a statement he made regarding those who continually commit abortions and about the evil heart of man. It is not that what he said is so profound; it is the fact that tragically, a minority of Christian pastors in America speak so strongly on this critical issue. While discussing those who approve of, support, or vote for abortion, Steve Smothermon simply stated:

"If you can kill babies, you're capable of anything."

If a person can endorse the taking of innocent life in a mother's womb, their heart is darkened, they do not value all human life, and there is not much that would be off limits to that person. The right to life is the most basic of our privileges and protections under the US Constitution.

Should a Bible-believing, God-fearing, obedient church tolerate the murder of preborn babies in society without praying, preaching, sharing on social media, cutting abortion funding, helping save lives, working to change laws, change minds, promote adoption, and helping single moms and pregnant women in crisis?

Sadly, many Christians are divided on the issue of life in a mother's womb. For decades, abortion has been a nonnegotiable platform of a major political party in the nation. Democrats can scarcely win an election without their candidate being pro-choice. Half of the voters in the US justify child sacrifice and making you help pay for it.

How did we get here? The legalizing of abortion in 1973 is just one glaring catalyst that led to decades of unprecedented immorality. This was a major demonic victory, causing untold millions to rebel against God, to devalue life, and see pregnancy as a problem to be dealt with rather than a precious gift of God to be received. The Bible refers to children as a blessing.

Had the American church been teaching truths about life in the womb, had we organized, mobilized, and protested *Roe v. Wade* at the time, we would be having a much different discussion right now. There were allegedly hundreds of thousands of Christian churches in the nation at the time the Supreme Court made its deadly, infamous decision.

Where were all the voices of truth? Where were those willing to stand up for the least of these?

Most of us know the story but maybe you haven't really thought about it in terms of life in the womb. Early in the gospel of Luke, Mary's cousin Elizabeth was pregnant with John the Baptist while Mary was pregnant with Jesus and arrived for a visit.

The Bible tells us Elizabeth heard Mary's greeting, and her baby leaped in her womb (Luke 1:41)! And—so that people would understand it wasn't a misprint or mistranslation, three verses later, Elizabeth says,

> "For behold, when the sound of your greeting reached my ears, the baby leaped in my womb for joy" (Luke 1:44).

The point is this: God's Word makes no distinction between the life of a child in the womb and a child outside the womb.

Did you know the meaning of the Latin word for "fetus" is offspring or little one? Through history, even up until recent years, a pregnant woman was considered to be "with child."

We know from Scripture that an immortal soul is created at the moment of conception, and personhood is established by the presence of that soul. A baby's gender has been determined at conception along with its genetic makeup. King David wrote,

"You [God] formed my inward parts; You wove me in my mother's womb" (Psalm 139:13).

A distinct and separate life is created, having a unique DNA and its own arms, legs, organs, and everything else that makes up a human body. Then, a little heart starts beating! So, within the mother's body there is a completely different— living, growing body.

But what have we fallen for? "My body, my choice!" And "a woman's right to choose." My question is—to choose what? Child sacrifice. Deuteronomy 30:19 says,

"So choose life in order that you may live, you *and* your descendants…" (emphasis added).

To be Gospel proclaimers and cultural influencers, we must recommit to the whole counsel of God, to living our faith out loud and not just talking a good game. We must kill complacency like a cancer. We better redirect if we hope to stir up a comfortable church and reach a secular culture whose gods are self, sex, power, money, and entertainment.

Precious preborn lives are a lynchpin issue for the church and country.

Another pastor I met at that Dallas conference was Dr. Scott Lively. He has been a faithful warrior on the front lines of these cultural battles for decades. He understands that we need to reach today's so-called Christians as well as those who have never been converted. He states:

"I will never give up trying to disciple the weak-of-faith majority in today's American churches, and to evangelize the deceived-unsaved pew-sitters among them."

The world is dark and needs the Gospel, but there should not be a debate about things such as abortion, gender, marriage, and socialism in Bible-believing Christian churches! We need to encourage the difficult work of confronting carnality, doing discipleship, and equipping the saints for ministry.

The enemy has diluted the Word of God and many churchgoers do not believe all that the Bible teaches. Since most *professing* Christians do not believe in fixed moral absolutes and think people can live their own truth, why are we surprised they can tolerate the horrific act of abortion?

We answer to an audience of One. If the risen Lord Jesus really is the Cornerstone of our faith, the solid ground upon which we stand, why are we so concerned about what the world thinks? Yes, Americans have generally become hostile toward the things of God. But we did not start out that way.

Noah Webster once stated,

"The Bible is the chief moral cause of all that is good, and the best corrector of all that is evil in human society; the best book for regulating the temporal secular concerns of men."

Abortion is evil. We have been deceived by Satan, the one the Bible says comes only to steal, kill, and destroy. But Jesus came to give us life. The church in America has been influenced by man-pleasing, worldly, feel-good philosophies promoted by today's mainstream media, the Democrat Party, Hollywood, Planned Parenthood, and government education.

Their godless, secular ideas such as reproductive freedom have been repackaged and sold to the public. Theirs is the wide path leading to destruction; a path Jesus said many will take. There are many deceived Christians today. Even the early church was warned:

> "See to it that no one takes you captive through philosophy and empty deception, according to the tradition of men, according to the elementary principles of the world, rather than according to Christ. For in Him all the fullness of Deity dwells; ...and He is the head over all rule and authority" (Colossians 2:8-10).

If Jesus is our final authority, why are so many of us Christians conforming to this world and its philosophies? We have bought the lie that this life is all about us and our happiness.

Therefore, a baby can be seen as inconvenient. This has led to justifying abortion for the mother (and in many cases, girl and boyfriend) to preserve a particular lifestyle. And to justify the removal of a human life, you have to convince yourself it is not living or human—yet.

If the morality of abortion hinged on the personhood of the fetus, that case should have been closed long ago from what we know Scripture teaches. But when *Roe v. Wade* was being decided in 1972-73, there was some apparent confusion over what was happening—or more specifically—what was growing in a pregnant mother's womb.

First, let's all agree that dead things don't grow.

Second, if it is not human life, what else would it be? We marvel at the thought of possible evidence of life on Mars, but some can ignore human life in a mother's womb. Reprobate minds suppress the truth.

In my book, *The Cost of Our Silence*, I detailed sections of the extensive *Roe v. Wade* court transcript. I want to revisit just five key statements from that discussion.

In that monumental case, the attorney arguing for abortion representing Jane Roe said *a pregnancy disrupts a woman's life*. Think about that for a moment. God calls a baby a miracle and a gift; Americans have been programmed to call it a disruption, a choice, or a problem.

Keep in mind, they did not have today's remarkable technology such as ultrasound, DNA, sonograms, etc. They did have the Bible, but they ignored its clear teachings on life. (Once again, however, science finally caught up with Scripture.)

The attorney for Jane Roe admitted that her argument might be different *if* it could be established that the fetus was a person. Guess what? Personhood has been established!

Supreme Court Justice Stewart responded by asking about personhood and constitutional rights of a baby in the womb. He stated:

> "Well, if it were established that an unborn fetus is a person with the protection of the Fourteenth Amendment, you would have almost an impossible case here, would you not?"

Listen to how Sarah Weddington responded:

"I would have a very difficult case."

Justice Blackmun then asked about the apparent uncertainty among doctors as to when life begins in the womb. (Remember, this was in the early 1970s.) He stated:

"Is it not true—or is it true, that the medical profession itself is not in agreement as to when life begins?"

Justice White then said:

"Well, if you're correct that the fetus is a person, then...the State would have great trouble permitting an abortion, would it not?"

District Attorney, Mr. Flowers, responded: "Yes sir, in any circumstances."
He continued...

"Gentleman, we feel that the concept of a fetus being within the concept of a person, within the framework of the United States Constitution and the Texas Constitution, is an extremely fundamental thing."

Please stop and reread these five quotes from *Roe v. Wade* in 1973. What's our excuse today?
Here are just two of the many Scriptures that reinforce our biblical fight for life.

"Listen to Me, O islands, and pay attention, you peoples from afar. The LORD called Me from the womb; From the body of My mother He named Me" (Isaiah 49:1).

"Before I formed you in the womb I knew you,
And before you were born I consecrated you;
I have appointed you a prophet to the nations"
(Jeremiah 1:5).

Fact: What God has declared immoral, man cannot make moral. But man did—in 1973.

For nearly fifty years, we have seen a drastic and downward shift in beliefs about morality in America. We justify things that cannot be supported by God's Word. As a result, the number of deaths caused by abortion worldwide was over 42.6 million in 2020 alone!

So, church, where is the outcry and why are so many pulpits in America silent?

In addition to contextual preaching and Gospel truth, if your pastor does NOT address the importance of life in the womb, creation, worldview issues, the role of civil government, and a Christian's responsibility to vote biblical values rather than support philosophies of this world, please encourage him to do so!

I am not suggesting churches need to be obsessed with culture, constantly focused on social issues, or spending less time in the Scriptures. With the Bible as our foundation, we must discern and apply what He taught to the issues affecting us today. You can find answers in God's Word to every so-called controversial subject.

Christians are to be set apart from the world and not to blend in or give in to good-sounding arguments. After all, they say, who would want to deny pregnant women a choice and refuse them healthcare when it comes to their right to commit an abortion? Democrats demand easy access to eliminating life and liberty from preborn human beings.

Regarding culture and the public square, we lost it. Christians were to infiltrate, not isolate! Seek out those leaders and believers who trust the Lord, those who have a firm foundation of faith and are willing to speak the truth and stand against evil. Salt and light.

The contrast in people's worldviews and between political parties is as glaring as it is disappointing. What makes this worse on a moral level is the fact too many professing Christians remain on the side of abortion, death, and destruction. Yes, I mean the Democrat Party.

I have not had much success converting liberals on the issue of abortion. Even presenting Scripture, talking about life in the womb from a standpoint of biology and science, and reasoning with them about when human life begins, I barely make a dent. Their consciences have been seared.

There are also some major problems with openly supporting abortion of babies based on race, sex, or disability. Were you aware of this? Democrats have consistently opposed legislation seeking to limit abortions based on these factors.

China was exposed in the past for their radical one-child policy and abortions based upon sex. They wanted male babies, so they committed infanticide on female babies. We look down our noses at China and then elect Kamala Harris, who promised to reverse any bans on abortion whatsoever (she endorsed the Women's Health Protection Act), and Joe Biden, who wants to strip states of their rights to restrict abortion.

Who would not want to protect the health of women? See how wordsmiths operate? Modern Democrats support late-term abortion methods, a level of evil not endorsed until the Obama administration, and they force American taxpayers to fund the slaughter. They oppose pregnancy center alternatives, which begs the question: are they truly pro-choice if they refuse women the choice to go to a health center that does not commit abortions?

Republicans are not angels nor are their policies perfect, but we should take issue with Democrat Christians in churches today that support this sin. They oppose conscientious objections for religious and pro-life medical professionals. The Democrat Party almost unanimously demands every doctor, nurse, or clinic worker be forced to commit abortion, even if they oppose the practice.

Joe Biden and Kamala Harris have gone on record pushing or endorsing legislation that would coerce Christians and other religious individuals to engage in activities that directly violate their faith and conscience. Their policies speak for themselves.

It is quite astounding. Though I disagree with Christians who refuse to vote in elections, I understand why some might make that decision. But with all that we know about how extreme and radical Democrat policies are, I have a hard time understanding the rationale behind people's decision to vote for open immorality or be silent.

If you claim to be Christian, conservative, or pro-life, it is bewildering you can vote for the Democrat Party. It is idolatry, plain and simple. For whatever reason, you have elevated your political party over God's Word. I am not saying Republicans never do the same; but if we profess to be Christians, we must not have any gods before Him.

Does God's Word endorse the murder of babies or infants at any stage? Absolutely not! It is just the opposite. Scripture consistently speaks against those who take innocent life and details the consequences of people's actions.

Another question is, does the geographic location of an infant (in or out of the womb) matter when it comes to choosing to terminate a pregnancy and do irreversible harm to a human being?

Have you ever heard of the SLED test on the viability of a baby in the womb? SLED is an acronym for Size, Level of Development, Environment, and Degree of Dependency. We know God has already declared every human life valuable, but what about society? How do they decide, apart from the Bible, what lives are worth keeping and what ones should be discarded?

Size does not determine value. Level of development does not determine value. Environment does not determine value. Degree of dependency does not determine value.

I have heard excuses like, "President Trump was not a godly example of a leader, so I had to pick Biden, the lesser of two evils." Seriously? There is so much that is wrong with this logic.

If you are a true Christian, it is one thing to say Donald Trump is bombastic, prideful, or personally offensive and you're not going to vote in an election. But to say Trump was *so* offensive that you were willing to abandon your convictions and faith, and then endorse an opposing candidate whose policies are diametrically opposed to all you claim to believe, seems counterproductive at best.

Something I have come to terms with regarding the hypocrisy and moral relativism in today's culture is what is known as cognitive dissonance. This occurs when a person's behavior does not align with their beliefs. The dictionary definition of cognitive dissonance is:

"The state of having inconsistent thoughts, beliefs, or attitudes, especially as relating to behavioral decisions and attitude change."

If you believe God's Word on everything else, but when it comes to voting you go against what the Bible teaches, you are in contradiction. This not only causes internal stress, but you must then make some sort of mental justification for claiming to be one thing but acting (voting) the opposite.

Just because you can't stand President Trump, are you really willing to allow the continued decay of culture under rulers with wicked policies? Do you not care about the removal of God and our history, attacks on pro-lifers, the dismantling of the Constitution, the expansion and funding of abortion, and discrimination against Christians?

Do you see where this evil is leading? How far are they willing to go to allow human life to be devalued? The left is now pushing population control under the guise of climate justice and environmental extremism because, you know, humanity must be reduced.

This is the cultlike nature of modern liberalism. As many of us are praying for revival and a spiritual awakening, we have seen a wicked awakening of the spirit of the antichrist!

Part of this rebellion includes the spirits of lawlessness, deception, and rebellion. But people have also been blinded to their own hardened hearts and hypocrisy. To prove my point, prior to the 2020 election, there was an actual group called Pro-Life Evangelicals for Biden. Wait, what? Talk about cognitive dissonance and denial!

Can you be an evangelical Christian, be pro-life, and support Joe Biden or any Democrat? Yes. Should you? Absolutely not—that is, if you care about obeying what the Scriptures teach.

Joe Biden is the most pro-abortion president in US history. He repeatedly stated he would "pass legislation making *Roe* the law of the land," which lines up with the Democrat platform to repeal the Hyde Amendment and codify *Roe v. Wade*. Half of our churches are okay with this evil?

Part of our problem in America is a disconnect from Scripture and the God of our founders.

The left says other issues outweigh the right to life for babies, but in their conscience, they know abortion ends preborn human lives. It is both unbiblical and unethical. But, they say, "Poverty kills millions every year." Jesus said we would always have the poor with us. Their general point is the church has not done a good enough job caring for the poor. Agreed.

The debate then, is about how can we do better at this important service to the needy among us. The left has a solution: more government and the redistribution of wealth. The Bible's solution: the church is responsible for helping the poor and serving the least of these.

Democrats are also working the globalist angle to decrease human population. One of their main parroted talking points has been, "Climate change is an existential threat!" Their website also states that, "Unless we quickly make major changes, devastating climate change will kill tens of millions." And you can prove this, how?

They cannot prove it. Intense scientific debate will continue. But the more you repeat something—even if it is a lie—the more people will start believing it. Just as they did a year ago as early reports on a new virus described a pandemic that is going to kill millions of people in America!

Fear, fear, fear. Panic, sensationalism, exaggeration, propaganda. Balderdash!

Poverty does kill, but fair-minded people would agree President Trump's economic policies helped alleviate poverty more than the Obama/Biden administration ever did. Moreover, both parties want good healthcare for all citizens, but Republicans disagree with Democrats, wanting to force us to pay for abortions.

How do media activists frame it? "Republicans want women to die with no healthcare!"

This alleged pro-life evangelical group is confused about policy and procedure. Posing as evangelicals, they went so far as to say, "Even as we continue to urge different policies on abortion, we urge evangelicals to elect Joe Biden as president."

These pro-life evangelicals voted for the party that has supported these barbaric procedures for years. Indeed, they are calling on other Christians to vote for the party that opposes the Born-Alive Abortion Survivors Protection Act (similar to the Born-Alive Infant Protection Act), which would guarantee medical care for a baby that survives abortion.

As senator, vice presidential candidate Kamala Harris voted against this act, and also voted against the Pain-Capable Unborn Child Act, which would have protected unborn babies from abortion procedures after the point at which they can feel pain (twenty weeks).

By ignoring the shedding of innocent blood, they are so out of touch with the Bible and reality that their position cannot be justified. Most of us are thankful President Trump was the most outspoken and strongest pro-life president in history. Period.

Pro-choice Democrats claiming to be Catholic or Christian tout diversity, tolerance, and the uniting of all religions, but they are more concerned about being liberal than biblical! Many live as if the Ten Commandments are merely ten suggestions.

Barna Research revealed that only 34 percent of American adults believe moral truth is absolute, with the lowest percentage of believers being between eighteen and twenty-five years old. If you can make up your own truth, you can call a baby or a pregnancy whatever you want to justify abortion.

What happens when you cave or compromise your morals and values is you then must follow it up with more compromise. You soon end up supporting a bunch of policies you never would have before you fell for Planned Parenthood's cultural conditioning and propaganda on abortion.

Author and teacher, Peter Heck was baffled last year by the illogical, absurd, and self-defeating stance taken by professing Christians and conservatives who endorsed Joe Biden. He stated:[31]

> "[P]lease, someone help me understand the argument that Trump is not conservative enough, so to fix that we should cast a vote for:
>
> • Abortion on demand
> • Rifle banning
> • Green New Deal
> • DC statehood
> • Economy-crippling lockdowns
> • Tax hikes
> • Liberal Supreme Court stacking
>
> I don't claim to be a smart man, but I need to understand in what universe that approach even borders on making sense."

This is a worldview issue. The left wants one without God, focusing on more government power and control, rather than a worldview that prioritizes God and focuses on life, marriage, family, and religious freedom. For believers, Jesus Christ is the

Cornerstone of our faith and His Word endures forever. The Bible says,

> "For no man can lay a foundation other than the one which is laid, which is Jesus Christ" (1 Corinthians 3:11).

If your faith is established on the word of truth, you will have a firm foundation. You will not have to worry about the hypocrisy of cognitive dissonance or being double minded. People's thinking must change. Then Lord willing, once hearts and minds are changed, behavior will follow.

A great spiritual and physical conflict for the soul of America has reached a boiling point. There is much at stake, including lives of preborn babies, eternal souls, truth, righteousness, liberty, and the future of our country. One reason is we are more divided than ever about how to govern the nation. The question is, are we beyond the point of repairing the fracture?

9

The Divided Church and State of America

"Can two walk together, unless they are agreed?"
(Amos 3:3)

"If a kingdom is divided against itself, that kingdom cannot stand. If a house is divided against itself, that house will not be able to stand" (Mark 3:24-25).

"There cannot be a peaceful coexistence of two completely different theories of life, theories of government, theories of how we manage our affairs. We can't be in this dire a conflict without something giving somewhere along the way."   —Rush Limbaugh

The future of the United States is in jeopardy for at least two reasons: this republic has been under constant attack from within; and Americans are more divided than ever before.

Lines have been drawn dividing the liberal left from the conservative right in our culture. These may not be battle lines, but opposing ideologies about which we used to simply disagree.

The left sees you and me as the problem because we stand for something true, hopeful, and eternal. We are dregs to the elites and secular humanists who think believers are idiotic, ignorant, intolerant, and even immoral. Can this be resolved or are we too far gone?

I enjoy reading author and senior editor at *The Stream*, John Zmirak. He wrote last year about the impending split of America barring another Great Awakening. He declares that, "the common ground we once shared is no man's land." He provides some sobering but insightful thoughts:

"Is there a truce possible between two halves of the country, when each side thinks the other so morally depraved they're a threat to innocent kids, even their own? It's not about having different religions. For 200 years we took our kids to church or not, or to synagogues, and agreed to differ. That's how a healthy, pluralist society works…

"But the men who founded our country, and governed it till around 1960, used to agree on basic truths of natural law, knowable by reason. They agreed that a basic, tolerant Christianity with its mores anchored our view of the common good. They agreed that unborn life is sacred, marriage is between one man and one woman, and homosexuality is an unfortunate aberration: at worst a deadly sin, at best a heavy cross. Certainly nothing comparable to a person's race or religion, which we must respect."[32]

The problem is we do not respect others enough to hear them out and we are a less patient, tolerant nation. If the 2020 election revealed anything, it was our national divide.

Glaring issues were exposed involving election integrity. The entire voting process and how to deal with the virus were both politicized. With so much happening, I certainly understand why people grow weary or get angry. Reasonable people see their country being hijacked and had a hard time dealing with the 2020 outcome.

If you were discouraged or think the system is rigged, you are not alone. Many fair-minded people are still struggling with frustration.

We were told to accept the election outcome and move on, but I am unconvinced about the extremely controversial results. There were too many problems with nearly every aspect of the election process in multiple states, not to mention servers and voting machines.

Though I personally believe there was fraud, I am trusting God that He allowed it to happen for some reason, for His purposes. It is also hard to understand all the issues with investigations and judges, but the dust has settled and we need to avoid wasting time stewing. Our hope must never be in government or in a man or woman. We need to guard against all forms of idolatry.

We must align with like-minded believers, conservatives, and patriotic Americans. We also need to face the sobering fact this country is just not the same. Aside from the cheating and fraud that happens every election, it is scary that half of US voters are still willing to support godless Democrats and their policies. We are more stubborn and divided than we may want to admit.

For example, there are Christians who have voted for one political party all their life—no matter the candidate or the issues. This is wrong. Platforms change. This is idolatry. If a major part of your platform opposes God's Word, stop sinning by approving of evil! Repent of your pride.

THE CHURCH: BIBLICAL VS. LIBERAL

While it is no surprise the nation is divided, it is disappointing the church is fractured as well. Believers have been divided over doctrines and principles, Bible prophecy, the deity of Jesus, inerrancy of Scripture, political issues, social justice, exposing evil, and even what it means to be the church in the context of America.

Politics is one thing, but sadly, we now need to define what it means to be saved or conservative. "We" means true, Bible-believing Christians, also known as disciples or followers of Jesus Christ; we are the remnant who believes Scripture is inerrant and literally God-breathed. We trust God's Word is true, living, authoritative, and is essential.

Since some are true believers, that means there are false converts or what may be referred to as professing believers. A pastor friend describes them as so-called Christians. The late Dr. D. James Kennedy confirmed this idea:

"The vast majority of people who are members of churches in America today are not Christians. I say that without the slightest fear of contradiction. I base it on empirical evidence of 24 years of examining thousands of people."

Only God knows a person's heart, and He has the final say about whether someone is converted, saved, and sanctified or not. But the Bible does tell us we will know them by the fruit they produce in their lives. Does a person have good fruit, rotten fruit, or no fruit?

Once a person is truly repentant and born again of the Spirit, attitudes and behaviors change. This is why we need undiluted Gospel teaching, more faith, and less fluff in our churches. We need more hard truths and less soft sermons preached from pulpits. In our emotion-driven, moral relativistic culture, we need to hear about the authoritative Word of God.

American churches have not been producing mature disciples of Jesus, but many do have very nice programs and beautiful buildings. Some churches are more like entertainment empires masquerading as churches. There are pastors who avoid the Old Testament, Revelation, Bible prophecy, and social issues. Therefore, we are also divided over methodology.

The essence of evangelism is a call for repentance, a call to go, to tell them the bad news about sin, the justice of a holy God, and wrath to come. Then, the good news can be happily received.

The great theologian and preacher of the 1800s, Charles Finney, once said,

"Evermore the Law must prepare the way for the gospel. To overlook this in instructing souls is almost certain to result in false hope, the introduction of a false standard of Christian experience, and to fill the church with false converts."

Do you see why we are divided? The test of time has proven Charles Finney to be right. The church is overpopulated with false converts. Barna Research, Gallup, Lifeway, Pew, and others have shown this again and again.

Modern so-called Christians are confused about what the Bible teaches, and some do not even believe it's true! As a result, we have majored in mediocrity, and rather than having great influence, we have been deemed nonessential. COVID-19 helped prove this sad reality.

On the flipside, there are also many wonderful churches led by amazing, unappreciated men who boldly lead the saints and teach the uncompromising Word of God. We need more like them! Since they are in the minority, I refer to them as remnant leaders or patriot pastors.

By the way, the modern-day every-head-bowed approach to altar calls, crusades, and revival meetings can also be less than productive long term. Real discipleship is often missing.

A. W. Tozer put it this way:

"It is my opinion that tens of thousands, if not millions, have been brought into some kind of religious experience by accepting Christ and they have not been saved."

In the emotion of the moment, a person invites Jesus into their heart, perhaps in response to a heart-wrenching song or pastor's plea. But if they do not follow through, are they really saved? One reason for our church divide is there are unbelievers within the ranks!

People tend to think division is always a bad thing, but the more we unite around Scripture and biblical Christianity, further divides will occur out of necessity. Sheep and goats. Division never seemed to bother Jesus, His disciples, or early church saints throughout the centuries.

Jesus—the Prince of Peace—came to provide salvation, which includes peace with God. We cannot be at peace with this world. The world system is antichrist. We are in the world, not of it. It is not until the Lord returns and sets up His Kingdom that there will finally be everlasting peace.

Jesus said He came to destroy the works of the devil (1 John 3:8) and to cast fire on the earth. He even warned that even families would be divided over Him:

"Do you think that I have come to give peace on earth? No, I tell you, but rather division. For from now on in one house there will be five divided, three against two and two against three. They will be divided, father against son and son against father, mother against daughter and daughter against mother, mother-in-law against her daughter-in-law and daughter-in-law against mother-in-law" (Luke 12:51-53).

Perhaps you understand this because you have unsaved family members. Maybe they are hostile toward your faith. Many families are split over religion and politics, issues that affect the afterlife (faith) and how we live now (government).

Doctrine divides, but we are not the dividers! People must decide what to do about Jesus and His Word. We are ambassadors for Christ, not secret agents. Believers are called to permeate society with the aroma of Christianity and the life-saving Gospel of repentance from sin.

Paul wrote to the Corinthians:

"But thanks be to God, who always leads us in triumph in Christ, and through us reveals the fragrance of the knowledge of Him in every place. For we are a fragrance of Christ to God among those who are being saved and among those who are perishing. To the one an aroma from death to death, to the other an aroma from life to life" (2 Corinthians 2:14-16).

He works through us to manifest the fragrance of Christianity in and on our culture. But the flavor of the preserving salt has faded. Evil has never been so prevalent, and the light is flickering. This is no time to back down or retreat!

In most other countries throughout the world, Christians are suffering greatly. Our brothers and sisters have been constantly threatened, persecuted, tortured, and killed for their faith. The church in restricted nations had to go underground. And they are still meeting together.

We have been spoiled in America. Christianity and the US Constitution are incredibly unique to the most blessed, envied, free, loved, hated, powerful, and prosperous nation in the world. We just thought it would last longer.

At the end of his life, the apostle Paul told Timothy about difficult times that would come in the last days (2 Timothy 3); times in which men will be haters of good (vs. 3); lovers of pleasure rather than lovers of God (vs. 4). Paul warned, "Men also oppose the truth, men of depraved mind" (vs. 8). Like it or not, we are in a battle.

In another outstanding chapter in the Bible, Paul wrote to the church in Rome about men who "exchanged the truth of God for a lie" (Romans 1:25) and referred to these lost souls as "haters of God" (1:30),

> "And just as they did not see fit to acknowledge God any longer, God gave them over to a depraved mind… being filled with all unrighteousness, wickedness, greed, evil" (Romans 1:28-29).

Tragically, not only will most of them reject God, but they will also take countless souls with them. So how should true, Bible-believing Christians respond?

In Psalm 119, David wrote about being afflicted by the arrogant mocking him, and yet he was comforted by God's Word. Catch this raw emotion he expressed due to his love for God.

"Burning indignation has seized me because of the wicked, who forsake Your law" (Psalm 119:53).

We, too, should have a hatred of wickedness. We can confront and expose deeds of darkness (Ephesians 5:11) while promoting truth and righteousness. Burning indignation should seize us! This is not the hour for weak witnesses and silent believers. Keep pointing to Jesus!

Founder of Life Outreach International, James Robison, said:

> "We must reject the thought that evangelism is to be separated from the importance of standing against evil. We weren't saved just to escape this world and go to heaven. Transformed people transform the culture while standing boldly against evil."

There is a spiritual principle that may be helpful here: the devil never gives back any ground he has already taken. We must stand! The godless left now runs the entire public education system. They control most news, Big Tech, social media, the entertainment industry, corporations, the courts, an entire political party, and they want to censor or control the church as well!

The battle is now at our door and we have a relentless foe coming against everything that is good, holy, and true. We must resist evil and those who advance it. Their worldview is anti-Christ, and their end is destruction. They did not see fit to acknowledge God; they hate Him, and those who represent Him. Their hearts have been hardened.

Jesus said love your enemies and pray for them; they have no idea hell is real and judgment is coming. He did not say compromise with them! The left refuse to live and let live. But we are blessed to have a constitution in which our freedoms are still protected—for now.

Educator and writer Emma Willard founded the Troy Female Seminary in New York in the early 1800s. About 200 years ago, she stated:

"The government of the United States is acknowledged by the wise and good of other nations, to be the most free, impartial, and righteous government of the world; but all agree, that for such a government to be sustained many years, the principles of truth and righteousness, taught in the Holy Scriptures, must be practiced."

We used to be wise, but we neglected the practice of truth and righteousness. We were a virtuous people, had much in common, and life was simpler. Agreeing that we as a nation were under God had a lot to do with our being united.

That was then. The heart of the nation has changed and many things divide us today, including:

Worldview. The Bible. US history. Socialism. Obama. Islam. Russian collusion. Clinton. Corruption. Big Government. Impeachment. The 2016 election. Tweets. Abortion. Religion. Nationalism. Religious Freedom. Trump. The 2020 election. America first. Capitalism. Liberal Media. Biden. COVID-19. Racism. Government shutdowns. The US Constitution. The Second Amendment. Harris. Feminism. Climate Change. Public Schools. LGBT Issues. Supreme Court. Israel. The United Nations…

A century ago we had fewer things to disagree about, and how to govern the country was not one of them! The catalyst was the falling away from God.

THE STATES: NO LONGER "INDIVISIBLE"

When two sides cannot agree on pivotal issues such as the existence of God, truth, freedom, our history as a nation, the value of life in a mother's womb, how to define family, gender, marriage, and the purpose of civil government, it can be nearly impossible to work together.

Worse, when one of those sides uses any means available to gain power, and when there are few standing in the gap to hold them accountable, options are limited. When typical checks and balances fail, what can be done? Since our founders already considered a separation of powers in government, it may be time for the people to consider political separation.

It may also be time to revisit the biblical and constitutional concept of interposition. This is when someone places them self between the oppressor and intended victim(s).

In our context, the victims are American citizens who oppose big government, communism, socialism, Marxism, progressivism, mask mandates, economic shutdowns, church restrictions, the unending power grabs of state governors, the Democrat Party, and Joe Biden's pen.

The Lesser Magistrate Doctrine teaches that when the superior or higher-ranking civil authority makes unjust/immoral law, policy, or court opinion—the lower or lesser ranking civil authority has both the God-given right *and duty* to refuse obedience to that superior authority; and if necessary, actively resist the superior authority.

One benefit of interposition is it reminds those in power that their authority has limits. The doctrine was first formalized by Christian men in Magdeburg, Germany, in 1550.

Matt Trewhella has been the pastor of Mercy Seat Church since 1988 and founded Missionaries to the Preborn. Writing about Interposition of Lesser Magistrates, he explained that evil, overreaching government officials count on the compliance of the lesser magistrates to obey their edicts and spread wickedness down into the fabric of society. Trewhella adds:

> "Magistrates are all those who possess public office, whether through election or appointment. The authority all magistrates possess is delegated to them by God. Therefore, they have a duty to govern according to his rule.

> "They are not to make law, policy or court opinion that is contrary to his law or Word. They are not to exceed the limits of civil government as revealed by Scripture."[33]

Obviously, we the people nor the lesser magistrates have stood in the gap. When men do not oppose lawless actions, the tyrant authority is free to build the next plank of his tyranny. This is how godlessness has been allowed free reign in a nation formerly united under God.

Is the US Constitution, a miraculous document inspired by God, still the law of the land? Many concerned citizens are wondering about the fate of our fractured nation. This republic is hanging on like the American flag after the battle of Fort McHenry in 1814.

If the last four years have taught us anything, and if the eight years prior to that taught us anything, we have been fighting a cultural and legislative civil war in government, the courts, schools, and the public square. We have seen fierce debates and uncivil exchanges.

America looks less like the land of the free and home of the brave, let alone the Christian nation our great grandparents knew. It does, however, resemble a secular nation the left wants to control.

Author Matt Walsh of the *Daily Wire* recently did an unscientific social media poll with 52,000 people responding. Not surprisingly, over 60 percent support a plan to break up the United States so that the left and right can live in separate countries.

Let me be clear that repentance and a renewed America is preferable to secession, but a kind of national separation may be where we are headed. We must now discuss options in the hopes of preserving the country! Inevitable and unavoidable conflict looms and yet, few have thought through practical plans or solutions. History is a good reminder of where we need to go for help!

In 1787, delegates met to debate and draft the Constitution of the United States. During a spirited discussion, it was one of the least religious statesmen at the convention who appealed to Scripture and counseled the delegates to seek the aid of Almighty God.

Benjamin Franklin stated that, "God governs in the affairs of men...that an empire cannot rise without His aid." Though it is clear from our founding documents the Lord built and blessed this great nation, Franklin also said that *without* God's continued aid,

> "We shall be divided by our little partial local interests;
> our projects will be confounded, and we ourselves shall
> become a reproach and bye word down to future ages."

We are divided in large part because we have forgotten God, we have not lived for Him, nor have we prayed for His guidance and help. Moreover, half the country wants nothing to do with God. Believers must cry out to Him!

Those brave men took Franklin's advice to pray, imploring the assistance of heaven and its blessings on their deliberations. Without God's help, this nation, its powerful Constitution, and the freedoms we enjoy would never have been born. The Bible says nothing is impossible for God.

Can we as a nation survive much longer? President Abraham Lincoln asked similar questions in 1863 in his national declaration of prayer and repentance. The church must take the lead and respond before it is too late.

I am not being an alarmist, but right now at the federal level, two opposing parties are battling over a sinking ship.

For Christians, we must not unite with those who are advancing evil agendas diametrically opposed to biblical values. If we can no longer coexist politically, what are our options? These are serious questions with unpleasant, far-reaching implications. Yes, we keep the faith, share the Gospel of Jesus, make disciples, and pray, pray, pray as faithful pastors and believers have been doing.

But our country continues to splinter at an alarming rate.

THE SEPARATION

Today, when citizens are asked, "What is America?" it is not that they cannot answer. The problem is there are two conflicting responses—almost as if we are discussing two different countries! Ask young people this question and their views are even further from God and our founding values.

Is it time for a separation of counties, districts, cities, or states? How in the world would it work? We keep referring to "One Nation Under God" when we know it is a lie. We are no longer under the one true, living God. Americans worship many false gods, follow countless philosophies, and have rejected Jesus, the way, the truth, and the life (John 14:6).

Pastor Dan Fisher (Fairview Baptist Church, Edmond, OK) travels to churches and shares the history of the Black Robed Regiment. Leading up to the Revolutionary War, pastors were known to preach a Sunday morning sermon, remove their black clergy robe, grab their gun, and head for the battlefield!

How might this apply to our present times? The left and right are diametrically opposed and cannot simply agree to disagree while moving in opposite directions.

I asked Dan Fisher about this topic and he said there are simply times when peace is not possible. Jesus told His disciples to shake off the dust from their feet and not allow God's peace to come upon those who reject God's truth (Matthew 10:13-14). Wow.

In a recent sermon called "Irrevocable," he preached about principles from the Bible that we might apply to our modern cultural battle with government over religious freedom and our God-given, unalienable rights. Fisher stated:

> "A large portion of our country's citizens want to turn our American Republic into something you are NOT going to like. Are you going to just stand by and allow it to happen? How many liberties are you willing to forfeit? I'm calling for a political separation, just as Thomas Jefferson did in the Declaration of Independence."

Our Founding Fathers envisioned a nation ruled by the people, not a one-party big government system of corrupt, left-wing politicians—telling the church how they can now worship.

They also envisioned a free press having integrity, and who would hold powerful people accountable. But sadly, the Democrat media pledged their undivided allegiance to the left, and they look with disdain on Christians, conservatives, and patriotic Americans.

Scripture does not teach that we can or even should agree with *everyone*. Yes, we need to try living peacefully with all people, but some simply do not want peace. Believers should pursue the things which make for peace (Romans 14:19), but God's Word does not elevate peace as the highest of virtues. We must not pursue peace at the expense of eternal truth and liberty!

Disagreeing is one thing. We should be able to do so respectfully. The left, however, owns cancel culture. They no longer simply oppose us; many want to destroy people's lives. They do not just think we are wrong; they think they know what is best for the whole country. We are at a stalemate.

In the last year I have read some good articles on this topic of separation. Opinions, solutions, and speculations are many, but Scott Morefield over at Townhall says it would be much better than living under a Democratic socialist, one-party state. He quoted George Mason University Scalia School of Law professor F.H. Buckley who argues that secession could be a reasonable way to resolve unbridgeable partisan differences.

Last year, Buckley wrote a book, *American Secession,* about the US being ripe for a national breakup, and says a constitutional split could occur with no bloodshed at all. As one example, Buckley writes about the velvet divorce of the Czechs and Slovaks in 1993:

> "Distinct in religion, language and culture, they had been combined in a country created in 1918 after the collapse of the Austro-Hungarian Empire. The

Slovaks were conservative and agricultural while the Czechs liked avant-garde plays and rock music. Czechoslovakia suffered through Nazi and Soviet rule, and then split apart into Slovakia and the Czech Republic upon the fall of communism. The two new countries, both Western and liberal, solved questions about their border, the division of assets and assumption of public debt through negotiation, and they've since maintained the friendliest of relations."[34]

I realize this is impossible to imagine for most people over fifty, but a political divorce may be what is needed. Where will we end up if we do nothing? At the very least, states should vote on it.

We might estimate there are close to 200 million people in the US who do not approve of God being removed from our culture. They still love the American idea. The founders assumed a virtuous, Christian citizenry who would pray and vote for moral and godly men who would then serve the best interests of the people.

But somehow, the church became powerless to stop the immoral, authoritarian freight train in our nation. John Adams, a leader in the American Revolution and the second US president, said it well:

"Our Constitution was made only for a moral and religious People. It is wholly inadequate to the government of any other.

"[I]t is religion and morality alone which can establish the principles upon which freedom can securely stand. The only foundation of a free constitution is pure virtue, and if this cannot be inspired into our People in a greater Measure than they have it now, they may change their Rulers and the forms of Government, but they will not obtain a lasting liberty."

A country rejecting God and without redeeming virtue has led to a Congress lacking character and truth. Citizens are responsible for our leaders, and we the people have tolerated recklessness and corruption. I shake my head thinking about today's corrupt Congress. We lost our moral compass.

And yet, even though we are reaping what has been sown, the vast majority does not want globalism, socialism, or communism. Most Americans do not endorse BLM violence in the name of political virtue or abortion on demand. They do not want the LGBT agenda normalized to the point boys will be girls and religious freedom will be history.

The sad truth, however, is the career politicians who are rich, powerful, or well known have the most influence, the loudest voices, and of course, the megaphone of the liberal media on their side. They have become enemies of God, of Christians, of freedom, and of America.

Other than our humanity and citizenship, we have next to nothing in common with left-wing progressives in politics, Hollywood, Wall Street, Big Tech, and power elites. We now have extremely limited influence even in local government, but this is one area in which we must be more involved: at the local and state level.

I just heard news about California, that a report stated over 5 million people have moved out of CA in recent years, unhappy with bloated government, astronomical taxes, and other awful policies. We see this across the country: two philosophies of government that are polar opposites.

At what point are the stark differences beyond irreconcilable? The political division in the United States being fueled by the left is extraordinary. I am a man of faith and trust God in all things. But I do not see a way around the inevitable fall of our nation unless drastic measures are taken. It is hard to imagine enough people having the will to resist the growing oppression and tyranny.

The decline of morality and government corruption in this country are more daunting than a few elections could possibly fix. If there is any chance of reversing course, millions more evangelical Christians must vote in upcoming elections. Why? We must win by massive margins due to voter fraud. If not, the liars and cheaters will always find ways to squeak out slim victories.

I also believe we must face new realities when it comes to information and communication since we are dealing with a one-party liberal media conglomerate. Considering Big Tech censorship, government schools, Democrat media, universities, corporate sports, and entertainment, how do we combat all the godless influences and misinformation out there?

It may very well happen that Republican candidates—at least on the presidential level—will never be treated fairly again. Do not be naïve when it comes to political battles. It may be helpful to consider the adage, "People who cannot be reasoned with can only be fought." We must fight on our knees, then with our voices, peaceful activism, and votes.

One argument the left uses is America is an evil nation of systemic or institutional racism. In 2008, Obama/Biden campaigned for hope and change, and in 2020, Joe Biden again promised change and to bring healing to Washington. Joe Biden has been in elected office since 1972!

If it is true that we are such a racist country, why has he not been able to do anything about it all these years? In my opinion, he has only divided people and made things worse.

He speaks out of both sides of his mouth. He said in an interview, "If you vote for Trump, then you ain't black."

If we are a nation with such deep-rooted racism, what have old Joe and the accusers of the brethren done to improve things? For many decades, Democrats have controlled every major institution in America. If we are divided and more racist today, why is no one holding them accountable?

Over at *American Thinker*, Selwyn Duke said the time for talking is long past. He writes that in a saner world, people seeking truth and common ground could talk things out, but "morally nihilistic leftists scoff at absolutes and have thus turned themselves into glorified animals," and they will not stop. I agree with him and others who have concluded most Democrats have become so divisive and vitriolic, they seem to be ensuring that we cannot talk things out.

It is a Saul Alinsky tactic to justify saying and doing anything to achieve their ends; "no lie is too great, no theft too grand, no contradiction too bold," and as we observed with COVID, "no sacrifice of life too unpalatable." See NY Gov. Andrew Cuomo (D-NY).

Duke warns conservatives to accept these hard realities, and then lists some accomplishments of the liberal, progressive, secular-socialist left in recent years. He writes:

"They have

- continually attacked us traditionalists and fomented unrest at our political events while accusing us of authoring violence;
- visited career and reputational destruction upon those who dare speak unfashionable truths while accusing those truth-tellers of intolerance;

- used government agencies such as the IRS and FBI to persecute us while accusing us of endangering the republic;
- played the identity politics card and demonized whites while accusing conservatives of being divisive, racist and bigoted;
- conspired with foreign powers to undermine our nation while accusing us of treason;
- enabled China, an imperialistic foe and a clear and present danger to our country;
- endeavored to steal an election after having wrongly accused conservatives of thus doing in 2016;
- abetted an invasion of our nation in order to raise an alien electoral army;
- mismanaged a pandemic and caused death while using it as a pretext for stripping our liberties, "locking down" the country and destroying people's livelihoods;
- corrupted our children with perversion and scarred their bodies, minds and souls;
- facilitated the murder of the unborn while accusing us of indifference to the vulnerable;
- prosecuted conservatives on trumped up charges;
- called truth "hateful" or "misinformation" and censored it via Big Tech while presenting convenient lies as "fact";
- encouraged violent mobs to create mayhem;
- attacked our history and heroes and destroyed our cultural heritage;
- indoctrinated the young in schools to transform them into leftist foot soldiers;
- attacked our nation's foundational faith, Christianity, while spreading corruptive moral relativism and destructive theologies"[35]

This is not to discourage you, but for you to know the enemy we are dealing with and to consider how we might rally the remnant and strengthen true believers for battle. I have been praying for wisdom more frequently in the last few years than I have in all my life. The Bible says,

"The fear of the LORD is the beginning of wisdom,
And the knowledge of the Holy One is understanding"
(Proverbs 9:10).

The Bible also says, "The fear of the Lord is to hate evil" (Proverbs 8:13). We must not be ignorant of evil, nor should we allow evildoers to go unchecked and unchallenged!

Not much should surprise us any longer. The left is capable of anything at this point. In January of this year, discredited liberal media personality, Katie Couric, recently said those who supported President Trump need to be reprogrammed!

Her exact words were:

"How are we going to really, almost deprogram these people who have signed up for the cult of Trump?"[36]

Who is "we"? The left. Power elites, including globalists, and Democrat socialists wanting control of the country. They are the godless cult of liberalism.

Wake up, friends. In the last few months, I have read, heard, or have seen headlines with many others asking the same thing. These include Hollywood celebrities, leading Democrats, liberal media entertainers, LGBT advocates, public school teachers, university professors, and Don Lemon.

Hillary Clinton said Trump supporters are deplorable and domestic terrorists, but at least she didn't say anything (on record anyway) about deprogramming or reeducation camps. Who would stop them?

We no longer have a justice department that follows the law and is unbiased; the DOJ is loyal to Democrats and the deep state. We were reminded again in events following the 2020 Election.

No administration was more corrupt than the Obama administration that for eight long years led an all-out assault on Christianity and conservative values. Who can forget how he flaunted executive orders, weaponized the IRS, and punished his enemies? The activist media, FBI, and DOJ covered for Obama/Biden in ways we will never fully know.

And now, it is the O'Biden/Harris administration's turn. Last year, the left kept the pressure on citizens to ensure a constant crisis mode under President Trump. Divisive and destructive rhetoric was injected to tear us apart, and if that were not enough, they added riots and cheered shutdowns.

The left introduced or has redefined concepts such as: tolerance, diversity, inclusion, political correctness, climate change, reproductive justice, social justice, identity politics, toxic masculinity, cancel culture, white privilege, woke, and being on the wrong side of history.

Author, political commentator, and media host, Ben Shapiro, wrote about how the left have used disintegrationist history to deprogram and divide people. They have successfully pushed the claim that any good in this country must have come from poisonous seeds.

In his book, *How To Destroy America In Three Easy Steps*, he explains the bottom line is those who hate the country insist we were born in sin, so to speak. Shapiro writes:

"Disintegrationist history teaches three fundamental principles: first, that America was founded in evil; second, that America is irredeemably divided and can never escape her past absent dismantling her founding principles; third, that America has been, on net, terrible for her citizens and terrible for the world.

"The third principle, in particular, is provably false; But Disintegrationists simply assume the third principle by the virtue of the first two: America was born in sin and can never be redeemed."[37]

Since the right and the left are in gridlock, how can we coexist with those who hate our God, suppress the truth, and are radically changing the nation we love? Today's Democrats are not liberal; they are progressive. The left has become authoritarian! Now what?

There are possibilities to consider rather than surrender or unlimited submission to the left. We are still blessed in America beyond the imaginations of most people around the world, but God only knows where we go from here.

No matter what happens in Washington DC, most of us can do something locally. And one morally reprehensible institution that must be addressed is the government-run school system. That's next.

10

Anti-Christian, UnAmerican Education

"The great enemy of the salvation of man, in my opinion, never invented a more effectual means of extirpating [extinguishing] Christianity from the world than by persuading mankind that it was improper to read the Bible at schools."   —Benjamin Rush

"Education is a weapon; whose effect depends on who holds it in his hands and at whom it is aimed."
                                                              —Joseph Stalin

"In my view, the Christian religion is the most important and one of the first things in which all children, under a free government ought to be instructed."
                                                              —Noah Webster

What did we expect? After more than a half century of teaching kids in America that there is no God, truth changes, and that their country is evil, we are reaping what has been sown. We have seen much rotten fruit produced by the so-called education system. Sadly, this generation of young adults generally has more disdain for America—but knows far less about actual US history.

They do, however, know all about LGBT causes, climate change, abortion and Planned Parenthood, gender ideology, Black Lives Matter, socialism, and that they are supposed to support Democrats and hate Republicans. These are things they have been convinced of.

Education has become a weapon in the hands of the left who hijacked public schools and universities. We now know what happens when kids are programmed and told to believe lies. Young people have been given clear marching orders.

For example, during the 2020 protests, riots, and mob violence, communities were destroyed, thousands injured, and many lives were lost forever. But the damage, destruction, and downside of these stories barely made the news. The average protestor age? Twenty-five.

Historic statues in cities across the US were defaced or torn down. Instructions were even sent out on how to topple monuments. And did you hear that the occupation of some of those who faced felony charges across the country were schoolteachers? I am not saying the violence, chaos, and division was all the fault of government-run schools, but decades of groundwork had been laid poisoning a generation against God, country, parents, religion, and history.

Students were trained to gather and protest on their school campuses, they signed petitions for far-left causes, and attended political rallies for socialist candidates. Tens of thousands of high school and college students either joined or supported Antifa and Black Lives Matter, as many of them marched, protested, and shouted obscenities from coast to coast.

They have been indoctrinated around ideas such as the threat of climate change, open borders, abortion is health care, global government, social justice, Republicans hate women, children, and minorities, Trump is bad, Marxism is good. A generation has been groomed as social activists.

How did we get here?

For nearly a hundred years, the United States has been in the process of being fundamentally and radically transformed as the left infiltrated government education. Christianity was declining while high numbers of young people became more open to socialism.

Our great grandparents once said, "It could never happen in America."

But it did—and we are now living with the consequences of pursuing happiness while surrendering the education of our children. In hindsight, we now understand one of the anthems of the left: win the children and control the future. It was easy to program young minds when they knew so little about their own history.

In his 1988 farewell address to the nation, President Ronald Reagan warned that, "Because we're a great nation, our challenges seem complex. It will always be this way. But as long as we remember our first principles and believe in ourselves, the future will always be ours."

Reagan said that the people tell the government what to do, not the other way around. He said when government expands, liberty contracts. But when he transitioned to education, he asked if we were doing a good enough job teaching our children what America is and what she represents in the long history of the world.

We could have nodded in agreement with President Reagan as he said many of us grew up in a very different America because we were taught what it means to be American! He continued:

"We've got to do a better job of getting across that America is freedom—freedom of speech, freedom of religion, freedom of enterprise. And freedom is special and rare. It's fragile; it needs protection; …If we forget what we did, we won't know who we are. I'm warning of an eradication of the American memory that could result, ultimately, in an erosion of the American spirit. Let's start with some basics: more attention to American history…"[38]

Is it too late? I personally believe so but hope I am wrong.

The roots of anti-American teaching began over seventy-five years ago at our universities with the help of Fabian socialists coming over from Europe. Many of these leftists were well educated, upper-class elites who entered our major universities, and the transformation of academia was underway.

The public school takeover began even earlier with the help of atheists like John Dewey, the so-called father of modern education. The contagious virus of godless socialism has now spread into all levels of learning and throughout our culture. At the college level, radical professors attack the ideals of Western civilization and the Judeo-Christian values America was founded upon.

Progressives such as Dewey were very influential in the development and direction of the modern education machine and believed in preparing children for a desired new world order. Opposed to the Christian faith and religion in general, Dewey coauthored the 1933 *Humanist Manifesto,* favored Marxism, and wrote an essay saying capitalism restricted freedom.

Dewey also declared that there is no such thing as God or the human soul, and so he concluded there is no need for religion and no room for truth, natural law, or moral absolutes!

No wonder Christianity was expelled from schools. The left could not have infiltrated education and caused such a decline in morality, producing a generation of Democrat disciples without first removing pillars of truth: God, prayer, the Bible, and the Ten Commandments. Schools have never been the same. The doors were then flung open to everything else. The void was filled with an ABC philosophy—anything but Christ. The NEA became hostile toward Jesus and Christians.

Years ago, students in America were optimistic about their future and had a deep appreciation for the freedoms they enjoyed. Most generally had traditional beliefs and family values, a respect for authority, and were confident in their identity. Today, however, many students are angry, anxious, depressed, entitled, and divided. They do not share their grandparents' values, they have no religion, and are more concerned about global warming, inequality, injustice, political correctness, racism, and capitalism.

This kind of shift in basic thinking and worldview has had tragic results. Generations of kids grew up, and we have seen the negative impact in nearly every aspect of society.

We already discussed the Great Reset, but it is important to point out that millions of young people worldwide would not be accepting of such radical economic, social, and technological change had they not been prepped and programmed. To them, a new world order is for the greater good of mankind globally.

Tag teaming with public schools, Big Tech has aligned with Hollywood and the liberal media to mold a generation to be politically active, Democrat voters. These minions are convinced the agenda against capitalism, America, and Christianity is a good thing and they are willing to take what they have learned to the streets.

Writing for *Off Guardian*, Winter Oak explains:

"Youth activism is increasing worldwide, being revolutionized by social media that increases mobilization to an extent that would have been impossible before. It takes many different forms, ranging from non-institutionalized political participation to demonstrations and protests, and addresses issues as diverse as climate change, economic reforms, gender equality and LGBTQ rights. The young generation is firmly at the vanguard of social change. There is little doubt that it will be the catalyst for change and a source of critical momentum for the Great Reset."[39]

The worldview parroted throughout academia that capitalism and religious freedom are rooted in evil is central to the globalist, socialist cause.

In a way, we no longer have capitalism in its truest form, but a technocracy including a top-down approach with big government in bed with Big Tech. Big Tech is the behemoth that the left uses to promote and support Democrat policies. Therefore, surveys and Bernie Sanders voters now indicate about 70 percent of millennials would vote for a socialist candidate.

Socialism is a centrally planned economy in which the government controls all means of production. Forty percent of all Americans now have a favorable view of socialism. Is this historical amnesia, or did they not learn true history in the first place?

CANCEL CULTURE AND COMMUNISM

Thirty-six percent of millennials support communism. For those keeping score at home, that's one in three youngsters. Not surprisingly, these same millennials believe President

Donald Trump is a bigger threat to world peace than North Korea's Kim Jong-un and Russia's Vladimir Putin.

In its fourth annual report on attitudes toward socialism, the Victims of Communism Memorial Foundation revealed some alarming trends among young people in the United States of Entertainment. Ready? Only 57 percent of millennials believe the Declaration of Independence better guarantees freedom and equality over the Communist Manifesto. And, only 62 percent of future world shakers believe China is a communist country.

Marion Smith, executive director of Victims of Communism Memorial Foundation stated:

"When we don't educate our youngest generations about the historical truth of 100 million victims murdered at the hands of communist regimes over the past century, we shouldn't be surprised at their willingness to embrace Marxist ideas; we need to redouble our efforts to educate America's youth about...the dangers of socialism today."[40]

Most of us don't understand how kids can go through junior high and high school and not come away with at least a basic understanding of economics and world history. We remember the Soviet Union and Red Communist China, and today, we see a few obvious examples in Cuba and Venezuela.

This growing love affair with socialism coincides with a foggy understanding of economic philosophies and is a result of globalist, ideologically driven public school curriculums. How else can you explain why 10 percent of millennials say Trump is responsible for more deaths and human rights abuses than Russian leader Joseph Stalin, who murdered tens of millions of people, or Nazi dictator Adolf Hitler?

The same way we can explain how 87 percent of high school students flunked a five-question test of basic knowledge about American history. These same students were also least likely to identify the four presidents on Mount Rushmore. Only 35 percent got it right.

In addition, many kids graduate from high school or college not knowing specifics about the US Constitution, world history, including the Holocaust, and universities do not require the study of American history. Those man-on-the-street interviews with clueless young people are real, and there has, in fact, been a deliberate dumbing down of students for many decades now.

Conversely, our founders had quite a different approach.

The true father of American scholarship and education, Noah Webster, believed children ought to be acquainted with their own country and to rehearse the history of their own country. Webster was a textbook pioneer, English-language spelling reformer, editor, and prolific author. He was a revolutionary soldier, judge, legislator, and the creator of *Webster's Dictionary*.

In 1832, Webster took on what he called "the most important enterprise of my life"—transcribing the 1611 King James Bible into language more understandable to American readers of his day. He served in the Connecticut General Assembly, the Massachusetts Legislature, and four years as a judge. He was one of the first Founding Fathers to call for a Constitutional Convention.

In addition to the quote at the beginning of this chapter, Webster stated:

"No truth is more evident to my mind than that the Christian religion must be the basis of any government intended to secure the rights and privileges of a free people."

All you need to do is look up quotes from just about any American founder and patriot, compare what they say about faith, education, and government, and you will come away wondering how things turned upside down. You do not have to look too hard to see the damage done by the US Department of Education and the National Education Association.

Please understand that I was raised in a family of teachers, from both parents to my sisters to an uncle and cousin. In most cases, people going into teaching had good intentions and genuinely cared about children. But it is obvious the system was hijacked by the left many decades ago.

Today, public schools are practically an arm of the Democrat Party. In fact, when it comes to campaign money, 98 percent of donations by teachers' unions go to Democrats.

This presents quite the dilemma for a teacher who is a true believer in Christ, conservative, or Republican. People of faith must oppose revisionist history and the emotional and psychological manipulation that has been so effective in brainwashing generations of kids.

This brings us to recent years and the emersion of cancel culture. A person can get canceled today if they do not adhere to the ideology and worldview of the left. You must support modern liberalism, the Democrat Party, socialism, globalism, and progressive policies or you can be ostracized, bullied, shunned, threatened, and even fired from your job.

Activists enforce it while others go along with it by their silence. One explanation of cancel culture in schools is the editing, reconstructing, or rewriting of American history by ignoring or eliminating parts of our past that do not align with the Marxist values of the left. Then, graft in new interpretations of history and behavior while encouraging political activism. Christian influence must be downplayed or erased.

But considering this nation's rich history, with our outstanding Constitution, Bill of Rights, and Declaration of Independence, how did we get to the point where we practically have two vastly different Americas? When did it become acceptable and fashionable to criticize and even repeat blatant lies about the country, our founders, their intentions, and their legacy?

Short answer? Education was weaponized by radicals and used to chip away at biblical values. We were nowhere near a perfect, sinless nation. But using code words such as diversity, inclusion, health, equality, sex education, tolerance, white privilege, and wokeness, most schools proudly promote anti-Christian and anti-American ideas today.

I'm not saying there aren't some good teachers out there, but their hands are tied, and their frustrations are at a tipping point—just like our country.

As government schools continue down this path, the homeschooling movement is rapidly growing for obvious reasons. Public schools have become toxic. Yes, some Christian students do escape with their faith intact, but after years of secularization and social instruction, the majority is thoroughly programmed to conform to the world.

Surveys indicate students have generally been told what to think, especially when it comes to politics, religion, history, and morality. About ten years ago, the architect of Common Core openly said that teachers will "teach to the test." What does this mean? A handful of educators determine the outcome by creating testing materials, and students learn whatever is required to get the right answers on the tests.

In keeping up with the cancel culture that she helped create, House speaker Nancy Pelosi gave orders to remove from the walls of the US Capitol building four portraits of former House speakers who served in the Confederacy. Please understand what is really going on with all this.

Dr. Andy Woods of Sugar Land Bible Church in Texas addressed this in a Facebook post:

> "The deliberate erasure of history is a Stalinist, Maoist tactic for purposes of destroying one civilization so that they can bring in their 'higher' social order (Communism, Marxism, statism). Beyond that, if you want to get rid of all vestiges of racism in the history of the United States, you would also have to also get rid of the Democratic Party itself, which is the party of the Jim Crow South, the KKK, and Robert Byrd."

Students, however, are not learning the whole truth about racism and slavery because it is inconvenient to modern virtue-signaling liberals. Activists deemed themselves justified for tearing down statues of people they knew little about last year during the BLM purge.

In a Monmouth University poll last year, 58 percent of respondents with a four-year degree said rioting and vandalism are either fully or partially justified because of racism.[41] Another poll showed that 62 percent of young people are okay with looting—which is theft of someone else's property! Hard-working people lost businesses and property in cancel culture 2020.

I would not expect most people under thirty-five to know this, but Matthias Baldwin was a Christian and abolitionist that lobbied against slavery for three decades. Ironically, Black Lives Matter protesters, aka Joe Biden voters, tore down a statue of Baldwin in Philadelphia. Remember, the issue is never the issue. The issue is the revolution.

A college professor at the University of Alabama actually provided online instructions on how to tear down monuments that allegedly promote nationalism and racism. UA's Sarah Parcak tweeted a detailed description of how to pull down a monument, complete with a Black Lives Matter hashtag and advice to "let gravity work for you," watch it topple, and get out of the way.

In Mississippi, a junior high teacher faced felony charges after being arrested for the destruction of a Confederate monument at the University of Mississippi. The suspect has been identified as former UM graduate, Zachary Borenstein.

Taking a cue from Kamala Harris, who helped raise money to bail out rioters in Minneapolis, a fundraiser was launched to bail him out. Arielle Hudson, a 2016 UM graduate, said Borenstein was arrested "after making a strong stance against oppression and racism." In other words, way to go, Zach! More than 600 Democrat donors contributed to raise $20,000 for the felon.

To spark discussion last year, a public school teacher in Detroit wore a sweatshirt that boldly declared, "Columbus was a murderer." Hmm, I do not recall that in history classes growing up. She is not alone. In Rhode Island, middle school teacher, Derrick Garforth, was arrested for vandalizing a statue of Christopher Columbus. He teaches social studies.

Are you noticing a common thread here?

In the southwest, the University of Arizona offers academic credit for internship with anti-capitalist, far-left extremist groups. An arm of Black Lives Matter, The Alliance for Global Justice is one option listed under the university's Public Management and Policy Internship's site. Part of its campaign is to, drumroll please: Defund the Police. Another project cofunded by the alliance, Refuse Fascism, actively and openly worked to overthrow President Donald Trump and Vice President Mike Pence.

This is part of the modern university system.

Most of us were disgusted, not only when college students across the US were attacking unarmed statues, but many school administrators went right along with it. Biden/Harris voters went from assaulting police, stopping traffic, burning down buildings, blowing up cars, and breaking windows, to tearing down federal monuments and statues of historical figures.

But would minions of mayhem obey the marching orders of radical and racist Shaun King, a leader in the BLM movement?

A social justice activist, King unleashed a firestorm on social media when he said statues of Jesus Christ are a gross form of white supremacy and must be taken down.

The New Testament describes Jesus as Jewish, being from Bethlehem in Judea, but Shaun King insists Jesus is a European. He said:

" 'I think the statues of the white European they claim is Jesus should also come down. They are a form of white supremacy. Always have been…Tear them down.' He continued, 'All murals and stained glass windows of white Jesus, and his European mother, and their white friends should also come down. They are a gross form of white supremacy. Created as tools of oppression. Racist propaganda.' "[42]

A majority of college-educated people under thirty-five have a disdain for Jesus, the Bible, Christians, Israel, and the Jews.

Some students seemed to follow King's advice. Last July, Catholic churches across the US and Canada suffered a wave of arson and vandalism during Black Lives Matter and Antifa protests. The weeklong spree included spray-painting or beheading statues of Jesus and Mary.

Someone set fire to Queen of Peace church in Ocala, Florida, another arsonist torched a statue of the Virgin Mary in Boston, and yet another fire broke out at Mission San Gabriel Arcángel in Los Angeles, destroying the building's roof and interior. Vandals beheaded a statue of the Virgin Mary and knocked the monument off its pedestal at Saint Stephen Church in Chattanooga, TN.

I wonder what would have happened had law enforcement been freed up to arrest and fine rioters, looters, and vandals from coast to coast. We will never know.

Democrats also forced New York City officials to fall in line and agree to remove the bronze statue of Teddy Roosevelt from outside the Museum of Natural History. The statue has stood there in the Theodore Roosevelt Rotunda facing Central Park since before the Second World War. Roosevelt was a hero to millions of Americans.

In fact, in 1901, he invited (black author and educator) Booker T. Washington to dinner at a time when no African American had ever eaten in the White House. Democrats roared with rage and because Roosevelt had a meal with a black man, they attacked Teddy Roosevelt and his wife for the rest of their lives.

Ironically, Shawn King supported the campaign of an old white man, Bernie Sanders. How does that make any sense? It doesn't have to if you are a Democrat. One Christian teacher pointed to the education problem in the US by declaring last year, "We are planting the root and then are surprised by its fruit."

PUBLIC SCHOOLS PROMOTING ISLAM

Another observation about the public schools over the last decade or so is the acceptance of Islam. It seems the separation of church and state only applies to Christianity.

Even Joe Biden quoted the prophet Muhammad while speaking to Million Muslim Votes last summer. He went so far as to approve of Sharia Law and used a word, perhaps to pander to Muslims, that means, "If Allah wills it." Biden referred to Islam as a "great" faith and said, "Muslim American voices matter."[43]

Naturally, Emgage Action, the country's largest Muslim-American political action committee, endorsed Biden for president. And as far as government-run education, he said that he wishes "we taught more in our schools about the Islamic faith." None of this is surprising coming from a former VP of the most pro-Muslim administration in US history.

Even if you are neutral about religion in public schools, perhaps the following news stories will convince you there is a problem with pro-Muslim bias and indoctrination in education today.

In Michigan in 2019, when public schools started up, over 400 teachers had just completed mandatory training that exalted Islam but denigrated Christianity, America, and white males. (Surprise, surprise!) The training gave the impression that Islam is the peaceful, true religion while Christianity is a man-made, inferior, false religion.

In Maryland, La Plata High School students were required by a teacher to profess what is known as the Shahada, the Islamic conversion creed. ("There is no god but Allah, and Muhammad is the messenger of Allah.") The school did not allow a Christian student, Caleigh Wood, to opt out, and failed her for refusing to submit.

The Thomas More Law Center submitted a petition asking the Supreme Court to take up her case. For the record, when Caleigh's father complained, he was banned from the school campus.

In West Virginia, as part of a class on world religions, Mountain Ridge middle school students in Gerrardstown were asked to practice writing the Islamic declaration of faith in Arabic calligraphy. The class is said to have included a thirty-page section, "Islam in the World Today," and required seventh graders to also read segments of the Qur'an, learn Muslim prayer poses, and understand the Five Pillars of Islam.

One parent reportedly asked, "We cannot discuss our Ten Commandments in school, but they can discuss Islam's Five Pillars?"

Students apparently received packets on Buddhism, Christianity, Hinduism, and Judaism. The Islam packet contained passages from the Qur'an, but no Bible verses were included in the packet on Christianity. Parents were understandably outraged, especially after hearing students would be given a detention slip if they didn't do the assignment. The teacher later claimed the assignment was optional.

In New York City, parents were outraged after a public school held a moment of silence in 2018 for the people killed in Gaza. A Beacon High School public address announcement urged students to pause and honor those who died in the clash at the Israeli border during protest of the US Embassy in Jerusalem. The terrorist organization Hamas confirmed fifty out of sixty-two who died were members of their militant Islamic group.

In Olmstead Falls, Ohio, parents had tried to raise awareness and get the school board to change some school lessons and history textbooks that stated Muslims historically practiced religious tolerance by requiring Christians and Jews to pay extra taxes. There was no mention that the alternative was often death!

Jenny McKeigue was notified by her oldest son that during class his teacher played a reality TV episode of *30 Days: Muslims and America* about a Christian converting to Islam.

In Washington State, several school districts were promoting Islam through a Ramadan policy of giving Muslim students special privileges. One district ordered employees to greet Muslim students in Arabic.

In New Jersey, two mothers were accused of being Islamophobes after attending a school board meeting and requested changes to Chatham Middle School curriculum in which students were required to learn about Islam. No similar courses were taught on Christianity or Judaism. The two moms were also labeled as bigots and attacked on Facebook.[44]

According to *The Daily Wire*, superintendent Michael LaSusa refused to correct or eliminate the course because "it is part of the New Jersey curriculum core content standards to teach students about the various religions of the world." He also refused to meet with the moms, Gayers and Hilsenrath, who were then interviewed by *Fox News'* Tucker Carlson.

In Newton Massachusetts, a school district was exposed over charges that teaching materials about the Middle East were funded by Saudi, Palestinian, and other Arab states. According to reports, one of the books that Newton schools recommend as reading material included extremist writings by Muslim Brotherhood leaders Sayyid Qutb and Yusuf Qaradawi.

Newton school officials have continuously refused to make school curricula and teaching materials available to residents. Public pressure previously forced the high schools to discontinue using the Saudi-funded *Arab World Studies Notebook*, which makes spurious charges against Israel. Other districts had rejected the notebook.

There have also been similar stories in California, Georgia, New York, Oregon, Texas, Tennessee, Virginia, and others—all receiving extremely little attention in the politically correct, progressive media. This is a form of cultural jihad.

In 2012, ACT for America analyzed thirty-eight textbooks used in grades 6-12 in public schools and found that since the 1990s, discussions of Islam are taking up more and more pages (and class time), while the space and time allowed to Judaism and Christianity have simultaneously decreased.

Discriminating against those holding to the biblical Christian worldview while promoting other religious views is unconstitutional. Where is the Freedom *from* Religion foundation when it comes to Islam being taught in schools?

Parents across the country also objected to Access Islam, a Department of Education program. According to the Clarion Project, the federally funded program is directed at children from grades 5-12 and is also featured on various websites, including *PBS LearningMedia*.[45] The Smithsonian also promotes the course as does the United Nations.

A video from the course features a Christian convert to Islam, who emotionally declares how he found the true religion without any intermediaries. Concerned parents have noted the US Department of Education provides no comparable study or promotion of any other religion.

One high school homework assignment obtained by a news outlet revealed the question: "How did Muslim conquerors treat those they conquered?" The correct answer was, "With tolerance, kindness and respect." So, invading armies annihilated their enemies with tolerance, kindness, and respect? Wow.

The prophet Muhammad was a violent warrior who led the slaughter of many people. Islam means "submission," and many were executed because they did not submit to Allah. Millions of Christians have been slaughtered by Muslims through the centuries, women are still treated harshly and with disrespect in many Muslim countries, and homosexuals are executed in others. For those open to truth, just do a little research.

Note: while researching Islam-related articles, including articles I personally had written, a few of the sources referenced did not come up in searches or are no longer available online.

But it is not only Islam.

The American Center for Law and Justice (ACLJ) gathered over 87,000 signatures from concerned citizens after receiving complaints from parents in eleven states (at the time) about the growing practice of teachers incorporating Buddhism-based mindfulness meditation into everyday curriculum of elementary school-aged children.

Elementary-aged children. Buddhism. In school.

Those promoting mindfulness clearly understand the religious connection to Buddhism because many of them have been caught on tape admitting it. Why school representatives do not care is beyond me. They will argue that meditation helps kids settle down, but that is not the point! It is religious practice—in secular schools.

One proponent of mindfulness described the program as stealth Buddhism, and in an interview, the audience laughs at the intentional deception, saying such things as mindfulness will transform students whether they want it or not. One program developer admitted that they tried removing the chanting and religious references to Buddhism to slip it into public school classrooms.

According to the ACLJ, students are required to participate in up to three meditation sessions each school day.

"Some sessions last 3 minutes; others last approximately 15 minutes. Most of the programs—Mind Up, Inner Explorer, Calm Classroom, and Mindful Schools—include audio recordings encouraging children to empty their minds or watch their thoughts float away on a cloud. Other audio recordings encourage children to be one with the universe.

"In conjunction with these audio recordings, some schools have incorporated Buddhist art and craft projects, encouraged the use or oracle cards, and printed t-shirts of the school's mascot assuming a Buddhist pose; ...several teachers, upon learning of the undisputable religious connection between mindfulness and Buddhism, have ceased using the curriculum and practicing mindfulness in their classrooms."[46]

Christian-based teachings, however, have been practically expelled from public schools. What is astounding is, other than Judaism, no other religion had anything to do with America's founding principles of morality.

Does it make sense to allow all of this in schools—in America—and not allow children to pray to Jesus? We could do a whole chapter answering this question, but public prayer was first banned in government schools in the early 1960s. You didn't think the left would stop there, did you? From speeches in classrooms to school graduation ceremonies to high school sports, prayer was expelled.

You may remember Coach Joe Kennedy, a former US Marine of twenty years who coached high school football in the state of Washington. He was fired in 2015 for publicly praying on the field after football games. His players asked to join him, and this was what offended people. The case was not just about one football coach, but also about the rights of all believers and public employees.

I have read stories of students being warned not to pray in the school lunchroom, at recess, in the hallway, or anytime during school hours. Our complacency and compliance have again paved the way for the values of the left to overtake Christian values. Few of us fought back—so they knew they could get away with it.

To us, the thing to do in a crisis, for example, is pray. To others, prayer is a waste of time; it is foolishness. But it is the fool who says in his heart, "There is no God" (Psalm 14:1). Also,

"For the foolishness of God is wiser than men, and the weakness of God is stronger than men" (1 Corinthians 1:25).

I am not suggesting the Christian faith should be the only one allowed in public schools—although that is what took place for over a hundred years in America when our country was vastly different morally and spiritually. But I thought equality was a value of the left?

Part of the solution is to inform concerned parents, many of whom have little idea about school curriculum, the radical agenda of the NEA, and what is really being taught and discussed in classrooms. Aggressive citizen action and engagement is critical in our churches, public dealings, and at the voting booth.

Pray for those who cannot see through their own contradictions, hate, and virtue signaling. Pray for well-meaning

Christians who have been caught up in liberalism, secularism, and social justice movements. Pray for Christian teachers, and for parents to understand the gamble they are taking by sending their children to public schools.

And pray for this nation. Individuals can still be saved, but the education system and major institutions in the US are past the point of redemption or reform. They are anti-Christ. The battle lines have been clearly drawn.

Jesus offers a solution no one else can, and if we do not tell young people the good news about a Savior that loves them and offers them salvation, they certainly will not hear it in school. Tragically, this is a complete reversal from how the education philosophy in America began.

Like education, the media in America is another institution that began with truth as its goal. Those days are long gone.

11

Beyond Bias: A One-Party Media/ Big Tech Conglomerate

"Progressive politicians, Wall Street, the media, academia, Hollywood, and professional sports are all on the side of the mega-rich tech cartels. Partnering with Big Tech is both politically useful and financially lucrative. So the values of the 19th-century rail and oil monopolies are back. But now they are married to the 20th-century leftist totalitarianism of George Orwell's *1984*. And they are further powered by the 21st-century instant reach of the internet."

—Victor Davis Hanson

In addition to the education system in America, two of the biggest pillars of progressive propaganda are the liberal media (aka the mainstream media, aka Democrat media, aka media activists) and the Big Tech conglomerate. These news and social media giants are for all practical purposes, arms of the Democrat National Committee.

Since most news corporations and social media outlets in America clearly support one political party, then we no longer have a fair, free press. What we find instead is commentary and opinion masquerading as journalism. And during elections, the media practically campaigns for Democrat candidates.

I wish it were an exaggeration, and I wish there were reasonable solutions, but the left is so driven by liberal ideology they do not even try hiding their bias any longer. The danger, however, is most people have accepted that this is the way it is, and yet, still use these biased news sources! This is not to say there are not any fair and conservative media outlets, but they are few and far between.

Studies have shown that broadcasters, journalists, and most of the news industry generally agree with Democrats and predominantly support their policies. In terms of dollars given from media corporations and employees (including social media giants), the campaign donation ratio is 100-to-1 favoring Democrats over Republicans.

More concerning to Bible-believing Christians is the fact the media generally opposes our values. These gatekeepers of information are influencing the public rather than informing them. And this is not just about how they report on politics. The liberal media conditions people to think less of Christianity and minimizes its positive contributions to society.

Another concern is the fact that the media and Big Tech are censoring, deleting, flagging, shadow banning, and silencing believers and conservatives without apology.

How can we have a free republic and open discourse with these threats to our First Amendment? Does this not sound more like communism? If I lost you, or if you think this is all an exaggeration, I am not sure what country you live in or where you get your information. But I am not surprised.

Research shows 70 percent of Democrats think the media is doing a good job. Ultimately, God is sovereign over all things, but as we know, those who control information have won the future. This is why education and media have become so influential.

It was George Orwell that stated:

"Whoever controls the image and information of the past determines what and how future generations will think; whoever controls the information and images of the present determines how those same people will view the past. He who controls the past commands the future. He who commands the future conquers the past."

I am not asking those in Big Tech, broadcasting, and journalism to have the same worldview as I do; nor am I asking them to favor the Christian worldview in their reporting. I am demanding they allow both sides, cover the facts, and report fairly so the people can process the news and make up their own minds.

During the Trump administration, the media became the most hateful, hostile, and disrespectful in our country's history, and after supporting two impeachment attempts, there is no going back. We must recognize this information war for what it is, and realize President Trump was right to call out the fake news outlets run by China, the deep state, far left, and socialists.

Some people are ignorant or naïve, or maybe they just do not want to admit things have gotten this bad. The truth is, censorship is one of the most un-American things you can do to a person's speech or to religious expression, and yet it has become its own pandemic with no cure in sight.

One reason this is such a problem is the anti-American left has been successful at shaping public opinion. It is too late when people's minds are made up! Decades have gone by and we let media activists get away with a form of treason. (*Treason is the crime of attacking a state authority to which one owes allegiance. This typically includes acts such as participating in a [form of] war against one's country, attempting to overthrow its government, etc.*)

Along with the media campaigning against President Trump and Republicans, they also have disdain for those who voted for him to the point of blatant mockery and condescension. Leftist ideology has blinded them to the point they have become enemies of half the country.

Since we have forgotten why a free press was established in the first place, it may be helpful to revisit five of the key principles of journalism.

1. The first obligation of journalism is to tell the truth. Truth is exclusive, objective, immutable, absolute, universal, and authoritative. Many in today's media reject biblical truth and fixed moral absolutes. The health of America depends on citizens having reliable, accurate facts and truthful information delivered to them in an unbiased manner. Journalistic truth is a process beginning with the discipline of assembling facts.

2. Its first loyalty is to American citizens. This is a problem when most media have aligned with the great reset version of a global worldview over a nationalist one. Even though news organizations answer to advertisers and shareholders, liberal producers and news editors, real journalists must maintain allegiance to citizens and the larger public interest above any other.

3. The essence of journalism is the discipline of verification. In the Internet age of instant news at your fingertips, the temptation to be the first to break a big story often gets an organization into trouble. Facts are not always verified. The treatment of this principle of verification differs depending on the subject, especially political reporting. (If the subject is a Republican shown in a negative light, report the story first; verify if possible.)

4. Its practitioners must maintain an independence from those they cover. Think about the Obama/Biden administration years. Media had an open invitation to the White House parties and other functions and seemed like lapdogs that were all too eager to serve Obama rather than the people. During the Trump administration, however, it was quite the contrast! The media enjoyed being attack dogs and received accolades from the halls of liberalism for doing so.

5. Journalism must serve as an independent monitor of power. Just the fact that the media viewed President Trump as a power-hungry, fascist dictator while allowing President Obama to rule virtually unchecked speaks volumes. They saw President Trump as a threat to freedom of the press while Obama/Biden had media reps visit the White House regularly and signed countless executive orders as the liberal press barked on cue.

Ben Shapiro is a best-selling author and editor-in-chief of *DailyWire.com*. In a December 2020 article, "Revenge of the Lapdogs," he pointed out how the press went into protective mode constantly covering for Joe Biden. As you know, the media rarely asked Biden any challenging questions and Americans were in the dark about much of the Biden/Harris agenda.

On the flipside, they drilled and grilled President Trump on and off the campaign trail as he worked feverishly, drawing massive crowds of over tens of thousands almost daily. Biden, conversely, was free to take days off, stay home, and not be accessible to the press for huge blocks of time. When he did attend small events, he stayed close to home and attendance was often sparse.

Shapiro explained the media's general role briefly comparing presidencies:

"During the Obama era, scandals went underreported; egregious seizures of power were portrayed as inevitable byproducts of Republican intransigence; and Obama's political opponents were treated as deplorable remnants of historic American bigotry.

"President Donald Trump was presented as the single-greatest factor in the rise of COVID around the nation. Barrels of ink were spilled over his supposed support for white supremacy. Reams of paper were wasted claiming that Trump presented a threat to the integrity of the election itself."[47]

Remember when the Democrat media gave Joe Biden a pass for wanting to beat the hell out of Donald Trump? Don't miss the irony: Biden talked about assaulting Trump—while speaking at a rally against sexual violence! Imagine if a Republican said the same thing.

For four entire years, the coverage of President Trump across the board was upwards of 92 percent negative. Even if you are not a Trump supporter, don't the people deserve better, honest reporting? A USA Today poll of Americans in 2016 found that by a 10-to-1 margin, the media wanted Hillary Clinton to win the election.

Sadly, the rare objective journalists—and I use both words sparingly—simply do not survive if they fail to follow their boss's orders and national media narrative. But it is not just a blatant bias that has emerged; there is a level of animosity for those who do not hold the liberal view.

This animosity for those who oppose the Democrat Party goes back even prior to the selection and anointing of President Barack Obama. Remember the media malpractice openly exhibited back in 2008? Postelection polls revealed that by an

8-to-1 margin, voters said the media wanted Obama to win. By another 10-to-1 margin, liberal media activists "Tried to Hurt Palin."

I researched and wrote extensively in a chapter for my book, *ERADICATE*, about the left's relentless assault of Sarah Palin, why they love to hate her, and why it should have been something that fair-minded Americans would not forget.

But people forgot. Here is a quick reminder that prior to TDS, or Trump Derangement Syndrome, we sadly witnessed Palin Derangement Syndrome.

I will spare you the details as they would likely infuriate you, but what happened in the presidential election cycle of 2008 should be taught in journalism classes and should go down as the final nail in the coffin of media objectivity. The character assassination, personal attacks, and brutal political assault on former Alaska governor Sarah Palin should never have been allowed to happen.

Where were the feminists and #MeToo and the antibullying crowd back then? They only support liberal, pro-choice, progressives and Democrats (all the same, I know). I had never seen so much hatred toward one person trumpeted by Democrats, Hollywood celebrities, late-night comedians, and liberal media activists—until 2016 when Donald Trump announced his run for president.

The media do not care that we know exactly what they think of us: ignorant, uneducated, behind the times, deplorable, mouth-breathing Neanderthals that simply do not know any better.

Remember the Tea Party back in 2010? As the media made excuses and even promoted the Occupy Wall Street movement funded by communists and the radical left, tens of millions of American patriots mobilized in efforts to hold government in check. They flew their flags at peaceful rallies, they were proud of our founders, and they respected our Constitution. They really love America.

CNN accused them of rabble rousing. The Democrat National Committee called them rabid right-wing extremists. ABC said they were a mob. Harry Reid called them evil mongers. Nancy Pelosi said they were artificial Astroturf and un-American. We could go on, but fast-forward to today. Trump supporters have been disdained and treated even worse.

BIG TECH DEMOCRATS, GLOBALISTS, AND CULTURE SHAPERS

Most Americans would admit there were issues with the 2020 election, including ballot harvesting, voter fraud, cyber warfare, foreign interference, and the use of questionable servers and voting machines. Add it all up and you get a questionable, unacceptable, unfair election.

But here is one major story that was lost in the chaos: Big Tech and the Democrat media did more to help Biden and Harris than documented election fraud did. For starters, according to Open Secrets, Big Tech employees at Microsoft, Amazon, Apple, Facebook, and Alphabet, Google's parent company, donated over $15.1 million to Joe Biden's presidential campaign.

Quick review: many Americans knew something was wrong leading up to the 2020 election.

We were told not to believe our eyes; that for the first time in history, a candidate for president did not even need to campaign to win! Just ignore the small crowds for Biden and him taking days off to stay home. Ignore massive rallies for President Trump. Forget all the enthusiasm for him and his policies, including historic job numbers and a booming economy.

What happened in the early morning hours after Election Day 2020 may go down in history as a miraculous Biden comeback tainted with doubt, suspicion, controversy, anomalies, and asterisks. The amazing flip included an unprecedented shift in vote-tallying momentum to favor Biden. He gained votes while Trump lost votes.

And this all happened in the face of an overwhelming red wave of Trump voters that caught Democrat operatives and media completely off guard, making it nearly impossible to cheat or commit fraud without any suspicion. They underestimated Trump again.

Tragically, the country will never be the same—at least when it comes to trusting the election process. We will likely never know the whole truth. And that is a sad indication of the power of politics in America.

Here is where the Big Tech media conglomerate again helped the far left. Hoping Joe Biden would be certified president of the United States, Big Tech ramped up its censorship of Republicans, conservatives, and Christians even more toward the end of 2020. People wanted to share news reports of lawsuits, recounts, and election challenges, but the Democrat machine would have none of that.

The networks and Big Tech partners pulled out all the stops. They downplayed and refuted any story favoring President Trump or anyone saying Biden was not president yet. (He wasn't.) Many Americans have no idea there is no such thing as The Office of President Elect. Barack Obama made that up when he was elected but not yet inaugurated.

Even though it was unconstitutional (a country cannot possibly have two presidents at the same time), his narcissism could not wait. So, what did Joe Biden do? He hauled out the faux presidential podium and official-looking seal of the nonexistent Office of President Elect, and made it appear he was in power during the controversy and lawsuits.

What made things worse was the election results were being challenged and disputed in several key states and vote counts were up in the air for many weeks following the election. Nonetheless, Biden gave teleprompter speeches behind his phony podium and, with the promotion of the media, half the nation went along with the charade.

Constantly in attack-Trump mode, the media lied for years as Big Tech suppressed the free speech (blogs, videos, posts, and tweets) of those not submitting to the liberal party. As a result, postelection surveys showed indisputable proof that Democrat voters were clueless about actual Biden corruption scandals while President Trump was censored hundreds of times on Twitter alone.

Trump administration attorneys worked to expose voter fraud, but who in Congress or in a position of influence was taking a closer look at the role of Big Tech?

Last November, while media activists reported about Joe Biden's dogs, his broken foot, his wife the doctor, and the wonderful (radical is more accurate) cabinet appointments he was making, the old joker still had not been censored, flagged, or suppressed on any social platform.

What does this tell you? It was not only the Democrat media mob, Big Tech, and social media controllers were also complicit. They had been in on the Marxist coup to remove a duly elected president at any cost. I agree with those who say today's mainstream media and Big Tech conglomerates are enemy combatants, and the modern battlefield is information and technology.

According to the MRC (Media Research Center), Twitter had censored the Trump campaign 325 times, but never once did they censor Biden. And they did not stop after the election! Through Thanksgiving, they worked feverishly to flag and suppress tweets from Trump and his campaign.[48]

Twitter had slapped labels on more than sixty Trump tweets, including those saying he was being suppressed by the Fake News Media and freedom of the press is gone, and that they refuse to report the facts of the 2020 election. These were all true statements—so they were censored. And YouTube began deleting videos and any content that did not support Biden's alleged victory.

When I write articles or books, I often know what I am looking for when it comes to a news story, quote, or reference. While using search engines, however, I would have to scroll through several pages of search results to find what I needed because typically, all the liberal and secular-progressive sites are listed first.

Washington Times columnist Robert Knight pointed out that Google accounts for more than 90 percent of Internet searches. America has a handful of corporate technocrats controlling information. This, of course, can easily determine elections by adjusting algorithms to favor the Democrat Party! Here are a few conclusions he made in his column, "The Digital Election Heist:"[49]

- Regardless of the extent of vote fraud, Google, Facebook, and Twitter fixed the election for Joe Biden over President Trump. There should be no doubt in any honest observer's mind.
- Undercover operatives for Project Veritas caught a Google executive on camera last year boasting that only Google could prevent the next Trump situation (reelection).
- Facebook regularly either censored conservative material or added caveats on posts.

He also mentioned behavioral psychologist Robert Epstein, who for years warned the US Congress about Google's search algorithm that can shift the voting preferences of undecided voters! They even had a name for it: Search Engine Manipulation Effect (SEME).

The bottom line is they have been doing this without anyone knowing it because search-ranking bias can be masked so that people have no awareness of the manipulation. Mr. Epstein told Tucker Carlson on Fox News that he believed the SEME technique cost President Trump a bare minimum of at least 6 million votes. How was he so confident about this?

He had 733 field agents in three swing states—Arizona, Florida, and North Carolina—and his team recorded discrepancies such as voting reminders that were sent only to liberals on Google's home page. Not a single field agent received a reminder to vote so he blew the whistle on the Big Tech giant. It was then they began sending reminders to everyone.

Mr. Epstein's team surveyed about 1.5 million search results and over a million web pages, and "just based on the first 150,000 searches that we've looked at…we're finding very substantial pro-liberal bias in at least nine out of ten" Google search results on the first page.

Hollywood and corporations did their part as well. When celebrities did get-out-the-vote videos, who do you think they were primarily reaching? Democrat voters. When cable news and other networks such as MTV, Freeform, BET, USA, and VH1 aired commercials featuring young people or liberal celebs telling everyone to vote, what audience were they mobilizing?

All this was going on as President Trump, Ted Cruz, and others warned about the danger and potential for fraud as Democrats kicked their early voting plan into high gear. Since there was an unprecedented amount of absentee ballots and people voting early, the sheer numbers created a crisis. Out of

156.8 million, more than 100 million ballots were cast before election day.

There are a handful of influential people still working on solutions while raising awareness about the extensive problem. Brent Bozell with the Media Research Center wrote a letter in December 2020 to Congress about the dangers posed by Facebook.

Since it dominates the market of social media and has such power over the processing of information, Bozell is concerned about the lack of accountability. He said if its protection from liability is not curtailed, Americans will no longer vote for their elected representatives—Facebook will decide who our political masters are.

I agree with Bozell. The possibility is very real for voting in future elections, that rather than being fairly elected by citizens, representatives will be chosen by Facebook, Twitter, Google YouTube, and our other technocratic overlords.

According to *NewsBusters*, Bozell is calling for Congress to rein in Twitter, Facebook, and Google after the Big Tech companies obviously teamed up to elect Joe Biden. Keep in mind that a swing state study showed one in seven Biden/Harris voters (14 percent) got their election information from Facebook and Twitter!

His letter was sent to the chairmen and ranking members of four major committees: the House Judiciary, House Committee on Energy and Commerce, Senate Judiciary, and the Senate Committee on Science, Commerce, and Transportation. Addressing Big Tech interference in the 2020 Election, Bozell's December 18 letter states:

"Big Tech, along with the traditional liberal media, did more than work together to elect Joe Biden. They abused their power to censor news that was bad for Biden or good for President Donald Trump.

"Twitter, Facebook, and Google YouTube proved they are emphatically not neutral 'platforms.' In fact, they are an indisputable and integral arm of the radical left. Big Tech companies worked intentionally and with extreme prejudice to do everything in their power to support Biden's candidacy and thwart Trump's campaign.

"...It is undeniable—Twitter, Facebook, Google YouTube, and a handful of other tech companies, are a radical leftist cabal—a very powerful technocracy with the ability to hand pick the president of the United States. They also have the power to shape and bend the public policy beliefs of the American electorate. Big Tech proved it could do both in this past election."[50]

Misinformation is only one problem with a deceitful media conglomerate. Another issue is purposely uninformed citizens, those who never heard certain stories. What do I mean?

Many Democrats get their news from the usual culprits, CNN, MSNBC, the three main networks, *New York Times*, *Washington (com)Post*, progressive sites, and social media echo chambers. Another voter survey was done after the election, and on various major news stories, Biden/Harris voters were in the dark.

Voters surveyed in seven swing states were asked what they knew about top news stories leading up to the presidential

What about ABC, CBS, and NBC? Immediately following the report of accusations against Brett Kavanaugh, they were all over it. In those first twelve days of Ford's false claim, the morning and evening news shows churned out 305 minutes of coverage—all assuming Ford was telling the truth and Kavanaugh was a guilty, lying, misogynist.

This was absolutely sickening. Three hundred five minutes. In just twelve days! So how many reports, articles, or interviews were done by the Democrat media in the first twelve days of Tara Reade's sexual assault charge against Joe Biden? Zero. None. Goose egg. Silence! This is not journalism; it is activism.

The Federalist's Mollie Hemingway provides a great contrast:

> When Christine Blasey Ford accused federal judge Brett Kavanaugh of nearly killing her and trying to rape her when she was in high school, she was unable to provide any evidence that the two had even met. That didn't stop media outlets from doing everything they could to destroy Brett Kavanaugh's life and keep him from becoming a Supreme Court Justice. When Tara Reade accused her former employer Joe Biden of sexually assaulting her when he was a United States Senator, media outlets buried the news.[51]

Then there's NPR, aka National Progressive Radio. Three years ago, NPR jumped to interview *Washington Post* reporter Emma Brown on the same day her first story on Christine Blasey Ford's accusations against Brett Kavanaugh was published. The same day! At the time, a Nexis search found 224 stories at NPR with Ford's name mentioned. Are you beginning to see the problem here? This was the agenda across the news outlets and into social media.

Where are the elite Hollywood celebs and voices that spoke out against Kavanaugh? Heck, Lady Gaga even did a PSA with Biden about sexual abuse! I know, awkward. And when he appeared at the 2016 Oscars to discuss sexual abuse, the crowd naturally gave Biden a standing ovation.

Fading actress, Alyssa Milano, was one of the main social media drivers of the mob fury toward Justice Brett Kavanaugh, so when she remained silent about the Biden sexual assault, a few fair-minded people began calling for her to address it. When she finally did say something, guess what? Not only did she endorse old Joe for president in 2020, but apparently, she also changed her mind about due process and said Biden should be given the benefit of the doubt.

You can almost write this stuff since it is so predictable.

Mr. Biden did plenty of interviews around that time as he was in better physical and mental condition in 2018. In a period of one month during what should have been a political scandal, Biden fielded about four-dozen questions from liberal media sycophants. Guess how many Democrat interviewers asked Joe about his newest accuser at the time, Tara Reade?

None. Zero. Nada. Goose egg. Nil. Not one. This should tell you all you need to know about the integrity of the agenda-driven media in America.

NBC's Chuck Todd used the Biden interview to trash President Trump about his administration's response to the coronavirus outbreak. With a straight face, Todd asked Biden if he thought there was blood on the president's hands, and CNN's Brooke Baldwin asked Joe the fondler if President Trump was responsible for the deaths of Americans.

Not one question to Joe Biden about Tara Reade and the serious sexual assault charges.

Flash back a few years. What did Biden say about the Kavanaugh accuser?

"For a woman to come forward in the glaring lights of focus, nationally, you've got to start off with the presumption that at least the essence of what she's talking about is real."

With no interest in pursuing truth, the left concluded that Biden's accuser was lying. And the public bought it because the media blocked it.

But here is how the story ended. We were approaching election season in 2020 and the Democrats did not want any negative press, even if the accusations were in fact true. A political correspondent at CNN finally offered a small web piece—but you won't believe her take. Okay, maybe you will. They were worried about how to handle the incident!

In other words, there was no compassion or sympathy for the assaulted woman who had the courage to come forward. (Alyssa Milano used to call people like Tara Reade, survivors.) There was no honest pursuit of the truth, but instead, a suppression of it. They were concerned about how to fix their inconvenient Biden PR problem. Here was the actual headline:

"Democrats grapple with questions about Tara Reade's sexual assault allegation against Joe Biden"

Kamala Harris also denied charges against Biden, but immediately believed and got behind the now discredited woman who accused Justice Kavanaugh at the time. Harris said Joe would never do such a thing.

Let's review. Ford could not remember the day, month, or year of her alleged assault. She never told anybody about it at the time, and not one person came forward to corroborate any part her story. Reade's story had details confirmed that the left could only have dreamed of.

Did Ford receive any jail time for lying under oath or bearing false witness? Nope. She did make the October 2018 cover of *Time* magazine and was hailed as a hero for "Her Lasting Impact."

Was Believe Survivors, then, just a bunch of BS and a catchy bumper sticker slogan, or perhaps a fundraising tool for Democrats? Having lost their credibility decades ago, most liberal media activists only care about how their Democrat heroes look.

The Daily Wire's Matt Walsh addressed reputations of the accused and summed it up this way:

> Reade is accusing a man [Biden] with a reputation for acting inappropriately towards women, while Kavanaugh, aside from the claims dug up during his nomination hearing, has exactly the opposite reputation; …[I]n the eyes of the media and many on the Left, the only evidence needed against Kavanaugh was the fact that he was nominated by a Republican. And the only evidence needed to vindicate Biden is the fact that he is the presumptive Democratic nominee for president.[52]

Media malpractice has been on full display recently as well, and I wish there was more pushback as they are almost never held accountable.

Leading up to the 2020 election, another *Daily Wire* writer, Ian Haworth, referred to an unfortunate truth that became clear: "The legacy media are the Democratic party's propaganda wing." In his December piece, he exposed three bombshell stories the media hid from Americans and as a result, declared that the Democrat media ushered in "a new age of blatant and shameless narrative control with the expressed goal of achieving partisan political objectives."[53]

What were those three big stories at the end of last year?

1. A woman came forward saying NY governor Andrew Cuomo sexually harassed her for years. The allegations were made by Lindsey Boylan, one of Cuomo's former advisers. No media interest.

2. Evidence showed China...had succeeded in infiltrating Western industries and governments, but for some reason, the Democrat media didn't cover it. A historic, major leak of official records uncovered 1.95 million members of the CCP (China Communist Party). US Government agencies were found to have members of the CCP employed, as well as Pfizer, AstraZeneca, Boeing, and Rolls Royce.

3. Democrat Eric Swalwell, one of the most vocal instigators in the Russia collusion hoax against President Trump, had a relationship with an alleged Chinese spy, a woman named Fang Fang or Christine Fang. Liberal media activists did not acknowledge the story's existence let alone report on it.

Haworth draws the same conclusion most fair-minded, truth-seeking citizens would. Imagine, had it been a Republican congressman who was accused of sleeping with a Chinese spy, this story would have been blasted as breaking news and parroted from the progressive AP and big three networks all the way down to local media outlets.

We can try demanding the media tell the truth and report fairly—and we should—but at this point I believe they are too far gone. The cat's out of the bag. They cannot stand Middle America and those who disagree with left-wing liberalism. It is clear they no longer serve all American citizens. Shut them off!

It is imperative we find new alternatives as well as new ways to communicate with each other.

The left spent four years attacking and lying about President Trump. Every problem in America was Trump's fault while the only reasonable solutions to the nation's ills naturally could only come from the Pelosi/Schumer Biden/Harris/Sanders AOC Democrats.

Without rampant bias, censorship, fraud, manipulation, and propaganda, elections would not even be close. But hopefully, we will learn from 2020 or this country may be history.

Finally, we cannot wrap up this chapter without discussing the media's glaring sin of omission with it comes to Christians being persecuted in record numbers around the world.

PERSECUTION IGNORED BY DEMOCRAT MEDIA

For those of us thinking we have it rough and persecution is ramping up in the land of the free, here is some much-needed perspective. The persecution of believers in Christ is at record highs around the world, and it is tragic the American media refuses to report on this injustice.

Christians have been slaughtered in many nations almost nonstop, and it seems only Christian organizations and a handful of nonprofits are helping with humanitarian efforts. Families are oftentimes left with next to nothing.

It is hard to provide you up-to-date numbers as they keep changing and increasing, but I reported in the past on stories such as over 300 Nigerian Christians slain in s a single month. The radical Islamic group, Boko Haram, has been responsible for killing thousands of Christians and displacing countless more in northern Nigeria.[54]

Over 2 million people have been forced to leave their homes due to severe persecution. In addition, the Muslim group known as the Fulani have maimed or killed over 6,000 Christian women, children, and elderly in two years' time. We have been a caring, compassionate country in the past. Why do we not hear about these stories from the American media?

I can offer some speculation. The liberal media, politicians, and world leaders took turns condemning the 2019 mosque attacks in New Zealand and denouncing the violence. And rightly so. It was front-page news for weeks. And rightly so.

But Christians are the victims. See where this is going?

There have been constant and simultaneous massacres of countless Christians, but since death comes by the hands of Muslim militants in Africa and the Middle East, it does not fit the PC media narrative. In some cases, families of over a hundred believers were killed in central Nigeria alone, and the murderers used machetes and gunfire to wipe out men, women, and children.

In the last several years, hundreds of houses have been burned down, along with churches and villages, as militants continue their mission of destruction and spreading terror. One instance took place in 2017 and Breitbart News covered the story while pointing out American news outlets who do not cover those types of stories: *NY Times, Washington Post, Chicago Tribune, Detroit Free Press, LA Times*, every other major paper, CNN, and MSNBC, and the Big Three networks.

Notice a pattern? Can we call the Democrat media racist for ignoring the slaughter of African Christians? I can just hear some executive in a newsroom dilemma saying, "Darn, I realize the victims are black—but they are also Christian," so it is not fit to print, so to speak. Plus, the perpetrators are Muslim, so the stories are off limits.

No excuse can be justified for not doing their jobs. I realize the constant murder of Christians by Muslims may not draw viewers or readers, but a white supremacist shooting up a mosque? That is right up the PC media's alley. I also realize it may be repulsive to think this way, so perhaps I have become a bit jaded with the media mob.

They have no worries about offending believers. The last accepted prejudice may be bias against Christians or bias against white American males. Still, we certainly are not experiencing the level of discrimination and persecution our brothers and sisters are around the globe.

Open Doors has reported that seven of the top ten countries are Islamic, where murder and violence are carried out by Muslims targeting Christians. To be fair, they are also killing other Muslims, but in far fewer instances. The highest mover on the list of countries wanting to stamp out Christianity is China, and get this: its Communist Party manages the nation's religious affairs.

The Barnabas Fund reports on persecution and the sad details of brutal rapes and beatings in Christian villages. Islamic gunmen engulf villages chanting, "Allahu Akbar!" according to reports, and ransacking homes. Too often, most of the dead were women and children, apart from elderly and blind men who were unable to flee.

Women and young girls are deemed less valuable in some societies, and among the abuses they face are kidnapping and forced marriage, lawful beatings, rape, having acid thrown in their faces, domestic violence, and honor killings. Where are the (liberal) women's group voices in America?

Is this hard to hear? Well, step back and imagine having to go through it yourself—and thank God if you live in a land such as this where religious freedoms are still protected—for now. Pray for our family members in Christ being persecuted around the world. Lord, protect them, increase our faith, and please, intervene, oh God!

We should all be committed to the truth. To conclude, there is an institutional bias in Big Tech and at major media networks. I am highly skeptical that news executives are interested or capable of operating fairly anymore after having gone all-in for the left long ago.

Because of this, there are no easy fixes and sadly, few practical solutions. Please support new, Christian, conservative, and independent outlets. Double-check your news sources. Email and message trusted friends. Call people or use texting.

Pray for the Gospel to advance, regardless of suppression or censorship. Pray that we somehow get back to having fair elections and freedom of speech in America for *all* people. And pray that more people wake up to the fact of communist influence, something they said would never happen here. But it did.

12

Sanitized Socialism Leads to Communist Policy

"We must understand something very thoroughly. If the state gives the rights, it can take them away— they're not inalienable. If the state gives rights, they can change and manipulate them. But the Founding Fathers believed there was a Creator and that this Creator gave inalienable rights—that is what has given us the freedoms which we still have. We are losing those freedoms and we can expect to continue to lose them if this other worldview continues to take increased force and power in our country."

—Dr. Francis A. Schaefer, 1982

When citizens of a country are banned from public platforms and their speech is censored, when churches are discriminated against, when immorality and depravity run rampant, and when one party practically owns the schools, corporations, the media, and controls the information, it sure sounds like communism rather than a constitutional republic.

Considering every major area of importance in America where Christianity was once prominent, history shows that truth has been replaced by lies. We can only fight more effectively once more people realize the United States of America is under siege—from within.

Without the freedoms a Christian worldview supports, we will not only be limited in sharing the Gospel, but the church will also be persecuted, eradicated, or forced underground as more socialist and communist policies are enacted.

It can be said the church was once the lighthouse of the nation. But since we have conformed to the world and drifted toward secularism, it is safe to assume a more drastic shift took place in the nation. Until we acknowledge the enemy, we will just keep on spiraling downward.

Earlier we discussed modern movements and how they have been influenced by Marxism, but do we understand how they became so influential? We have been programmed to accept new ideas, to not judge, and to live by the left's highest virtue, tolerance. We have unknowingly learned a new school of language in America and are being programmed.

For example, when you hear the words "political correctness," what comes to mind?

In his book, *Grave Influence*, author and founder of *Worldview Weekend*, Brannon Howse states:

"You probably think of PC words such as tolerance, diversity, multiculturalism, and feminism. But what hides behind these terms? Tolerance means that one person never expresses a judgment about someone else's ideas, beliefs, and values...Tolerance demands that you not only accept another worldview, but that you value it—unless, of course, the worldview is Biblical Christianity."[55]

We could include an entire chapter on how the left has hijacked language and redefined words, but colleges and more recently the K-12 school system have weaponized diversity (or sensitivity) training. Modern diversity is about normalizing the LGBT lifestyle while minimizing or tearing down the role of white Christian males. Multiculturalism is now the criticism of Western culture, and feminism is now about the destruction of the patriarchal structure and the traditional family.

Political correctness is cultural Marxism. It is advanced by every institution today, especially government. What is commonly regarded as mainstream political policy is further left than our great-grandparents would ever have imagined. It is driven by subversive elements; some of them hidden while others are in plain sight. What are some specific, modern examples?

One of our most listened-to podcasts from 2020 was my interview with author, speaker, and filmmaker, Trevor Louden from New Zealand.[56] For more than three decades, he has researched and exposed radical left, Marxist, and terrorist movements in America and their covert influence on mainstream politics. Louden explained that today's Democrats are endorsing communism in their policies including the following—which are consistent with far left and Islamist agendas:

Consistent defunding of the US military, Obamacare, the Iran Nuclear Deal, normalization of relations with Cuba, Islamic refugee resettlement, LGBT agenda and Cultural Marxism, abortion, $15 minimum wage, fracking bans, pipeline shutdowns, welfare, the push for illegal alien amnesty, and open borders. Communist policy.

In America.

People generally think Communism faded or fell off the world stage when the Cold War ended. They assume it died when, thanks in part to Ronald Reagan, the Berlin Wall came down in 1989. The truth is, behind the scenes America had been infiltrated by socialists, progressives, and communists nearly a hundred years ago.

A few quick questions. Did you know:

- Socialism is a natural and necessary step to achieve Communism?
- Strong, biblical churches and informed, active citizens are key obstacles to resisting socialism in America?
- America nearly had a Communist vice president in 1944?
- The environmental movement began, and environmental extremism emerged because world Communism failed?
- The agenda enacted by communists and Marxists in America over the last seventy-five years was largely financed by the Soviet Union?
- The American left and our government today continue to carry out Communist goals?

It could never happen in America—right?

Enemies of God have done quite a good job concealing their methods and motives to take down the United States and usher in communism. That's conspiracy theory material, they say, insisting the cultural, economic, and moral deterioration was natural and inevitable. But our culture has been compromised, and they have purposefully achieved their objectives, in part, through our major institutions.

In the last twenty-five years, radicals, and yes, communists, have been emboldened by allies in a progressive media, education system, and government that once looked out for the nation's citizens.

But we need to go back in history nearly one hundred years and mention the Frankfort School in Germany and you will see its impact on America. Created by a group of intellectuals, the intended name for the school was the Institute of Marxism, and its goal was to eradicate Christianity.

Dr. William Lind wrote about political correctness and Cultural Marxism and stated:

> "The Frankfort School blended Marx with Freud, and later influences (some fascist as well as Marxist) added linguistics to create 'Critical Theory' and 'deconstruction.' These in turn greatly influenced education theory, and through institutions of higher education gave birth to what we now call 'Political Correctness.' The lineage is clear, and it is traceable right back to Karl Marx."[57]

In 1933, when the Nazis took over Germany, members of the Frankfort School wanted out of Germany and were invited to America by a founding member of the ACLU, education guru John Dewey. A Fabian Socialist, Dewey was on staff at Columbia University in NY and targeted the media and education as institutions to infiltrate. He used his position to place Marxists from the Frankfort School into leading universities across the US.

Some historians believe socialists began slipping into the White House just prior to Reagan's presidency during the Jimmy Carter administration. Communism supposedly went down in Germany, but it wasn't out for the count. In fact, former insiders agree it was the Obama administration that dramatically sped up the fundamental transformation of America from a free Republic under God into a socialist-style global nation.

Two of today's most dangerous internal threats to America, threats that were once unthinkable, are Communism and radical Islam. Consider the fact it has been years since the government and media have been critical of socialism and

Islam. Prior to being elected president, half of the country did not seem to care that for most of Barack Obama's life, almost every friend, associate, and mentor of his had a Marxist or Muslim background.

I wrote about this Cultural Marxism in my 2012 book, *ERADICATE: Blotting Out God in America*. Two chapters that may be of interest include, "President Obama's Faith and Fruit," as well as, "It Could Never Happen in America."[58]

In December 2016, CNN announced controversial activist Van Jones would host a new show, *The Messy Truth*. A political mouthpiece for the far left, CNN did not care that Jones was asked to resign from the Obama administration in 2009 after Glenn Beck reported on his communist ties.

Describing how he evolved from a rowdy nationalist to an admitted communist, trying to be a revolutionary, Van Jones said, "I met all these young, [really] radical people of color... communists and anarchists," and then explained:

"I spent the next ten years of my life working with a lot of those people I met in jail..."

Jones has regularly smeared conservatives, law enforcement, white people, Christianity, and of course, Republicans. And now he gets paid to do it as a political commentator. This is CNN.

For those of you who don't watch the failing cable networks and haven't kept up with all the radicals and extremists from the Obama administration, Van Jones was the special advisor for green jobs at the White House Council on Environmental Quality.

Jones was recruited back in 2009 by none other than Valerie Jarett, Obama's senior advisor, who had very controversial ties herself. She admired the fact Jones signed a petition in 2004 calling for congressional hearings and an investigation by the New York attorney general into evidence that suggested high-level government officials may have deliberately allowed the September 11 attacks to occur.

Author, blogger, and commentator Michelle Malkin has been exposing left-wing radicals for over a decade, and declares both CNN and the Obama administration knew all about his record before they hired him. Jones obviously didn't accidentally slip through the cracks of vetters. If they were at all concerned about his past, why would CNN promote him with his own show?

It sure wasn't his expertise in political science, history, electoral trends, or even journalism that got Jones the job. It was his activism and his social justice résumé. Malkin writes:

> He rose to public prominence as a race-baiting agitator at the Ella Baker Center for Human Rights in Oakland, funded by the George Soros-supported Lawyers Committee for Civil Rights Under Law, the liberal Ford Foundation and the Rockefeller Foundation. He became a public fixture in the Bay Area after crusading to free convicted cop-killer Mumia Abu-Jamal for a Marxist organization and lambasting moderate civil rights leaders for objecting to politicizing the classrooms.
>
> …The progressives had nothing to say, of course, about Van Jones's own ad hominem attacks when he obscenely and publicly assailed Republicans as "a—holes" — and when he financed, produced and partic-ipated in cop-killer Mumia Abu-Jamal's rap album, which railed against "imperialist" America and white "mother———s" as the "true terrorists."[59]

We could expose at least two dozen former Obama administration staffers, but the purpose of this chapter is to provide an overall picture of anti-American infiltration, their agenda, and how much progress the left has made.

I was first reminded about the ugliness of communism in 2010 when the left held the Madison, Wisconsin, capitol building hostage during protests against Governor Scott Walker. Their failed recall efforts and election cost Wisconsin taxpayers millions of dollars. I saw protest signs featuring the blue-clenched Communist fist, and tables set up for Socialist Party of America recruitment efforts. Democrats loyal to the NEA encouraged teachers and students to skip school to join the protest—on the taxpayer's dime, of course.

Signs for the Communist Party USA were visible, union power on full display, cries of solidarity, "Walker is Hitler," as well as all the typical chants of "Shame! Shame!" Protestors intimidated and shouted down Republican representatives and blocked doors of the capitol building, denying them entrance. Their rebellious display of mob rule caused tens of thousands of dollars in damage.

But just like Black Lives Matter and Antifa in 2016-2020, since it was a liberal Democrat-approved cause, vandalism and violence were justified.

You might be asking, how have we allowed this to happen? Less than eighty-five years ago, six-time candidate for the Socialist Party of America, Norman Thomas, stated:

> "The American people will never knowingly adopt socialism, but under the name of liberalism they will adopt every fragment of the socialist program until one day America will be a socialist nation without ever knowing how it happened."

We have been seduced by socialist ideology, resulting in a more secular society where man is god, government manipulates outcomes, and the State is provider. Christians are not immune to the influence of this entitlement mentality that leads to the death of economic stability, biblical morality, and accountability in government. It has occurred, however, on our watch!

In the appendix of Milton Friedman's book, *Free to Choose*, he stated that most of the 1928 Socialist Party platform of Norman Thomas was already part of the federal establishment in America when President Reagan began his tenure. Some Democrats try to distance themselves from the word "socialism," but continue endorsing policies that march us down that road.

Most Americans under thirty are embracing socialism as recent polls have shown. Similarly, they generally reject capitalism and the free market system. According to one survey, only 16 percent of millennials could define socialism as government ownership of businesses (the means of production and distribution of goods). Since socialism is often depicted as a fair and compassionate system, many young people view it favorably.

In a poll done by the YouGov–Victims of Communism Memorial Foundation, seven in ten (70 percent) of millennials say they are somewhat or extremely likely to vote for a socialist candidate.

Though Hillary Clinton was always the champion of the left and expected to win the 2016 Democrat nomination for president, there was quite a competition at times thanks to Vermont senator, Bernie Sanders. It sure made that race interesting. Even in states such as Iowa, Democrats backed Sanders, including 84 percent of those under thirty! The

Democratic socialist came away with nearly 12 million votes in the primary to Clinton's 15 million.

The media has been veering to the left for decades, but it was quite revealing when during a debate with Sanders, MSNBC's Rachael Maddow asked Hillary Clinton if she is too far to the right for liberal Democrat voters. To them, the right means left of the political center.

Robert Knight of *The Washington Times* suggests today's young voters are part of the Free Stuff Army that Barack Obama cultivated during his reign. Knight states:

> "How could so many young people expect others to pay entirely for their college education, all their medical needs and their job training, which Mr. Sanders… promised; People falling for the siren song of socialism are not callously ignoring the many failures and atrocities committed in that doctrine's name; they're often blissfully unaware.
>
> "For the past several decades, government public schools and nearly all colleges have touted socialism's principles of redistribution, racialism and class envy while declining to connect the dots between socialism and tyranny, examples of which abound."[60]

How could this be? One reason is even adults tend to focus on the promises of socialism rather than the bloody history and destruction left in its wake. Many millennials have no clue about the Cold War or the collapse of the Soviet Union's evil empire because it occurred before the oldest of them were out of diapers and it is no longer taught accurately in schools.

In more recent years, soft totalitarianism (the confiscation of people's taxes and seizure/control of the media and private companies) has characterized socialist-led regimes in South America, including Argentina, Brazil, and Venezuela, where once-vibrant economies are struggling.

People debate world economics all day, but one thing is undeniable: during the twentieth century, Communist governments murdered over 150 million people, with Lenin and Stalin leading the way. Apparently, both brutal dictators were greatly influenced by Karl Marx. Before continuing, we should note ten steps to the destruction of a free enterprise system written by Marx.

First published in 1848, the *Communist Manifesto* was intended to seize power by inciting violent revolution and was a road map to tyranny. It led to brutal dictatorships that oppressed workers and slaughtered millions under Communist rule.

KARL MARX'S TEN PLANKS OF THE COMMUNIST MANIFESTO:

1. Abolition of Property in Land and Application of all Rents of Land to Public Purpose.
2. A Heavy Progressive or Graduated Income Tax.
3. Abolition of All Rights of Inheritance.
4. Confiscation of the Property of All Emigrants and Rebels.
5. Centralization of Credit in the Hands of the State, by Means of a National Bank with State Capital and an Exclusive Monopoly.
6. Centralization of the Means of Communication and Transport in the Hands of the State.
7. Extension of Factories and Instruments of Production Owned by the State, the Bringing Into Cultivation

of Waste Lands, and the Improvement of the Soil Generally in Accordance with a Common Plan.

8. Equal Liability of All to Labor. Establishment of Industrial Armies, Especially for Agriculture.
9. Combination of Agriculture with Manufacturing Industries; Gradual Abolition of the Distinction Between Town and Country by a More Equable Distribution of the Population over the Country.
10. Free Education for All Children in Public Schools. Abolition of Children's Factory Labor in Its Present Form. Combination of Education with Industrial Production.

Communism is basically a theory advocating elimination of private property; a system in which goods are owned in common and are available to all as needed; a totalitarian system of government in which a single authoritarian party controls state-owned means of production. Government ownership and control leads to a lack of freedom for the people, who are essentially employees of the government.

Citizens of a communist nation are told where they can live and in what government housing since no one can own a home, business, etc. In theory, the people share everything equally. In practice, those in power (the government or State) have ultimate control of everything and live lavish lives off the backs of the people. There is no incentive to work hard because everyone shares equally, and if you put extra effort to produce something, it is taken away and given to others.

People have no say on legislation and there is no choice of political parties. The Communist Party is the only ruling authority and elections may be held only to select one Communist leader over another. Since they don't allow for free thinking or faith in God, there is no moral authority, and the primary religion is atheism or humanism.

History has shown people will risk their lives to flee from Communist countries to go to a country where there is freedom. Regardless of the destruction, enslavement, and starvation of people, economic disaster, oppression, and murder, there are some today who fail to identify Communism as the cause.

Due in part to clever marketing in America, many people lack a true understanding of communism. Young voters have grown up in schools where capitalism was often a dirty word. They were told socialism is the great equalizer. It will be sad to see them wake up to reality.

In case you are not familiar with the Communist Goals, they were read into the Congressional Record (Congressional Record–Appendix, pp. A34-A35, January 10, 1963) during a session in the House of Representatives. The goals are from a 1958 book, *The Naked Communist,* by former FBI agent and university professor, W. Cleon Skousen.

The father of filmmaker, Curtis Bowers, published another book in 2011. James C. Bowers penned *The Naked Truth (The Naked Communist—Revisited).* This book is an analysis of the following goals and how they have been implemented or achieved. Keep in mind that Marxists have been successful at breaking down our culture and opening people up to socialism.

Written decades ago, some of these may not make sense to us. It is important to recognize, however, these goals were not accomplished by Communists, but by the liberal Democrats, progressives, and socialists in America. Some are still being carried out. (Notice goals 15-30!)

CURRENT COMMUNIST GOALS (FROM 1958)

1. US acceptance of coexistence as the only alternative to atomic war.

2. US willingness to capitulate in preference to engaging in atomic war.

3. Develop the illusion that total disarmament [by] the United States would be a demonstration of moral strength.

4. Permit free trade between all nations regardless of Communist affiliation and regardless of whether or not items could be used for war.

5. Extension of long-term loans to Russia and Soviet satellites.

6. Provide American aid to all nations regardless of Communist domination.

7. Grant recognition of Red China. Admission of Red China to the UN.

8. Set up East and West Germany as separate states in spite of Khrushchev's promise in 1955 to settle the German question by free elections under supervision of the UN.

9. Prolong the conferences to ban atomic tests because the United States has agreed to suspend tests as long as negotiations are in progress.

10. Allow all Soviet satellites individual representation in the UN.

11. Promote the UN as the only hope for mankind. If its charter is rewritten, demand that it be set up as a one-world government with its own independent armed forces. (Some Communist leaders believe the

world can be taken over as easily by the UN as by Moscow. Sometimes these two centers compete with each other as they are now doing in the Congo.)

12. Resist any attempt to outlaw the Communist Party.

13. Do away with all loyalty oaths.

14. Continue giving Russia access to the US Patent Office.

15. Capture one or both of the political parties in the United States.

16. Use technical decisions of the courts to weaken basic American institutions by claiming their activities violate civil rights.

17. Get control of the schools. Use them as transmission belts for socialism and current Communist propaganda. Soften the curriculum. Get control of teachers' associations. Put the party line in textbooks.

18. Gain control of all student newspapers.

19. Use student riots to foment public protests against programs or organizations which are under Communist attack.

20. Infiltrate the press. Get control of book-review assignments, editorial writing, policymaking positions.

21. Gain control of key positions in radio, TV, and motion pictures.

22. Continue discrediting American culture by degrading all forms of artistic expression. An American Communist cell was told to eliminate all good sculpture from parks and buildings, substitute shapeless, awkward and meaningless forms.

23. Control art critics and directors of art museums. "Our plan is to promote ugliness, repulsive, meaningless art."

24. Eliminate all laws governing obscenity by calling them censorship and a violation of free speech and free press.

25. Break down cultural standards of morality by promoting pornography and obscenity in books, magazines, motion pictures, radio, and TV.

26. Present homosexuality, degeneracy and promiscuity as normal, natural, healthy.

27. Infiltrate the churches and replace revealed religion with social religion. Discredit the Bible and emphasize the need for intellectual maturity, which does not need a religious crutch.

28. Eliminate prayer or any phase of religious expression in the schools on the ground that it violates the principle of separation of church and state.

29. Discredit the American Constitution by calling it inadequate, old-fashioned, out of step with modern needs, a hindrance to cooperation between nations on a worldwide basis.

30. Discredit the American Founding Fathers. Present them as selfish aristocrats who had no concern for the common man.

31. Belittle all forms of American culture and discourage the teaching of American history on the ground that it was only a minor part of the big picture. Give more emphasis to Russian history since the Communists took over.

32. Support any socialist movement to give centralized control over any part of the culture-education, social agencies, welfare programs, mental health clinics, etc.

33. Eliminate all laws or procedures that interfere with the operation of the Communist apparatus.

34. Eliminate the House Committee on Un-American Activities.

35. Discredit and eventually dismantle the FBI.

36. Infiltrate and gain control of more unions.

37. Infiltrate and gain control of big business.

38. Transfer some of the powers of arrest from the police to social agencies. Treat all behavioral problems as psychiatric disorders which no one but psychiatrists can understand [or treat].

39. Dominate the psychiatric profession and use mental health laws as a means of gaining coercive control over those who oppose Communist goals.

40. Discredit the family as an institution. Encourage promiscuity and easy divorce.

41. Emphasize the need to raise children away from the negative influence of parents. Attribute prejudices, mental blocks and retarding of children to suppressive influence of parents.

42. Create the impression that violence and insurrection are legitimate aspects of the American tradition; that students and special-interest groups should rise up and use ["]united force["] to solve economic, political or social problems.

43. Overthrow all colonial governments before native populations are ready for self-government.

44. Internationalize the Panama Canal.

45. Repeal the Connally reservation so the United States cannot prevent the World Court.

For most of these goals, no follow-up commentary is needed. We could estimate that between thirty and forty of these goals have been accomplished if not fully implemented.

Evil doesn't sleep and will not relent. Look at how far this nation has fallen!

In *The Naked Truth*, James Bowers details most of the goals listed above and he comes to several conclusions at the end of his book. One reason we are where we are today has to do with the apathy and busyness of Americans over the past several decades. This includes the church!

We've pursued happiness, entertainment, we've gone to work, taken vacations, established careers, taken care of the kids, attended church, and we've minded our own business. Americans have generally been ignorant of those dedicated to dismantling the nation.

How much of the progressive agenda has been achieved under the radar, so to speak?

David Horowitz is an author, professor, and former Communist who used to fight as a radical for the Left until realizing how dangerous the extremists were among the Democrats and the Socialist Party of America. The most dedicated travelers have always remained loyal to the cause.

Quoting Horowitz:

"My parents, who were card-carrying Communists, never referred to themselves as Communists but always as 'progressives,' as did their friends and political comrades. The Progressive Party was created by the Communist Party to challenge Harry Truman in the 1948 election, because he opposed Stalin's empire. The Progressive Party was led by Henry Wallace and was the vehicle chosen by the Communists to lead their followers out of the Democratic Party..."[61]

At the beginning of this chapter, I mentioned America nearly had a Communist as vice president. There have been times in our history when we nearly went off the cliff but were miraculously spared. One of those periods was 1944 during which America had a close call, according to Bower's father, who worked as an Army officer during WWII. His father managed an airport in Indiana, and one day received an unexpected visit by the Army chief of staff.

It was toward the end of the ten-year Great Depression and apparently, there was talk among top military brass that there was a chance President Franklin Delano Roosevelt (FDR) might use the crisis as an excuse to declare martial law. Military leaders secretly agreed among themselves they would ignore Roosevelt's orders and come out on the side of the people.

At the time, progressive-minded advisors, politicians, and newspaper editorial boards encouraged him to use more power due to the critical economic situation in America. Roosevelt's wife, Eleanor, also suggested America might need the leadership of a benevolent dictator. The term "dictator" did not carry the negative connotations it does today, and some saw the situation as needing a political general to lead the battle against the depression.

According to Discover the Networks:

"FDR chose to attack the depression with his so-called New Deal, a series of economic programs passed during his first term in office. These programs greatly expanded the size, scope, and power of the federal government, giving the president and his Brain Trust near-dictatorial status. …Roosevelt used the FBI and other government agencies to spy on domestic critics. He also authorized the use of the American Legion to assist the FBI in monitoring American citizens.

"The Civilian Conservation Corps (CCC) was perhaps the most popular program of the New Deal, mobilizing some 2.5 million young men to work mostly as a 'forestry army,' performing such tasks as clearing dead wood. In both substance and style, the CCC was essentially a paramilitary organization. ...In 1934 the Nazi Party's official newspaper depicted President Roosevelt as a man of 'irreproachable, extremely responsible character and immovable will,' and as a 'warmhearted leader of the people with a profound understanding of social needs.' "[62]

FDR was running for a fourth term in 1944 and in an incredibly rare move, he decided to drop Vice President Henry Wallace from the ticket, perhaps due to rumors many Americans were becoming skeptical of them. For whatever reason, after three terms working together to expand government power, Roosevelt replaced Wallace with Harry Truman as his VP running mate.

If Henry Wallace stayed on, he would have become president when FDR died, not Truman! Why is this important? Four years later, in 1948, Wallace ran as a candidate on the Progressive Party ticket against Harry Truman. Wallace was also endorsed by the Communist Party USA. The plot thickens! Bowers writes:

"A lifelong radical socialist with numerous communist connections would have become our president, if he had not been replaced as VP; ...At that time the USSR was in full swing to back Wallace at every turn. Also, there were no FOX [News] TV, talk radio, Tea Party and the Internet. The citizens would have likely never known what hit them until it was too late. Our country was spared a horrendous ending…"[63]

Like Roosevelt, another progressive president in US history that believed the Constitution to be a living, breathing, changeable document was Woodrow Wilson. Some consider Wilson a leader of the progressive movement in the early 1900s, preceding FDR by twelve years. A former New Jersey governor, Wilson was the first president to dramatically increase the size, scope, and control of the federal government.

Conversely, in the last one hundred years there have been only two American presidents who ever worked to reduce the centralized control of the federal government: President Calvin Coolidge in 1923 and President Ronald Reagan in the 1980s. Most of us remember the economic boom of the Reagan years, but few remember the hands-off approach to government and spending cuts by the Coolidge administration many believe to be largely responsible for the Roaring Twenties.

As for the Great Depression, the decade of misery lasted much longer than it needed to and certainly longer than the economies around the world. Many believe the policies of FDR's New Deal made things worse, and led to extremely high unemployment, inflation, and rationing.

There are major differences between the philosophies of conservatives and liberals, but many big government programs are run by advocates of progressivism. But even the Communists may not have dreamed that a certain government agency would be one of the greatest weapons in their arsenal: the Environmental Protection Agency (EPA).

They turned a legitimate agency into a tool used to suffocate and smother businesses and industry with endless regulations. Unfortunately, radical environmentalists are now using the EPA to impose harsh regulations, including those threatening property rights. Admittedly, we did need to change some habits and clean up air pollution and water problems, but good things are often abused by agenda-driven ideologues.

In August 2015, President Obama actually gave a speech warning about climate change, saying that, "no challenge poses a greater threat to our future, to future generations…" Today, how often do you hear the left complain that climate change is an existential threat to the world?

That same year, the Obama/Biden EPA expanded their control over virtually every waterway in the country, from major lakes and rivers to the smallest ponds and streams on farms and private property. CNS News reported that from 2009 when Obama was elected, 3,373 rules and regulations were published by the EPA covering greenhouse gases, air quality, emissions and hazardous substances, and others.

Passing two regulations a day, Obama and Biden ballooned EPA regulations to 29,770 pages in the *Federal Register*. According to CNS news:

"The EPA regulations have more than double the number of words as the massive Obamacare regulations, which have 11,588,500 words; 78 times as many words as the Obamacare law itself, which contains 381,517 words.

"The EPA regulations, to date, have 6,552 times as many words as the US Constitution, which has 4,543 words, including the signatures; the regs also have 20,418 times as many words as the Declaration of Independence, which has 1,458 words including signatures."[64]

It should come as no surprise that over the course of the Obama/Biden presidency, the EPA greatly expanded its regulatory overreach, and so have many other federal agencies!

James Bowers believes the idea of so-called global warming was initiated by communists and their progressive collaborators as a way to tax and regulate capitalism out of existence. He shares a quote from an interview with Greenpeace cofounder, Patrick Moore, and in a footnote, declares Moore's statement has the most far-reaching implications of any paragraph in his book. Here it is:

"Environmental extremism emerged because world communism failed, the wall came down and a lot of peaceniks and political activists moved into the environmental movement, bringing their neo-Marxism with them. They learned to use 'green language' in a clever way to cloak agendas that actually have more to do with anti-capitalism than with ecology or science."[65]

If academia was infiltrated by Marxist socialists back in the 1930s and 40s, why would we be surprised that they got into government as well?

Here's a quick question: What is the one primary benefit of living in this nation and the very reason patriots and pilgrims arrived on these shores to begin with? Freedom. And what is our first freedom? Religious freedom. Therefore, church and politics are incredibly important!

If you have never seen images of North and South Korea at night, do a quick Internet search for the "Korean peninsula at night," then click "images" and prepare for a stark contrast. What is the difference? The communist north is one of the poorest countries in the world and the people sadly have zero freedom, zero productivity, and Christianity is illegal. Just across the well-fortified border in the south, however, is a quite prosperous, free, somewhat Christianized nation.

Do you care about free speech and the ability to preach the Gospel of Jesus Christ? Then you must also care about politics, as well as maintaining our liberty and defending the US Constitution.

Many of us have taken life in America for granted. We have enjoyed exceptional blessings, but we've lived our lives without continuing to fight to maintain our freedoms. The left, however, has been working this whole time. As a result, we are now experiencing a period in this nation our founders— or our great grandparents—would have never imagined!

God has been rejected, truth redefined, sin celebrated, the church compromised, and the future of America is hanging in the balance. It is almost past time we start paying more attention.

13

Kamala Harris Redefines Radical

"[I]t is religion and morality alone which can establish the principles upon which freedom can securely stand. The only foundation of a free constitution is pure virtue, and if this cannot be inspired into our People in a greater Measure than they have it now, they may change their Rulers and the forms of Government, but they will not obtain a lasting liberty." —John Adams

"The same communists that gave us Barack Obama have given us Kamala Harris." —Trevor Louden

When Alaska governor Sarah Palin was selected by Republican presidential nominee John McCain in 2008, the other side was afraid of her for many reasons. They despised her faith in Christ, her strong approval rating, impressive accomplishments being a working mom, her ability to challenge both sides, Reagan conservativism, and her authenticity.

When she lifted a dull, establishment Republican and energized the McCain ticket, the entire left got their marching orders and viciously lashed out at her practically nonstop. One thing I heard from Democrat leaders at the time was, "This woman is trouble."

In 2020, Democrats kept Kamala Harris out of the spotlight and the public as much as possible. They kept pressure on Trump and relentlessly attacked him to divert attention from an aging, homebound Joe Biden and a caustic VP pick in Harris. The two answered very few questions from the fawning media, and the rare, hard questions were literally laughed at or dismissed.

For politicians supposedly campaigning for the highest office in the land, they certainly kept a low profile. Mission accomplished. Biden was limited to a couple gaffs a week, and few seemed to know the truth about Kamala Harris and her worldview. This woman is trouble—but in a different way than Sarah Palin.

Let me be clearer: This woman needs Jesus, and she is wicked. Pray for her.

She failed miserably, dropping out of the 2020 race for Democrat presidential nominee at number sixteen due to her unpopularity with the people. So why would Kamala Harris be selected to be president, I mean, VP of the country? Excellent question.

Before digging in and answering that question, some may wonder why there is no chapter about President Joe Biden. Though I detail plenty of his policies and background, he has been in political office since 1972! I am not going to convince people who supported the Obama/Biden administration, and they would likely not be reading this book.

But we knew little about the VP and what we do know is disturbing. Moreover, most people assume it is just a matter of time before Biden steps down or something happens with his health. Then what? President Harris and VP Pelosi, which may be exactly what the feminist, global, leftist cabal had planned all along.

Some of the Democrat media referred to her and old Joe as moderates during the 2020 campaign—and they did it with straight faces. So, what should people know about her?

Kamala Harris' views are even more extreme than Senators Bernie Sanders' or Elizabeth Warren's views. Harris was one of the most liberal Democrat senators in US history—and that is really saying something! She proudly supports abortion on demand—through birth, and she wants to force taxpayers to fund the slaughter of preborn babies.

Kamala Harris has redefined "radical." Then again, so has the Democrat Party.

While campaigning last year, she touted Medicare for All, and she also supports forcing taxpayers to fund transgender surgeries. These are just a few far-left policies, but she is really a political chameleon. Kamala is an opportunist willing to do and say whatever will help her gain power.

Kamala Harris was raised Hindu and her husband is Jewish. Her mother, Shyamala Gopalan, is from India; her father, Donald Harris, from Jamaica. Hard-core leftists, they met as graduate students at, drum roll, the notorious University of California, Berkeley.

Kamala's name means "lotus" in Sanskrit and is another name for the Hindu goddess of wealth and prosperity known as Lakshmi.

In the early 1960s, her parents were active in the Berkeley-based Afro-American Association. A former member said some of their heroes were Che Guevara and Fidel Castro. Of course. The leader of the association was Donald Warden, formerly known as Khalid al-Mansour, and mentored the two men who founded the Black Panther Party in 1966. They followed a Maoist philosophy and support Communist China.

Kamala's family, friends, husband, people she worked with, and even a radical protégé were connected to China, Democrats, Marxists, or radical groups.

Prior to last year's election, author, producer, and expert on the far left, Trevor Louden, laid out some of the communist ties of Kamala Harris in his article exposing her controversial history. Harris' 2020 chief of staff, Karine Jean-Pierre, was active with the New York-based Haiti Support Network in the early 2000s. The organization worked closely with the pro-China/North Korea Workers World Party, according to Louden, who added:

> "If Harris was to apply for a mid-level job in the Department of Agriculture, she would almost certainly fail the security background check. She owes her entire career to sympathizers or active enablers of the Chinese Communist Party.

> "Fortunately for her (and disastrous for the country), elected office-holders are not subject to the security clearance process. President Trump once said that 'if Joe Biden ever got elected, China will own America.' Biden picked the ideal running mate to help out."[66]

It is common knowledge that Harris began her career in an adulterous affair with former San Francisco Mayor, Willie Brown, who then appointed her to a couple of board positions that paid her something like $400,000 over five years (according to *San Francisco Weekly*). Brown was sixty years old and Harris was just twenty-nine at the time.

Kamala Harris, the strong, independent, outspoken feminist candidate, had quite a bit of help early in her career. Interesting.

A pro-life PAC, Women Speak Out, ran ads in seven battleground states blasting Biden and Harris as pro-abortion fanatics. Kamala Harris voted in 2019 with Senate Democrats to block a GOP bill requiring doctors to treat infants born alive after botched abortions. You read that right; her Party wants to just let the baby die on a table.

Many faith leaders spoke out in the hopes of informing Christian voters that the 2020 Democrat ticket of Biden/Harris was the most pro-abortion presidential campaign in history. President of Samaritan's Purse, Evangelist Franklin Graham, said as a follower of Jesus Christ, he is pro-life and believes "every life is precious to God, and that the extreme abortion-on demand ticket of Biden/Harris should be a great concern to all Christians."

Southern Baptist Theological Seminary president, Albert Mohler, said Harris consistently has chosen "the sexual revolution over religious liberty." More on that in a minute.

Many conservative outlets and Christian writers pointed out the new bold, unapologetic, radicalism of the modern left. To those who did their homework, Kamala Harris epitomizes exactly what the Democrat Party has become: anti-Christian, pro-abortion, hard left, and anti-American.

You may recall in 2015 when the Center for Medical Progress (CMP) released shocking undercover videos exposing Planned Parenthood's ghoulish practice of selling the body parts of aborted babies for medical research. David Daleiden and Sandra Merritt recorded public conversations in restaurants with Planned Parenthood employees where they haggled over the prices and methods by which the tissue would be harvested.

I reported a few years ago on Daleiden's court case against Planned Parenthood. Kamala Harris was CA State Attorney General at the time and get this: she launched an investigation—not into the trafficking of aborted baby body parts—but into the citizen journalists who exposed it!

It was one of the most shocking trials involving abortion and First Amendment rights. The testimonies were disturbing, and the repercussions of the case should have been devastating to the abortion giant. But the Democrat media activists refused to report on the case because it reflected negatively on the practices of the dark and gruesome abortion industry.

Planned Parenthood employees were caught—on tape—breaking federal laws, laws that prohibit the sale of fetal tissue for profit. And they were not prosecuted! Citizen journalists David Daleiden and Sandra Merritt were the ones forced to defend themselves against fifteen felony counts in the California lawsuit.

How could this happen, you ask?

Kamala Harris received over $81,000 in contributions from Planned Parenthood. Obviously politically driven, it was Obama administration Attorney General Loretta Lynch who initiated the prosecution of those who had the audacity to defend life and expose evil.

Harris personally met with executives from Planned Parenthood back in 2016 and ordered a search warrant to steal David Daleiden's videos and documents. Even though California law protects citizen journalists, the heavily armed raid was carried out anyway! The lead investigator under Harris testified that he did not examine the evidence. He simply did what he was instructed to do by the attorney general's office.

You can just smell the corruption here. But to Democrats and the media (I know, one in the same), there was nothing to see here—move along and get out the vote! According to the Hill, Planned Parenthood spent $45 million in 2020 to elect the Biden/Harris Democrats.

When Kamala Harris announced her run for president, David Daleiden tweeted:

"It's a bad joke for @KamalaHarris to say she's running for 'truth, justice, decency, equality, freedom, democracy' when she weaponized the powers of law enforcement to attack my 1st Amendment civil rights as a citizen journalist at the bidding of her @PPact donors and backers."

Where else does Harris stand on issues of concern to Americans?

Kamala Harris has even gone so far as to compare ICE to the KKK and seemed to unapologetically cater to her hard left, anti-Christian base. She supports the Green New Deal and mandatory gun buybacks. (That would mean surrendering guns would not be voluntary)

During a Democrat Party debate last year, Harris responded to a question saying that as president she would use the Justice Department to strike down state pro-life laws. She would abolish laws that were enacted by legislators—who were duly elected by the people. Let that sink in.

It was Kamala Harris who played the role of ringleader in the character assassination and attempt to destroy Justice Brett Kavanagh. Even a year after grilling and interrupting him during the SCOTUS confirmation process, Harris tried to impeach him. She called the Democrats in the House Judiciary Committee to open an impeachment inquiry into Kavanaugh.

This is how the radical left plays. Oh, and by the way, the *New York Times* referred to Harris as a "pragmatic moderate." Really. Times and values change, but wow!

She also believes that Catholics and Christians are unfit to serve in our nation's courts. In 2018, Harris attacked a district court nominee from Nebraska, Brian Buescher, about his membership in the Knights of Columbus, which has been an important charity in the US for more than a century.

In one of her questions to Buescher at the time, Harris stated:

"Since 1993, you have been a member of the Knights of Columbus, an all-male society comprised primarily of Catholic men. Carl Anderson, leader of the Knights of Columbus, described abortion as... 'the killing of the innocent on a massive scale.' Were you aware that the Knights of Columbus opposed a woman's right to choose when you joined the organization?"[67]

Harris kept pressing him, criticizing biblical teachings on basic moral issues, and asked Buescher whether he was aware that they also opposed marriage equality—same sex marriage—when he joined the organization. The audacity to believe the Bible! This is your Democrat Party today.

It should alarm us that Kamala Harris also co-sponsored one of the most dangerous pieces of legislation against Christians that has ever been considered by Democrats. Biden and Harris support the so-called Equality Act, a pet project of Nancy Pelosi's. The bill will openly discriminate against Christians and give other groups special rights, not equal rights.

The Equality Act (H.R. 5 and S. 788) would actually amend the Civil Rights Act of 1964 by adding sex, sexual orientation, and gender identity as protected classes throughout the federal code. The horrible bill would force public schools to allow transgender athletes to play the sport of their preferred gender. Translation: biological boys who identify as girls would compete on girls' teams and be free to use their locker rooms. (In Connecticut, two boys won fifteen track state titles.)

Those who identify as LGBT already have equality under the law, but the so-called Equality Act would give them special privileges at the expense of women, children, and people of faith.

Joe Biden promised that one of the first things he would do as president is pass the Equality Act. Sadly, with Democrat control of the House, Senate, and Executive Branch, there are no more restraints to the evil that is to be unloaded upon our country.

As of this writing, the revamped Democrat bill is being voted on in DC. If it passes it would:

- Impose sexual ideology and all things LGBTQ
- Compel speech and penalize dissenters
- Shut down Christian charities
- Allow more biological males to defeat girls in sports
- Coerce medical professionals
- Disagreement with LGBT will be considered discrimination
- Enable sexual assault

If you are a Never Trumper, or did not vote at all last November, this is what you have endorsed.

Next, Kamala Harris said in an interview last year she would legalize prostitution—as long as it was consensual. How does this protect women and young girls who are afraid to speak up against their abusers?

Having no problem discriminating against Christian businesses, Harris filed a brief with the US Supreme Court asking it to refuse Hobby Lobby's request to deny women coverage for contraception because of the store owner's religious beliefs. In the landmark decision, the Court ruled that family-owned corporations can't be forced to pay for insurance coverage for contraception under the Affordable Care Act if it offends their religious beliefs.

Kamala Harris started her legal career prosecuting child sexual abuse cases. Survivors of clergy abuse and their attorneys, however, say her tough-on-crime ex-prosecutor record fails to paint an accurate picture.

Even the liberal Associated Press reported at the time that for whatever reason, Harris was silent on the Catholic Church sexual abuse scandal when she was San Francisco DA and California Attorney General. Why? The love of money is a root of all kinds of evil and people in power love money. She received tens of thousands of dollars in campaign donations from PR firms linked to the Jesuit order of the Catholic Church in San Francisco.

Kamala Harris then sealed the records of sex abuse victims and refused to investigate pedophile priests. You can look this up for yourself, but it makes little difference at this point.

One victim ignored by Harris was Joey Piscitelli. He said she never responded to him when he wrote to tell her a priest who had molested him was still in ministry at a local Catholic cathedral. Other survivors abused by Catholic priests say Harris turned down requests to help them with their cases, and she refused to release church records on abusive priests.

Ironically, when running for president in 2020, she often tried using the Gospel parable of the Good Samaritan. She endorses social justice activism and said she hopes America will overcome injustices, but every time you put a word in front of justice, you're probably talking about something else.

Last year at a Democrat fundraiser she stated:

"Economic justice is on the ballot. ...Health care justice is on the ballot. ...Education justice is on the ballot. ...Reproductive justice is on the ballot. ... Justice for children is on the ballot. ..."

Justice for children—from a woman who has no regard for human life in the womb. To her, economic justice means progressive policies leading to socialism; health care justice means a government-run system and socialized medicine. For education justice, take a good look at today's curriculum, the political correctness, and at what Democrats have done to the school system. Now imagine it on steroids.

Next, you may remember news about Mexican national deported felon Jose Inez Garcia Zarate, who shot and killed Kate Steinle on a San Francisco pier. As CA Attorney General at the time, what did Kamala Harris do? She defended the sanctuary city policy that protects illegal aliens. Where is the justice for citizens?

Then, you may recall Syed Farook and Tashfeen Malik killed fourteen people and wounded twenty-two in San Bernardino, CA. A year later, Kamala Harris finally issued a statement on what she called a devastating and tragic terrorist attack, but failed to name the Islamic terrorists and their motive for the mass murder.

In 2020, Harris refused to denounce the violence and rioting in American cities, including the four dozen deaths—caused by leftist activists—since the George Floyd murder in Minneapolis. She was silent on mob intimidation by the protest arm of the Democrat Party.

Harris helped raise bail money for rioters in Minneapolis, helped promote the groups that aid domestic terrorists, and she applauded the release of violent criminals. Just one example is a man who was bailed out with Kamala's help and happened to be a twice-convicted rapist.[68]

The Minnesota Freedom Fund (MFF) is run by those who are against the entire bail system and received about $35 million immediately following George Floyd's death. MFF was used to bail out individuals including Darnika Floyd, who was charged with second-degree murder after allegedly stabbing a friend to death. Christopher Boswell was facing charges of sexual assault and kidnapping but was bailed out as well. The group put up $350,000 on behalf of Boswell.

To this day, Kamala Harris is proud of her efforts to help support arrested criminals. As Minneapolis and surrounding areas were in flames during the violent rioting, here is what Kalama Harris tweeted to help those who were arrested:

> "If you're able to, chip in now to the @MNFreedom Fund to help post bail for those protesting on the ground in Minnesota."

Late last year, Harris referred to November's election as "a moment of real consequence for America." I agree, because we all know elections have consequences. Harris blamed President Trump for mismanagement of the pandemic and accused him of plunging America into the worst economic crisis since the Great Depression.

For those who are paying attention, we understand how the left uses words as weapons, as warnings to opposition, and as code words of action to Democrat followers. Most of us are not falling for the narratives. Harris encouraged everything from peaceful protests to violent rioting and demanded change. She said at the time, "We're experiencing a moral reckoning with racism and systemic injustice that has brought a new coalition of conscience to the streets of our country."

A moral reckoning? Systemic injustice? Coalition of conscience? Whatever.

Finally, regarding her religion of choice, Harris was raised in Hinduism, occasionally attending a Church of God in Oakland, CA, and Harris visited predominantly black churches. She now considers herself a Black Baptist.

In past speeches, Harris has invoked liberation theology, which emphasizes social concern and political activism to liberate oppressed people. Obviously, it is Marxist in nature, assuming there are oppressed people and oppressors.

Black liberation theology focuses on the plight of poor, African Americans being liberated from social, political, economic, or religious bondage and injustice, *whether real or perceived.* This is the ideology of Jeremiah Wright and Barack Obama, who attended Wright's church for twenty years. It is the belief that black people are victims of white supremacy and must be freed. It attempts to interpret the Gospel and co-opt Christianity to promote a form of Marxism.

Both Harris and Biden can claim anything about their faith or religion. Apparently, Biden is still Catholic. The Bible tells believers to test all things, be discerning of spirits, and to not get caught up in worldly practices and philosophies. Jesus said it best: we will know people by their fruit (what they produce). Forget what they claim; look at their lives, actions, and politics.

Finally, you probably have not heard of the Secular Democrats of America. These enemies of God are demanding a secular America and saw an opportunity when Joe Biden and Kamala Harris allegedly *won the 2020 election. They sent a 28-page document to the Biden transition team advising him to strip First Amendment rights from Christians who advocate traditional biblical positions on the sanctity of life, marriage, education, and the nuclear family.

According to the document, the Biden administration must educate the American public, particularly those identified as the religious right, and they must keep their religious dogma (the Gospel or any Scripture) to themselves. Secular Democrats are calling for a purge of social conservatives from all levels of government, and even label them as white nationalists and conspiracy theorists.

The contrast was incredibly clear last November: law and order or lawlessness, religious freedom or discrimination against Christians, support of righteousness or endorsing godlessness, support Israel or oppose our great ally, tax cuts or high taxation and regulation, God or man.

I predict Kamala Harris will soon become president. Either way, she and the O'Biden Democrats will keep working to dismantle biblical morality, the Constitution, and America's heritage in order to keep on radically transforming this republic, formerly under God. They will also infiltrate more churches with social justice apostasy, progressivism, and political correctness.

Please pray for our churches and freedoms. I write this with a heavy heart.

We examined a fraction of the personal and professional life of Vice President Kamala Harris. I hope this provides some convincing evidence to anyone who was unaware of just how radical she is, especially naïve Christians who voted for her or believed the liberal media.

In the next chapter, we will briefly compare and clarify policies of the two major parties in America. Some of it might surprise you.

14

Policies, Platforms, and Procedures

"The time has come that Christians must vote for honest men and take consistent ground in politics or the Lord will curse them...Christians have been exceedingly guilty in this matter. But the time has come when they must act differently...God will bless or curse this nation, according to the course Christians take."

—Charles G. Finney

"The people are responsible for the character of their Congress. If that body be ignorant, reckless, and corrupt, it is because the people tolerate ignorance, recklessness, and corruption."　　—James Garfield

How do you respond when people are appalled that you voted for President Donald J. Trump?

We'll get to that in a minute. For me, I am unashamed of the Gospel of Jesus Christ and I am proud of having a biblical Christian worldview. I see church, culture, and politics through the lens of Scripture. The Bible is our guide, filter, and instruction manual.

When it comes to civil government and voting, I consider policy and platform first; character matters, yes, but personality has little importance. I am not ashamed to say I voted for Ted Cruz in the Republican primaries in 2016. And in the presidential election, I voted for Donald Trump.

I would have gladly voted for Dr. Ben Carson, Scott Walker, Marco Rubio, Rick Santorum, Mike Huckabee, or Rand Paul. Any of these men would have been outstanding presidents.

But hindsight is 2020, literally and figuratively. I honestly believe they may not have survived let alone thrived in the face of such intense, unfair, relentless opposition and hatred. Let's face it: very few people would have had the courage and strength to persist in the face of such negative, overwhelmingly hostile enemy combatants and news media activism.

I have a theory that the left unintentionally helped Donald Trump win the Republican nomination in 2016. If you recall, they seemed to rally behind the liberal RINO, John Kasich. The media loved him for some reason, and that should have been a red flag right there. It almost reminded me of the 2008 campaign season when Democrats helped John McCain win a few states, and then the Republican nomination. But they freaked out when Sarah Palin was picked to run as VP.

John Kasich was a moderate at best and had absolutely no chance of winning. He lost every state he competed in, by a lot! And yet, he remained in the race perhaps so that Ted Cruz would not win the nomination. But why?

Democrats and globalists making up the left believed Trump was a joke and had absolutely no chance of winning a national election. The process, it seemed, was just a formality since the highly favored queen of the left, Hillary Clinton, was preparing to be coronated. At least this is what they expected.

But Mike Pence joined the ticket as VP, which gave Trump some credibility and scored some points with conservatives and Christians. Then, the more the left heard candidate

Trump talk about draining the swamp, standing up for life, families, and religious freedom, giving the White House back to the people, and fulfilling his promises (unlike most politicians), their disdain grew.

It was game on! But many people knew an America First movement was building. Now here we are in 2021. As Paul Harvey used to say, "and now you know the rest of the story."

Little did the church in America know how fierce the spiritual battle would be, how severe the storm, and how blatantly the enemy would hurl nonstop accusations, arrows, and attacks at President Trump and his supporters.

I, too, had my doubts about Donald Trump and did not like his arrogance and lack of character. I knew he would help the American economy, but since he is a former Democrat, I wondered how he would govern on religious freedom and social issues, for example.

Even though I had concerns and disapprove of certain aspects of Donald Trump's conduct, I still voted for him and supported him as a candidate. I see no contradiction there, nor do I see anything morally wrong with his policies. Thankfully, we can now say those glaring flaws did not prevent him from accomplishing a ton and doing some great things for America.

By the way, President Obama accomplished a lot while in office that led to historic division, sexual anarchy, and weakness in our culture, education system, family, church, military, and economy. I prayed for him and was embarrassed by his arrogance and godless policies.

I do admit that I shook my head at the fact this nation elected as president two of the most narcissistic men possible in Obama and Trump. But our concern should be their policies and platforms as well as what they did for America while in office.

Back to the opening question. So how did you respond when people asked how you could vote for President Donald J. Trump?

People on both sides often give an emotional response. Hopefully, you responded with facts and policy, that is, if they are really willing to listen.

From what we now know, most Bible-believing Christian voters supported Donald Trump in 2016—not because they liked him as a person—but because of his policies. Please do not fall for the propaganda campaigns and tedious talking points about how horrible a human being Trump is. As Christians, we need to be better at researching, getting informed, and voting biblically.

I saw a great post last year on actor and author Kevin Sorbo's Facebook page about responding to a person who says something like, "I can't believe you would vote for Trump." Around the same time, I came across a great article by a professor of theology and biblical studies, Wayne Grudem, called, "Letter to an Anti-Trump Christian Friend."[69]

I have read many pieces on politics when it comes to Christians and voting. Both Sorbo and Grudem give you plenty of ammo when having conversations about worldview. Similar to defending the faith, we need to explain to people what we support and why, because too many people only talk about what they're against and do not give any explanation.

So, assuming elections still matter, the next time it comes up, throw people off-balance by patiently explaining politics from a broader perspective. In the case of Republican and Democrat, the contrast could not be more obvious! It was never about Trump or Biden.

TELL THEM WHAT YOU ARE SUPPORTING AND WHY:

I'm voting for unborn babies to have a right to live, for pro-life policies, and for valuing every single human life.

I'm voting for originalist judges and the next Supreme Court Justice to protect the Constitution and the Bill of Rights; for continued appointments of conservative judges.

I'm voting for the First Amendment, especially freedom of religious expression and freedom of speech. I'm voting for the Second Amendment and the right of citizens to defend our lives and family.

I'm voting for strong support of Israel because the Bible says God will bless those who bless Israel and curse those who curse Israel (Genesis 12:3); for the US Embassy in Jerusalem, and I'm voting for continued historic peace efforts in the Middle East.

I'm voting for school choice, for true history to be taught again, and for parents to have more rights when it comes to opting their children out of the sexual indoctrination in public school curriculum.

I'm voting for a rare president that did not start a war, who is strong on national defense, rebuilt the US military, and truly cares about our veterans; for an end of America's involvement in foreign conflicts and the return of our troops.

I'm voting for secure borders, for the wall, and to reform our immigration system.

I'm voting for the police to be respected once again and to ensure law and order in our cities and streets; for criminals to be prosecuted and not bailed out; I'm voting in favor of the defeat of ISIS and the killing of radical terrorists who hate America.

I'm voting for a free market economic system and against socialism; for lower taxes, and for our jobs to remain in

America and not be outsourced again to China, Mexico, and other foreign countries; for the president who ushered in a record high number of jobs for minorities and presided over historic low unemployment.

I'm voting to keep America first, for lifting up American workers and families, for fewer government regulations, and unleashing American energy production.

I'm voting for the Electoral College and the free republic we live in; to not be forced, fined, or taxed by government for not having health insurance or having the wrong kind.

I'm voting to expose evil and fight against child trafficking; for restrooms, locker rooms, and single-gender sports teams to be restricted to people of one biological sex or the other; for truth and science to prevail over delusions and moral relativism.

I'm voting for freedom of conscience because government should not force Christians to use their business or artistic skills to convey a message approving of same-sex marriage or to use their medical skills to perform an abortion, or to use pharmacies to distribute drugs that cause abortion.

I'm voting for the right to speak publicly, share my opinions, and not be censored.

I'm not just voting for one person, I'm voting for the future of my country, and God-willing, generations to come!

And if they're still listening, ask them, "What are *you* voting for and why?" (Note: "I voted for Biden because I hate Trump" is not an acceptable or reasonable answer!)

Wayne Grudem concluded a separate article last August listing some of the president's achievements that should have justified a second term. Like many of us, he was hopeful that the country would be able to expect four more years of the same type of White House policy:

"...more originalist judges, ongoing lower taxes and deregulation, continuing funding for a stronger military, further restrictions on abortion, more school choice, continued support for Israel, hundreds of additional miles of border wall, a humane and just solution to immigration, continuing protection of religious freedom and freedom of conscience, abundant safe energy production, continued protection against Islamic terrorism;

"a stronger NATO alliance, more free speech protections on college campuses, continued protection of separate boys and girls sports teams and locker rooms, more trade agreements that are fair to the US, accelerated renewal of our aging infrastructure, unflinching resistance to Russian and Chinese aggressiveness, continued isolation of Iran and multilateral containment of their hostile expansionist ambitions, normalization of relations between Israel and other Arab nations, and further solutions to the problem of high drug prices."[70]

Now, how about if we look at the other side. In what sane universe can an evangelical Christian or someone who believes in Jesus and the moral values taught in the Bible support a progressive Joe Biden, radical Kamala Harris, and the far-left, God-rejecting Democrat Party?

Once again: this is about policies, platforms, and procedures!

HOW COULD CHRISTIANS—IN GOOD CONSCIENCE—SUPPORT POLITICIANS, LAWS, AND POLICIES THAT:

- allow abortion up to the moment of birth, authorize the use of our tax money to pay for abortions and gender reassignment surgery;
- cripple our economy with ever-increasing government control and taxes, including expensive Green New Deal energy regulations;
- increase unemployment, weaken our military, and promote a Jimmy Carter-like foreign policy of appeasement, and most importantly, abandon Israel to fend for itself;
- nullify the Senate filibuster rule so all legislation can be passed with only fifty senators plus the vice president casting the tie-breaking vote;
- support the rising influence of judges who are not constrained by the original meaning of the words of the Constitution, perhaps even adding six additional seats to the Supreme Court to give the court a new 10-5 majority of such justices (this could be done with control of the House, the Senate, and the presidency);
- grant statehood to both Washington DC and Puerto Rico, thus adding four more Democrats to the US Senate;
- support draconian laws that compel an artistic professional or a counselor to affirm the validity of same-sex marriage even when that is contrary to the person's conscience;

- reinstate the Obama-era guidelines that required schools to allow biological males who claim to be transgender females to use girls' bathrooms, locker rooms, and showers (the guidelines were canceled by Trump);
- allow biological males to compete in women's sports, setting new statewide records in women's track events and other sports;
- pass multiple new, extremely strict green energy laws that will massively increase energy costs and therefore will also increase the cost of everything that is made or transported with the use of energy;
- seek to defund the police (to be precise, Biden has said he favors redirecting some police funding to other programs, which is a partial defunding of police, which will lead predictably to a substantial increase in crime);
- use violence and intimidation to nullify freedom of speech (in practice) for those who disagree with them politically; and
- support open borders and sanctuary cities in defiance of the law, and promote a complete federal government takeover of our healthcare system?

How can you support all this—*unless* you hate God, America, or are deceived? Please understand, the modern Democrat party is hostile toward biblical values and Christians in particular.

The above policies and principles shape the platforms of two competing belief systems. One political party supports the Christian worldview; the other disdains it. One side views the Bible as an ally, the other as an adversary—and the left is overflowing with proud devil's advocates.

If you were unsure how the Biden/Harris administration would govern, look no further than the two long terms of Barack Obama. We may as well refer to today's presidency as the O'Biden administration. Informed believers who have been paying attention to legislation and politics through the years agree the Obama years saw the most biblically hostile policies in US history.

The spirit of antichrist is on the move and it is becoming clearer. We must not be ignorant of the enemy's schemes or surprised at how rapidly lawlessness is increasing across the nation and throughout the world. It is prophetic!

Most prophecy experts agree that God never pours out His wrath without warning—and America has had many. Yes, we need more watchmen sounding the alarms, but we must not let up on calls for repentance, beginning with the church. People need the Gospel now more than ever.

Some may wonder how the open hostility toward the Judeo-Christian worldview became so accepted and normalized. Having read this far, I trust you are no longer wondering.

Writing for the American Family Association, Don Feder explains why Christians and Jews are Public Enemy #1 for progressives. The culture war is between the left's neo-Marxist worldview—which has come to dominate the Democrat Party—and the Judeo-Christian ethic.

In an article, "Why the Left Hates Religion," he declares this clash was inevitable.

1. Judeo-Christian (or Biblical) morality teaches objective ethics—applicable for all time and in all places. Leftism teaches that morality is subjective (in a constant state of flux) and that anything can be justified if it advances the revolution.

2. Religion puts God above the state. Leftism says the regime is God—the source of all blessings.

3. Judeo-Christian ethics says the natural family is essential for social cohesion. Leftism says the family is whatever we say it is, and is really not that important, anyway.

4. The Judeo-Christian worldview says God created man and woman and intended for them to complement each other. Leftism says male and female are meaningless concepts, and that to believe otherwise is bigotry.

5. Judeo-Christian morality encourages procreation as the First Commandment. Leftism says that in a world of global warming, having children is irresponsible and should be limited by law, if individual choice isn't enough.[71]

Please share this with open-minded, reasonable people who need to hear the truth and who care about our country. I tried condensing what could be so much more extensive and detailed.

American citizens decide what kind of country they want to live in. Do we want Christ or chaos, liberty or liberalism, discipline or destruction, religious freedom or reprobate revolution, truth or tyranny?

Make no mistake: the left's hatred for Christianity is also its hatred for America itself, what she stands for, and what she was founded upon. Sorry for being redundant, but if the body of Christ does not engage and wake up to these facts, there may be little hope for a free America.

Regarding policies that affect every one of us, as I have been writing this book, an invisible virus has continued to be greatly feared. Governors and governments have implemented COVID-19 lockdown policies and restrictions that have severely affected our freedoms, the economy, our relationships, the elderly, school children, access to food and banking, our movement and travel, our church services (some more than others), national debt, the suicide rate, and more.

Health concerns should not be political issues, but here we are. Whatever your thoughts and conclusions about the source of the coronavirus, vaccines, masks, and mandates, the left has used them to force change and advance a global agenda. This happened with our approval.

We have exhausted key problems up to this point in the book and to be sure, there are not many solutions outside the spiritual. Keep the faith. Believe! Love. Pray. Stand. Vote. Warn. May God save the United States of America.

The battle, however, continues and the opposition will not relent, so we must find ways to keep working for the Lord and be prepared to fight at the same time.

*Still unconvinced about what policies to support or what President Trump did while in office? Check out the extensive listing from the Family Research Council documenting over a hundred Trump Administration Accomplishments (FRCaction.org) on life, family, religious freedom.[72]

15

Working for God, Ready for Battle: Nehemiah 4

"[H]ave the courage to walk toward the fire and not run away from the flames. God has brought us to this cultural moment, and our future cannot be taken for granted. As has been said, 'In a time of universal deception, telling the truth is a revolutionary act.'"

—Dr. Erwin Lutzer

"who by faith conquered kingdoms, performed acts of righteousness, obtained promises, shut the mouths of lions, quenched the power of fire, escaped the edge of the sword, from weakness were made strong, became mighty in war" (Hebrews 11:33-34).

I believe it will be helpful to give you some historical, biblical examples of faith in the midst of opposition that can be applied to our cultural battles today as we live for Christ in the face of evil.

Opposition is guaranteed and Scripture is full of true stories of believers enduring trouble and persecution. But it is also filled with amazing testimonies of God's faithfulness as He often prepares, strengthens, and sustains His children.

When Paul wrote to Timothy telling him to "Fight the good fight of faith" (1 Timothy 6:12), the idea was about a marathon battle, not a sprint to the finish line. We get the word "agonize" from the Greek word for "fight." These words were used in athletic contests as well as military endeavors to describe the concentration, discipline, and effort required to win.

A good fight, however, is one in which we win in the end.

The battle lines have been drawn between Satan and his kingdom of darkness and Jesus and the Kingdom of light. Those of us who know God's Word, are informed, and have been praying, recognize that the day of the Lord is approaching. The reality of these last days is as sobering as the task ahead is daunting for Christians, but no matter what hell can bring against us, God is for us and the victory is His.

Due to recent world events and the implosion of America in 2020, more Christians now understand the reality of spiritual warfare and why Paul would write about the armor of God and taking a stand against the enemy. It is also no surprise that over and over in the pages of the Bible we are reminded to "fear not." The Lord knows we need reminders!

But we must discern healthy fear versus unhealthy fear.

Dietrich Bonhoeffer once said:

"He who fears the face of God does not fear the face of man. He who fears the face of man does not fear the face of God."

Fear is a basic human response to a threat, but it should not immobilize us. Historically, people of God have faced tremendous opposition. But we have a great cloud of witnesses that have gone before us, and many examples to encourage our faith and inspire us in the times in which we live.

Men of God gained approval by exercising their faith in the Lord. I am not sure who said it first, but when godly men take stands for Christ and righteousness, it stiffens the spines of others. If we hope to be essential as a church, consider Jesus, the perfecter of our faith, and commit to persevering, no matter what.

Many have gone before us that we can learn from and who can give us perspective and encouragement. The enemy seeks to bully believers and prevent us from doing God's work. Once again, we have been warned!

> "Be of sober *spirit*, be on the alert. Your adversary, the devil, prowls around like a roaring lion, seeking someone to devour. But resist him, firm in *your* faith, knowing that the same experiences of suffering are being accomplished by your brethren who are in the world. After you have suffered for a little while, the God of all grace, who called you to His eternal glory in Christ, will Himself perfect, confirm, strengthen *and* establish you. To Him *be* dominion forever and ever. Amen" (1 Peter 5:8-11).

Notice the focus on enduring through trials, not knowing how long we will have to suffer or fight. God equips those whom He calls, and yet Christians can expect many hardships in this life. So do not retreat or give up. We serve a mighty King and Warrior!

We should be honored and privileged God has called us into service. Part of that call for Christians in America, I believe, is to work on preserving this republic. Yes, the church must repent and yes, we must pray and be better at making disciples as we evangelize the lost, but we are dangerously close to losing both our religious freedoms and our nation.

What do we do then? The left already has a stranglehold on America. If they gain even more power as they advance godless policies, free speech and preaching the Gospel will be severely limited.

Like the brave patriot pastors of the Black Robed Regiment in the late 1700s, we should not hesitate to fight on secular battlefields for victories in this world that preserve the freedom to advance the Gospel. Social media and the voting booth are examples of secular battlefields.

The church must be alert, prayerful, and prepared to fight. Part of the preparation is the work of equipping the saints for ministry—and this is key for the present time—and defending against opposition as we rebuild what the enemy has dismantled.

Last September, the Holy Spirit led me to preach a Sunday sermon from the book of Nehemiah. The focus was on faith in God and working in the face of opposition. It may be a good model for us to follow. Look at some of the parallels.

The work was daunting and exhausting, and people of Jerusalem were overwhelmed by the task to rebuild the walls around the city. Then, their enemies threatened them. Nehemiah saw fear in the faces of the people and told them not to be afraid, but to remember their great, awesome God. Oh, and he also told them to prepare to fight. Check out what happened next.

Half of the people worked at construction while the other half worked security. They "held the spears, the shields, the bows, and wore armor…" And not only that, it describes each builder of the wall having a sword at his side and, "with one hand they worked at construction, and with the other held a weapon" (Nehemiah 4:16-18).

Here we find a key concept for the success of the church: the people doing the work not only had a tool in one hand and a weapon to fight in the other hand, but others were armor ready as they held the weapons and battle gear. They joined together and were united in God's work.

Not to get too political (smile), but Nehemiah would eventually become governor of Jerusalem. God had him in a unique position to lead the people to do a great work for Israel. It is inspiring to read about the huge job of rebuilding the city walls and the creative strategies implemented by Nehemiah and the people.

Scholars suggest the book of Nehemiah was clearly drawn from Nehemiah's personal diaries, even though Ezra is the author. The primary theme of the book is "the good hand of the Lord," as it is clear to see God leading and guiding His people to do a great work.

Themes of the book include giving careful attention to the public reading of God's Word, Nehemiah's obedience in the face of astronomical odds, and enemy opposition. Today's Christian church must exalt the Word of God to its proper place again.

Some 400 years before the birth of Jesus, the nation of Israel and the Jewish people were in a desperate state. Their nations, the northern kingdom of Israel and the southern kingdom of Judah, were destroyed. Jerusalem was completely conquered by the Babylonians and the once-glorious temple of Solomon was demolished.

The Babylonians deported almost everyone from the city and surrounding region, and for some seventy years Jerusalem was sparsely inhabited. It could have ended up like many other ancient cities, completely forgotten except to history.

The book of Nehemiah explains he started out as a cupbearer serving King Artaxerxes of Persia, and the book opens with him receiving a sad, surprising report from Jerusalem, which was about 800 miles away. The report was about God's people living in fear and rubble in the demolished city. It grieved Nehemiah to the point of tears and mourning.

His heart of compassion and concern lead to this great prayer:

> "And I said: 'I pray, Lord God of heaven, O great and awesome God, *You* who keep *Your* covenant and mercy with those who love You and observe Your commandments, please let Your ear be attentive and Your eyes open, that You may hear the prayer of Your servant which I pray before You now, day and night, for the children of Israel Your servants, and confess the sins of the children of Israel which we have sinned against You. Both my father's house and I have sinned' " (Nehemiah 1:5-6).

Notice his confession of national sins and his reminding God of His promise to gather the people of Israel and bring them back to Jerusalem *if they return to Him and keep His commandments*. His prayer continued to ask the Lord to hear "the prayer of Your servants who desire to fear Your name" and to grant Nehemiah mercy in the king's presence.

God gave him favor with King Artaxerxes, who approved the mission to travel to Jerusalem and inspect the walls of the city. The king even provided Nehemiah with supplies to begin the work. We know from history that God uses pagan kings, presidents, and prime ministers, even when the people were apathetic and unfaithful.

This should be an encouragement to us today.

We do not know if the Lord will continue being patient with America and keep withholding the judgment we deserve, but we can trust the God of second and third chances.

In the face of opposition today, too many church leaders have backed down, but Nehemiah showed great faith when enemies of God mocked and threatened the rebuilding project. Sanballat the Horonite, Tobiah the Ammonite official, and Geshem the Arab heard about the plans and "they laughed at us and despised us."

Christians in America can relate to scoffers and those who despise us.

Nehemiah's enemies ridiculed the work of God and tried discouraging the workers. Not much has changed today as far as the tactics of the enemy. If he can discourage us from living for the Lord, building up other Christians, sharing the Gospel, speaking the truth, or impacting our culture by shining light in the darkness, he wins before we even get started!

One thing Satan seeks to destroy is a believer's assurance of salvation. Discouragement is such a powerful weapon because it is somewhat the opposite of faith. Where faith believes God's love and His promises, discouragement believes the worst—and tends to forget about who God is, what His Word says, and what He has promised to do!

Just as in Old Testament times, Peter warned early church believers about mockers in the last days (2 Peter 3:3), following their own lusts and denying the power and even the existence of God.

Sometimes, however, when we try impacting culture for Christ and resisting enemies of God, opposition can even come from within. There are many professing Christians today that think we should keep to ourselves and not fight these cultural and political (moral) battles. Some of these are well-meaning critics who judge the conscience of others and often miss what God is doing.

The context in Nehemiah is the work of God and the secular resistance to it. Christians in America can relate! The spiritual walls have been torn down in our churches and country, as we have been playing church for too long.

What else can we learn from Nehemiah? Prayer was a first resource, not a last resort. When times of opposition come, God wants us to depend on Him—and the purest way of expressing our reliance on God is through prayer.

Nehemiah's prayer gave God a reason to show mercy to the people and to come against his enemies. Nehemiah recognized that this was God's cause, not his own, and because the people worked together, the wall surrounding the vast expanse of the city was built up to half its height.

They were halfway done and had connected all the gaps in the wall. This made the enemy furious.

Ezra tells us one main reason for their progress: *the people had a mind to work*. A mind to work is a gift from God, and no significant job can be accomplished without a proper mindset. To do great things for God, we must work together.

But our churches and nation are divided over many things. Part of our problem is a misunderstanding of what the Bible teaches and a failure to stand on the essential doctrines of the faith, including basic teachings on sin and repentance. Then there are the cultural issues.

As the cult of liberalism has infected our churches in America, communists and socialists have permeated society. Like the proverbial frog in slow-boiling water, it happened so gradually we hardly noticed. By conforming to the world, desiring to please man, and by watering down Scripture, the church lost its essential influence and standing in society.

It's important we analyze the causes and learn from the past.

Whether it be blatant false teachings, post modernism, liberation theology, gay Christianity, or social justice, disciples of these doctrines can be found in many churches today. The apostle Paul warned about those masquerading as Christians, "holding to a form of godliness, although they have denied its power; Avoid such men as these" (2 Timothy 3:5).

Political liberalism is one thing; we know *exactly* where godless leftists stand by the politics they endorse. Think Nancy Pelosi. But religious liberals are dangerous, because they generally believe the same thing as secular progressives and yet claim to be Christian. We must no longer be surprised by those who oppose us. Preach the Word, expose heretics, and call out apostasy.

You might be wondering how Christians can have the same focus and mission if we cannot agree on foundational biblical teachings. How can the church be essential if less than half of us are willing to speak the truth at any cost and work to rebuild walls the enemy has dismantled?

God never calls us to do anything without supplying His power, protection, or provision. When it is a just cause, He gives us a spirit of discipline and unity with which to do the work.

One important takeaway from Nehemiah's prayer (Nehemiah 4:4-5) is that he asked God to judge his enemies and "turn their reproach on their own heads," but God answered by taking care of His people. See the difference? Nehemiah asked God to "not let their sins be blotted out."

How many of us have prayed for God to take out our enemies or judge those who hate us because of Jesus? This is another example of how God's ways are above our ways. He does not always stop our enemies, judge them immediately, or remove us *from* the battle; He gives us the strength to fight and endure *in* the battle!

The work of God makes the enemy angry, causing him to attack us. If we are making an impact for Jesus Christ while confronting evil at the same time, we are on the devil's radar.

This can be a lonely work and at times, overwhelming. Keep moving!

Another thing we need to recognize is that sometimes our enemies do not actually attack us. They use accusations, intimidation, and threats to try wearing us down. They call us hateful, intolerant, racist, or whatever.

It is interesting to note that Nehemiah's enemies did not actually attack—they were all talk. Sanballat and Tobiah were hoping that the *threat* of attack would be enough.

Satan uses the same strategy against us, hoping to cause us to back down. If we become worried or paralyzed by it, the threat worked. If the enemy can make us think a bigger threat or a fight is coming, fear could get the best of us.

In some cases, the enemy never intended to go to war, but just wanted to create confusion. This is an important strategy—to create chaos and disunity among the people of God. The enemy is the author of confusion and father of lies.

In Nehemiah's time, God seemed to allow opposition to continue because He was delighted that His people drew closer to Him with a deeper trust. God did His perfect work both in building the walls around Jerusalem *and* in strengthening His people.

We should also observe how the Jews prepared for battle and defended themselves.

"We set a guard against them day and night" (Nehemiah 4:9).

They strategically set guards and watchmen around the city 24/7. This crucial decision sent a powerful message, not only to the people, but also to their enemies. We need more watchmen!

The work of rebuilding the walls included not only construction but also cleaning up debris and hauling away the rubbish. The ruins of the walls lay there for 100 years. Clearing the area had to be done. The destroyed parts of the wall and the accumulated rubbish had to be moved so the walls could be rebuilt upon their foundations.

If they did not do this, the walls would not have stood at all.

It is interesting that in our Christian life, nothing great can be built for God's glory unless the rubbish of the past is cleared away. What needs to be removed from your life? It is harder to work let alone fight when we have excess baggage in our lives.

Another point is the determination to organize a defense. After the challenge from their enemies who apparently planned a surprise attack, the response was, "Hold the line!"

"Therefore, I positioned men behind the lower parts of the wall, at the openings; and I set the people according to their families, with their swords, their spears, and their bows. And I looked, and arose and said to the nobles, to the leaders, and to the rest of the people, 'Do not be afraid of them. Remember the Lord, great and awesome, and fight for your brethren, your sons, your daughters, your wives, and your houses' " (Nehemiah 4:13-14).

Remember our awesome God! Prepare for battle as we do practical things.

Nehemiah could have panicked and done nothing, but he wisely and calmly trusted God amid the storm and did the practical things necessary for him to obtain the victory. Notice the result of their courageous stand. Their enemies shrank back!

Their hearts sank when they heard that Nehemiah and the people were fighting to protect Jerusalem and knew about their plans, "that God had brought their plot to nothing" (Nehemiah 4:15). Perhaps they understood it had to be the Lord who thwarted their agenda.

What happened next? The people returned to the wall and eventually finished the work. Are we armed with the same attitude today, and heart for the Kingdom of God?

There will be constant warfare against those who claim the name of Christ. Expect confrontation. Prepare for opposition from within and without. We need to be ready to fight and clothed with the armor of God. We must also be rapture ready, watching for His return and listening for the final trumpet blast. His appearing may be much sooner than we think.

In the meantime, we have work to do. This is no time to retreat, shrink back, or hunker down. Don't isolate. Infiltrate! Let us be a force for good and against evildoers.

We also need wisdom. Some past efforts may be lost causes today. In many cases, Christians need to move on, and fight battles we have a chance of winning. How can Christian families thrive when they are so greatly influenced by a godless culture? We certainly have some decisions to make as individual believers, as parents, as Americans, as consumers, and as citizens of heaven.

Remember the earlier chapter about the tremendous impact of Christianity on the world? With God, all things are possible, but we are in danger of waving the white flag rather than fighting. This is one reason we must take a cue from Nehemiah and many others throughout Scripture.

For now, we can learn from the past and work together for God's purposes. Remember:

> "For whatever was written in earlier times was written for our instruction, so that through perseverance and the encouragement of the Scriptures we might have hope" (Romans 15:4).

There exists across North America a solid remnant of true believers in Christ. Find those near you and lock arms with these brothers and sisters. Notice the important balance of perseverance and encouragement; we need to do both, and we need both in our lives.

One final point of clarification for those hoping we get back to normal in America or times of peace on earth. Jesus Himself told His followers He did not come to bring peace on the earth (Matthew 10:34). In fact, He came to divide.

Jesus brings a sword. What? The Prince of Peace? Wasn't He all about love and meekness?

We have romanticized the baby in a manger around Christmastime. We forget the fact that Jesus is going to return as prophesied, as a conquering King, speaking the Word and ready to rule.

> "And I saw heaven opened, and behold, a white horse, and He who sat on it *is* called Faithful and True, and in righteousness He judges and wages war. His eyes *are* a flame of fire, and on His head *are* many diadems; and

He has a name written *on Him* which no one knows except Himself. *He is* clothed with a robe dipped in blood, and His name is called The Word of God. And the armies which are in heaven, clothed in fine linen, white *and* clean, were following Him on white horses. From His mouth comes a sharp sword, so that with it He may strike down the nations, and He will rule them with a rod of iron; and He treads the wine press of the fierce wrath of God, the Almighty. And on His robe and on His thigh He has a name written, 'KING OF KINGS, AND LORD OF LORDS' " (Revelation 19:11-16).

As prophecies are fulfilled and world events converge, we need to be ready and watchful as we do the Lord's work. The question is, do we have the will to endure, stand strong, and fight? If we trust God, He will be with us, help us, and complete the work He began in us.

To Him be the glory.

Conclusion

"We as Bible-believing evangelical Christians are locked in a battle. This is not a friendly gentleman's discussion. It is a life and death conflict between the spiritual hosts of wickedness and those who claim the name of Christ."   —Francis Schaeffer

"We are not to be living specimens of men, well preserved, but living sacrifices whose lot it is to be consumed."   —Charles Spurgeon

The Bible and the Christian faith have blessed and shaped Western civilization more than any other literary work or religion. Christianity has improved life dramatically in every way, including health, family, freedom, government, law, equality, human rights, science, hospitals, education, art, literature, music, charity, social agencies, societal norms, work ethic, and values.

And the left will hold nothing back to purge truth and cancel the Christian church from culture.

I think it is important to be reminded that though we are on the side of a winning battle, there are always injuries and casualties. People around us may not make it. Some in our families or in our own churches may quit or fall away. But God is still on His throne; set your mind on things above!

As I was preparing to write this conclusion to the book, I came across an email I printed out. It was by a friend who died of cancer and had spent his final years on this earth preaching the glorious Gospel of Jesus and being a herald of the coming Kingdom.

His life, along with the lives of so many redeemed saints and martyrs through church history, inspire me in the faith. My friend ended his email with a reminder from Scripture to set our hearts and minds on things above, and to resist worry, fear, and anxiety, as we trust in God's provision. He shared these two verses:

"But seek first His kingdom and His righteousness, and all these things will be provided to you. So do not worry about tomorrow; for tomorrow will worry about itself. Each day has enough trouble of its own" (Matthew 6:33-34).

Admittedly, this can be difficult, especially in 2021 with all we are faced with as believers and considering all that has transpired over the last several years. Still, it is a day at a time.

God said His people perish for lack of knowledge (Hosea 4:6), and He commended the sons of Issachar who understood the times and how to respond (1 Chronicles 12:32). Believers must not be clueless when confronted by cultural evil. This is another reason we need the Lord's wisdom.

People must be warned and informed. They must be reminded of our history, where we are now, and where we are headed as a church and nation.

Every believer in Christ, every pastor and church leader, every conservative, patriot, and every concerned citizen is responsible for their sphere of influence. We each must engage culture because we have passed a point of no return. I used to warn about the culture war, but that ship has sailed. We must now reclaim the church while attempting to preserve the country.

Yes, we are to be godly influencers as permeating salt and light, but is there a point when we shake the dust off our shoes and move on? And what does that look like?

In New Testament times, shaking the dust off your feet was a common sign of protest. Jesus told His disciples to do this whenever people did not listen to their words or receive the Gospel (Matthew 10:12-15). Our nation has generally rejected God and His laws.

The Savior, Jesus, is the Living Word, and we know the Gospel is the power of God. Keep sharing the truth and be listening for the Lord to tell us when to move on. It matters little we are mocked, scoffed at, discriminated against, and considered foolish. The godless will face judgment in the end. I pray they turn to Jesus before it is too late.

Our purpose has not changed and the Word of our God endures forever (Isaiah 40:8). This world, however, is constantly changing and will pass away. Seasons change, people change, rulers and presidents change. Great Reset or not, Jesus is Lord over all creation, leaders, and nations.

The globalist left and the Chinese Communist Party have been loosed. It also appears mainstream media is in bed with China as well as the Deep State in our government. Even corporations are helping build up China, who now has the US administration it wanted in power.

Be prepared as the Biden/Harris administration unleashes even more wickedness. It is what radicals do. For those who love the country and are grieved by all this, do not lose heart. Lord willing, the 2022 midterm elections will flip control of the House or Senate back to Republicans, but that would only be a temporary fix.

Looking ahead with an eternal perspective, hearts must be challenged and changed for Christ.

Last year, I interviewed Pastor Shane Idleman from California when churches there were being severely mandated, restricted, and their liberties were being infringed upon by CA governor Gavin Newsome. Idleman said we must resist, but no Christian should incite unbiblical rebellion or disobey local and state ordinances—*if* they are realistic and fairly enforced across the board.

But that was not the case in California and many other states. And yet, some of us saw it as good for the church. The threat and reality of an unknown virus exposed our weak spots. He stated:

"In one fell swoop, COVID-19 has dethroned many of our idols. We are finally realizing what is really important. In this sense, I am incredibly encouraged since this is fertile ground for revival. Revival thrives in brokenness, repentance, humility, and passionate prayer. I am concerned that America is fearful but not repentant, anxious but not surrendered to God, worried but not worshipful, confused but not diligently seeking Him."

We must not be anxious, confused, or fearful.

In this book, we have examined possible outcomes for the church and for America, but certainly did not exhaust the possibilities. It is imperative we continue to fight. Since the warfare is clearly intensifying, saints must first wake up, and immediately take up the whole armor of God!

We must also do our best to wean ourselves off secular influences, stand up for truth, and stop conforming to the world. Let us live counterculture and love Jesus more than this life.

The apostle John wrote:

"Do not love the world nor the things in the world. If anyone loves the world, the love of the Father is not in him. The world is passing away, and *also* its lusts; but the one who does the will of God lives forever" (1 John 2:15, 17).

We must redirect immediately. It must be all about Jesus again! Not about us, not about church growth, not about buildings, tolerance, numbers, programs, our comfort, or pleasing people.

The church is a battleship, but too many seem to think we are on a cruise ship.

The left is out to win! We must combat the lies, overcome cancel culture, and respond to deception with truth. Regardless of the ongoing purge of biblical Christianity, we press on!

It is time to count the cost and be willing to sacrifice. It is time to join forces with dedicated, like-minded believers. Today is the day of salvation, and we must redeem the time. Stay the course, my friend. Fight the good fight, run the race, and keep the faith!

A crown awaits.

About the Author

David Fiorazo is an author, associate pastor, media contributor, and talk show host of the *Stand Up for the Truth* podcast. He has been involved in the broadcasting and entertainment industries for over thirty years and in Christian ministry for over twenty-five years.

In his travels across the country, David became concerned about fading family values in America and growing complacency among Christians. He also saw churches conforming to the world while hostility toward Jesus Christ increased in every aspect of our culture. One of the catalysts that led him to start writing, eventually inspiring four books, was what David calls "a corrupt, anti-Christian, biased media and entertainment industry who refuse to report the truth and tolerate the free expression of Christianity."

He penned *ERADICATE: Blotting Out God in America*, *Redefining Truth*, the top-selling, *The Cost of Our Silence*, and now, *Canceling Christianity*. David is a culture observer some may call a watchman. He loves the Word of God, and strives to defend and proclaim the truth of Jesus Christ without apology or compromise.

Endnotes

1 Michael Haverluck, "Barna: 5 things you want to know about the Church in America," *One News Now*, 2.27.2020, https://onenewsnow.com/church/2020/02/27/barna-5-things-you-want-to-know-about-the-church-in-america

2 Clark, Heather, Christian Research Group: US 'Moving Toward Elimination of Biblical Worldview as Cornerstone of Society' Nov. 13, 2020, https://christiannews.net/2020/11/13/christian-research-group-us-moving-toward-elimination-of-biblical-worldview-as-cornerstone-of-society/

3 Heather Clark, "Survey Finds Many Americans Reject Moral Absolutes, Including Some Who Identify as Christians," 5.17.2020, https://christiannews.net/2020/05/27/survey-finds-many-americans-reject-moral-absolutes-including-some-who-identify-as-christians/

4 Peter Heck, "New study shows 74% of American teens and young adults embrace moral relativism," DISRN, 2.1.2021, https://disrn.com/news/new-study-shows-74-of-american-teens-and-young-adults-embrace-moral-relativism

5 Dr. Richard G. Lee, *The Battle for the Soul of America*, 2020, There's Hope America, Cumming, GA, page 11

6 Faithwire, Number of Christian Voters Decreasing, Study Finds, Nov 6, 2020, https://www.faithwire.com/2020/11/06/number-of-christian-voters-decreasing-study-finds/

7 Tre GoinsiPhillips, "Katie Couric Says Trump Supporters Need to Be 'Deprogrammed,' Faithwire, 1.19.2021, https://www.faithwire.com/2021/01/19/katie-couric-says-trump-supporters-need-to-be-deprogrammed/

8 Dr. Richard G. Lee, "The General Principles of Liberty," *In God We Still Trust*, Thomas Nelson, 2010, page 185

9 Anders Nygren, "Luther's Doctrine of the Two Kingdoms," Journal of Lutheran Ethics, 8.1.2002, https://elca.org/JLE/Articles/931

10 Noah Webster, "Faith of Our Founders," http://www.faithofourfathers.net/webster.html

11 Tony Perkins, "Nadler on God: He's 'No Concern of This Congress," Family Research Council, 3.1.2021, https://www.frc.org/updatearticle/20210301/nadler-god

12 Heather Clark, "Survey Shows Christians' Desire for Pastors to Address Abortion, Homosexuality, Persecution From the Pulpit," Christian News, 7.31.2020, https://christiannews.net/2020/07/31/survey-shows-christians-desire-for-pastors-to-address-abortion-homosexuality-persecution-from-the-pulpit/

13 Susan B. Anthony, "Marriage and Family," *The Revolution*, 8 July, 1869, 4.

[14] Alvin J. Schmidt, *How Christianity Changed the World,* Zondervan, 2004, pg. 273.

[15] Robert Velarde, *What Christianity has done for the World,* 2007 Rose Publishing, Torrance, CA

[16] Caleb Parke, Fox News, "California pastor defies coronavirus orders despite threat of arrest: Newsom 'not the head of the church,' 8.4.20, https://www. foxnews.com/media/california-pastor-coronavirus-church-newsom-order

[17] Liberty Counsel, "California's Outrageous Thanksgiving Restrictions," 10.28.20, https://lc.org/newsroom/details/102820-californias-outrageous-thanksgiving-restrictions

[18] Breck Dumas, "Socialist Seattle council member vows to replace capitalism with socialism worldwide," The Blaze, 7.7.2020, https://www.theblaze. com/news/ready-socialist-seattle-council-member-vows-to-replace-capitalism-with-socialism-worldwide

[19] John Binder, "John Kerry Talks 'Great Reset': 'We're at the Dawn of Extremely Exciting Time,' Breitbart News, 11.19.2020, https://www.breitbart. com/politics/2020/11/19/john-kerry-talks-great-reset-were-at-the-dawn-of-extremely-exciting-time/#

[20] Donald Trump, "Remarks by President Trump to the 74th Session of the United Nations General Assembly," UN Headquarters, New York, NY, 9.25.2019, https:// www.whitehouse.gov/briefings-statements/remarks-president-trump-74th-session-united-nations-general-assembly/

[21] Alex Newman, "You'll Own Nothing": UN-backed "Great Reset" Is Feudalism," *The New American,* 12.5.2020

[22] Keegan Fernandes, "The Plannedemic and the Great Reset," November 2020, https://www.rapturecountdown.com/the-plannedemic-and-the-great-reset/

[23] Reverend Jacob Duche, "First Prayer of the Continental Congress," Office of the Chaplain, 9.7.1774, https://chaplain.house.gov/archive/continental.html

[24] Abraham Lincoln, "Proclamation Appointing a National Fast Day," Abraham Lincoln Online, 3.30.1863, http://www.abrahamlincolnonline.org/lincoln/speeches/fast.htm

[25] Allen West, "Lt. Col. West Slams BLM for Attacking Nuclear Family and Ignoring Fatherlessness," *CNS News,* 6.29.2020, https://www.cnsnews.com/blog/andrew-davenport/lt-col-west-slams-blm-attacking-nuclear-family-and-ignoring-fatherlessness

[26] Elizabeth Vaugh, "Donations to Black Lives Matter Go to 'ActBlue' - The Activist Arm of the Democrat Party," *Red State,* 6.12.2020, https://redstate.com/elizabeth-vaughn/2020/06/12/854023-n241617

[27] John MacArthur, "Who's to Blame for the Riots," *Grace To You,* 6.7.2020, https://www.gty.org/library/sermons-library/81-80/whos-to-blame-for-the-riots

[28] Kyle S. Reyes, "The Real Numbers Of "Police Brutality" in America That You Need To See," 2.18.2019, https://www.lawenforcementtoday.com/police-brutality-race-numbers/

29 Joshua Lawson, "You Can Be a Christian, You Can be a Marxist, But You Can't Be Both," The Federalist, 6.11.2020, https://thefederalist.com/2020/06/11/you-can-be-christian-you-can-be-marxist-but-you-cant-be-both/

30 Brenda M. Hafera, "1619 Project's real goal? Target middle America with identity politics," WND, 12.20.2020, https://www.wnd.com/2020/12/1619-projects-real-goal-target-middle-america-identity-politics/

31 Peter Heck, "Opinion: Explain to me how 'conservatives for Biden' can be a thing," DISRN, 10.4.2020, https://disrn.com/opinion/opinion-explain-to-me-how-conservatives-for-biden-can-be-a-thing

32 John Zmirak, "Short of Another Great Awakening, America May Split Up … Or Worse," The Stream, 4.24.2020, https://stream.org/short-of-another-great-awakening-america-may-split-up-or-worse/

33 Matt Trewhella, "3 Beneficial Results of Interposition by Lesser Magistrates," DefyTyrants.com, 1.9.2021, https://defytyrants.com/3-beneficial-results-of-interposition-by-lesser-magistrates/

34 F.H. Buckley, American Secession: The Looming Threat of a National Breakup, Encounter Books, New York, 2020, https://www.amazon.com/American-Secession-Looming-National-Breakup/dp/1641770805/

35 Selwyn Duke, "The Time for Talking with the Left is Long, Long, Past," American Thinker, 12.10.2020, https://www.americanthinker.com/articles/2020/12/the_time_for_talking_with_the_left_is_long_long_past.html

36 Tre Goins Phillips, "Katie Couric Says Trump Supporters Need to Be 'Deprogrammed'," Faithwire, 1.19.2021, https://www.faithwire.com/2021/01/19/katie-couric-says-trump-supporters-need-to-be-deprogrammed/

37 Ben Shapiro, How To Destroy America In Three Easy Steps, HarperCollins, NY, 2020, page 181

38 President Ronald Reagan, "Farewell Address to the Nation," National Archives, Presidential Library and Museum, 1.11.1989, https://www.reaganlibrary.gov/archives/speech/farewell-address-nation

39 Winter Oak, "Klaus Schwab & His Great Fascist Reset," Off Guardian, 10.12.2020, https://off-guardian.org/2020/10/12/klaus-schwab-his-great-fascist-reset/

40 Victims of Communism Memorial Foundation, "U.S. Attitudes Toward Socialism, Communism, and Collectivism," 2020 Annual Poll, https://victimsofcommunism.org/annual-poll/2020-annual-poll/

41 Tim Ciccotta, "Poll: 58% of Young, College-Educated Americans Say Riots Are Justified," 6.3.2020, https://www.breitbart.com/tech/2020/06/03/poll-58-of-young-college-educated-americans-say-riots-are-justified/

42 Adam Ford, "Leading BLM activist Shaun King says 'tear down' all paintings, statues of light-skinned Jesus: 'They are a gross form of white supremacy'," DISRN News, 6.22.2020, https://disrn.com/news/blm-activist-shaun-king-says-tear-down-all-paintings-statues-of-light-skinned-jesus-gross-form-of-white-supremacy

[43] David Fiorazo, "Joe Biden: More Islam in Public Schools," 7.23.2020, https://davidfiorazo.com/2020/07/joe-biden-wants-more-islam-taught-in-public-schools/

[44] Aaron Bandler, "New Jersey School District Teaches Islam But Censors Christianity," Daily Wire, 2.21.2017, https://www.dailywire.com/news/new-jersey-school-district-teaches-islam-censors-aaron-bandler

[45] Meira Svirsky, "Pro-Islam Indoctrination in Public Schools?" Clarion Project, 8.28.2017, https://clarionproject.org/pro-islam-indoctrination-public-schools/

[46] Abigail A. Southerland, "Buddhist Indoctrination Update: Achieving Victories as We Expose the Intent Behind "Mindfulness" Programs in Public Schools," American Center for Law and Justice, 2.2018, https://aclj.org/religious-liberty/buddhist-indoctrination-update-achieving-victories-as-we-expose-the-intent-behind-mindfulness-programs-in-public-schools

[47] Ben Shapiro, "Revenge of the Lapdogs," One News Now, 12.16.2020, https://onenewsnow.com/perspectives/ben-shapiro/2020/12/16/revenge-of-the-lapdogs

[48] Corinne Weaver, "Twitter Censors Trump, Trump Campaign 325 Times, But Never Biden," NewsBusters, 11.30.2020, https://www.newsbusters.org/blogs/techwatch/corinne-weaver/2020/11/30/twitter-censors-trump-trump-campaign-325-times-never

[49] Robert Knight, "The Digital Election Heist," 12.1.2020, https://onenewsnow.com/perspectives/robert-knight/2020/12/01/the-digital-election-heist

[50] NB Staff, "Bozell Urges Congress to Address Big Tech Interference in Election," NewsBusters, 12.18.2020, https://www.newsbusters.org/blogs/nb/nb-staff/2020/12/18/bozell-urges-congress-address-big-tech-interference-election

[51] Mollie Hemingway, "CNN Flooded Zone with Kavanaugh Coverage. Hasn't Mentioned Biden's Accuser Once," The Federalist, 4.16.2020, https://thefederalist.com/2020/04/16/cnn-flooded-zone-with-kavanaugh-coverage-hasnt-mentioned-bidens-accuser-once/

[52] Matt Walsh, "WALSH: There Is Way More Evidence Against Biden Than There Ever Was Against Kavanaugh," Daily Wire, 4.27.2020, https://www.dailywire.com/news/walsh-there-is-way-more-evidence-against-biden-than-there-ever-was-against-kavanaugh

[53] Ian Haworth, "China, Spies, And Sexual Harassment: 3 Bombshell Stories The Legacy Media Are Hiding From You," Daily Wire, 12.18.2020, https://www.dailywire.com/news/china-spies-and-sexual-harassment-3-bombshell-stories-the-legacy-media-are-hiding-from-you

[54] David Fiorazo, "Media Refuses to Report on Christians Being Slaughtered," 3.27.2019, https://davidfiorazo.com/2019/03/media-refuses-to-report-on-christians-being-slaughtered/

[55] Brannon Howse, Grave Influence: 21 Radicals and Their Worldviews that Rule America from the Grave, 2009 Worldview Weekend Publishing, page 129

[56] Trevor Louden: "Marxism in America infecting Government, Church and Culture," *Stand Up for the Truth*, 11.16.2020, https://www.standupforthetruth.com/2020/11/marxism-in-america-infecting-government-culture-church/

[57] William S. Lind, "The Roots of Political Correctness," The American Conservative, 11.19.2009, (original source taken off line, "Further Readings on the Frankfort School" chapter VI, [Free Congress Foundation], https://www.theamericanconservative.com/the-roots-of-political-correctness/

[58] David Fiorazo, *ERADICATE: Blotting Out God in America*, 2012, Life Sentence Publishing, Abbotsford, Wisconsin, pp. 107, 229.

[59] Michelle Malkin, "The Messy Truth about Race-Baiting, Radical Demagogue, Van Jones," Dec. 6, 2016, http://michellemalkin.com/2016/12/06/the-messy-truth-about-race-baiting-radical-demagogue-van-jones/

[60] Robert Knight, "Keeping a lid on the truth about socialism," *Washington Times*, Feb. 7, 2016, http://www.washingtontimes.com/news/2016/feb/7/robert-knight-keeping-a-lid-on-the-truth-about-soc/

[61] James C. Bowers, *The Naked Truth: The Naked Communist Revisited,"* Schwartz Report Press, Manitou Springs, CO, 2011

[62] Discover The Networks, "Progressive Era Legacy: FDR'S New Deal," (no date), https://www.discoverthenetworks.org/organizations/progressive-era-legacy-fdrs-new-deal/

[63] James C. Bowers, *The Naked Truth: The Naked Communist Revisited,"* Schwartz Report Press, Manitou Springs, CO, 2011

[64] Ali Meyer, "Obama's EPA Regulations: 6,552 X As Long As The Constitution, 46 X As Long As Bible," CNS News, June 8, 2015, http://www.cnsnews.com/news/article/ali-meyer/obamas-epa-regulations-6552x-long-constitution-46x-long-bible

[65] James C. Bowers, *The Naked Truth: The Naked Communist Revisited,* Schwartz Report Press, Manitou Springs, CO, 2011

[66] Trevor Louden, "Why is No One (Except the President) Calling out Kamala Harris's Communist Ties?" *Epoch Times*, 10.16.2020, https://www.trevorloudon.com/2020/10/why-is-no-one-except-the-president-calling-out-kamala-harris-communist-ties/

[67] Alexandra Desanctis, "Kamala Harris's Anti-Catholic Bigotry," 8.11.2020, *National Review*, https://www.nationalreview.com/corner/kamala-harriss-anti-catholic-bigotry/

[68] Tyler Olsen, "Biden VP pick Harris promoted group that put up bail for alleged violent criminals," *Fox News*, 8.12.20, https://www.foxnews.com/politics/biden-vp-pick-harris-promoted-group-that-put-up-bail-for-alleged-violent-criminals

[69] Wayne Grudem, "Letter to An Anti-Trump Christian Friend," *The Stream*, 8.12.2020, https://stream.org/letter-to-an-anti-trump-christian-friend/

[70] Wayne Grudem, "List of 30 Good Things President Trump Has Done for America," 8.21.2020, http://www.waynegrudem.com/list-of-25-good-things-president-trump-has-done-for-america

71 Don Feder, "Why The Left Hates Religion," 10.15.2020, American Family Association, https://www.afa.net/the-stand/culture/2020/10/why-the-left-hates-religion/

72 Family Research Council, "Trump Administration Accomplishments on Life, Family, and Religious Freedom," FRC Action, 2017-2020, https://www.frcaction.org/accomplishments

CPSIA information can be obtained
at www.ICGtesting.com
Printed in the USA
BVHW080539191021
619151BV00001B/1